CITIZEN MOORE

The Life and Times of an American Iconoclast

ROGER RAPOPORT

RDR Books

Berkeley, California • Muskegon, Michigan

Citizen Moore

RDR Books
1487 Glen Avenue
Muskegon, MI 49441
phone: 510-595-0595
fax: 510-228-0300
www.rdrbooks.com
email: roger@rdrbooks.com

ISBN: 1-57143-163-2
After Jan. 1, 2007: 978-1-57143-163-9

Library of Congress Control Number: 2006908603

Design and Production: Richard Harris
Typesetting: Becky Eastling, MICR Graphics Printing
Additional Design: Mary Sexton
Production: Jeanette Bury
Cover Photo: Amy Graves, WireImage.com
Back Cover Photo: Duffy Arnoult, WireImage.com

Distributed in the United Kingdom and Europe by
Roundhouse Publishing Ltd., Millstone, Limers Lane,
Northam, North Devon EX39 2RG, United Kingdom

Printed in the United States of America

For John Ferriby
Boy Genius
Man of the Hour
Our Hero

CONTENTS

LOOKING FOR MICHAEL IN ALL THE WRONG PLACES

"Listen, a picture, all it is is an expensive dream."
—*Jack Warner*

"MY FIRST CONVERSATION with Michael Moore was on the phone for over an hour," said his former Beverly Hills manager Douglas Urbanski. "Whenever you have a client who wants help, the conversations are often similar. Michael was in trouble. He couldn't seem to get his new movie, *The Big One* sold. He was doing a pilot for a late night talk show that wasn't getting off the ground. He was trying to get money from the BBC for *The Awful Truth*. If you asked what he was going to do, you would get a Chinese menu of answers. He would tell you that he belonged on a sitcom, that he should be the biggest star since Jackie Gleason, that he should be organizing labor unions and that he should be a fictional screen writer. It was like the weather in San Francisco. If you wait long enough, you get a little of everything.

I asked him, "Michael, who are you? I want you to tell me."

"Can I call you back tomorrow? I need to call my friends and ask them."

A KODAK MOMENT WITH THE DIXIE CHICKS (PLUS HIS HOLINESS)

Michael Moore Wins an Oscar

"I want to take an ad out in Variety *and plead with academy voters to not vote for this film. It is a critical mistake to put me live on that stage."*

—*Michael Moore*

DARK-HORSE ACADEMY AWARD NOMINEE Michael Moore watched anti-war protesters being arrested as he arrived at the Kodak Theater in his studio limousine. On the way over, he'd nursed doubts that he would actually win an Oscar. Not since Woodstock won the Best Documentary award in 1971 had a big-box-office film been chosen in this category. Moore was pretty sure that no nominee since then had shown up at the ceremony wearing a tux from Sears.

But this was March 24, 2003, just five days after George Bush had gone to war in Iraq. As he watched the demonstrators and listened to antiwar comments by his fellow nominees, Moore realized this might be a very good year for a film that took on the American gun lobby.

The shock and awe of bombs bursting in air over Baghdad—and the possibility of attacks on America's film kingdom—had persuaded the Academy to dampen the glitz and cut back on the pomp. None of the nominees were dropped off at the Kodak Theater's towering Hollywood portal. Instead of moving down the red carpeted Awards

Walk framed by backlit Best Picture plaques, the Oscar candidates were dropped off unannounced and unphotographed at a secure entrance. The only autograph seekers allowed belonged to a Los Angeles Police Department SWAT team and the U.S. Department of Homeland Security. Airspace over the Kodak Theater was closed.

"I am really glad they cut back on the red carpet, that'll send them a message," host Steve Martin told the celebrity audience. Other performers made it clear Bush's attack had not won the war for Hollywood. At a Miramax party before the ceremony, Michael Feinstein couldn't persuade anyone to join him in a "God Bless America" sing-along. At the main event, peacenik after peacenik took to the stage calling for an end to the war. Gael Garcia Bernal of *Y Tu Mama Tambien* introduced a *Frida* song nominee and told the crowd, "We are not alone. If Frida (Kahlo) was alive, she would be on our side, against war."

U2's Bono rewrote the lyrics from a *Gangs of New York* song to add to the Hollywood Academy Awards antiwar chorus that included Adrien Brody and Susan Sarandon.

> "Late in the spring, yellow cloud on a desert skyline,
> Some father's son, is it his or is it mine."

Moore might not have been a Hollywood insider, but as a veteran super-reporter he knew a "buzz" when he heard one. After all, he was a real-life Clark Kent, wasn't he? Okay, so maybe he looked more like an Irish cop on a hunting trip than a superhero in an eyeglasses disguise, and maybe he'd have a hard time changing clothes in a phone booth. But like Clark Kent, Moore had grown up in a small town-in his case, Davison, Michigan, where kids rode their bikes to school and no one had heard of Kryptonite locks. Their careers as reporters had taken them inside prisons and the lairs of corrupt officials, master criminals and megalomaniacs. Look, up in the sky, it's a bird . . . it's a plane . . . No, it's the Big Bopper of investigative journalism!

Like Clark Kent, Michael Moore worked hand-in-hand with his own "Lois Lane," Kathleen Glynn, a producer and co-author with curly red hair and a legendary sense of humor. Their romance, which led her to leave her first husband, Wallace Rose, not long after the birth of her daughter Natalie, was Kismet. And Moore, like Kent, had his trademark disguise to help him blend in: jeans, a union jacket, running shoes and a Michigan State baseball cap worn the right way-the trappings of a blue-collar factory worker. It was the perfect uniform, one that even disarmed Klansmen and Michigan Militia members who proudly showed off their latest semiautomatics to him.

Beneath his meek, mild-mannered garb, his super-reporter powers were formidable. He was patient with his subjects, deferential, a good listener. Sitting down for a talk with Michael Moore was a little like taking a seat in a confessional—with cameras. When Moore returned to the editing room to look at the day's rushes, he mentally sorted his interviewees into two categories: those who'd been honest with him and those who wished they hadn't.

Now, inside the Kodak Theater on Oscar night, Moore believed that his time had definitely not come. He had only been kidding about that Variety ad and confessed to friends, "I'm going to sit there and lose."

He was convinced that the Academy was not going to let a ruffian like him in front of a microphone that would reach a billion people from Beverly Hills to Bangladesh. Even if he did win, Moore was convinced someone at Price Waterhouse would fix the results. When Diane Lane opened the documentary award envelope and announced the winner—*Bowling for Columbine*, written and directed by Michael Moore—he motioned for his fellow nominees to join him on stage.

The director began the longest walk of his life, relieved that he had sprung for that knockout gown that looked perfect on Kathleen. For United Artists chief Bingham Ray, who had never let his anger boil over while Moore badgered the UA staff for months to make sure *Bowling for Columbine* shattered all documentary box office records, this triumph was something to celebrate. But like everyone else following the Academy Awards, it was hard to predict what Moore was going to say. Top prize at Cannes, a documentary on the way to an unheard-of $20-million-plus gross, and the director would, in all likelihood, never even acknowledge UA's hard work on his behalf. For this was Hollywood, where you were only as good as your next Oscar acceptance speech. As he began walking down the aisle to the stage, Meryl Streep and Julianne Moore both gave him a "Go Get'em Mike" look as they reached out to touch the winner. Tuning out the applause, he began hearing voices.

"Just blow them a kiss and walk off the stage," said the first one.

"You have to say something."

"No, you don't have to say anything. Oscar good. Thank your hairdresser, your wardrobe designer and your agent and walk off the stage."

"No, no, you must say something."

"Shut up."

"Don't listen to him."

"Yes, listen, Oscar bad, Hollywood fake."

"No, Hollywood good. Hollywood lets you make more movies."

"Shut the . . ."

Looking out at Hollywood's Oscar lovers, illuminated by an oval tiara of light chandelier, Michael Moore knew what he had to do. His family was counting on him. So were the nuns who raised him, the sisters of St. Joseph watching the Oscars back home in Nazareth, Michigan.

And there was someone else, a man whose name had come to mind that morning during mass with his father and sister at Beverly Hills' oldest house of worship, the Church of the Good Shepherd. A former seminarian raised in the tradition of Catholics like the Berrigan Brothers and John F. Kennedy, Moore had been sitting in the same sanctuary where Elizabeth Taylor married her first husband, Nicky Hilton, the place where Rod Stewart and Rachel Hunter said their vows, when he had been reminded of the Vatican's position on the war in Iraq.

"I have invited my fellow documentary nominees on the stage with us . . ." Moore declared to the Oscar audience. "They're here in solidarity with me because we like nonfiction. We like nonfiction and we live in fictitious times. We live in the time where we have fictitious election results that elect a fictitious president. We live in a time where we have a man sending us to war for fictitious reasons. Whether it's the fiction of duct tape or the fiction of orange alerts, we are against this war, Mr. Bush. Shame on you, Mr. Bush, shame on you. And anytime you've got the Pope and the Dixie Chicks against you, your time is up. Thank you very much . . ."

"Cut him off!" Oscar producer Gil Gates yelled to his director, Louis Horvitz, who called for the orchestra conductor to lower his baton as Moore's microphone telescoped into the floor.

Backstage Moore heard three little words. "Champagne," said a young woman. "Breath mint," asked a young man next to her. As he grabbed his champagne flute and mint from the interns, an angry stagehand charged up to him and shouted, "Asshole." Moore claimed that the crowd applauded and only stagehands booed his remarks. But several local television commentators offering live coverage of the Academy Awards gleefully replayed Moore's Kodak Theater moment and tossed out the penalty flag. "That's the end of Michael Moore. Oh boy, he really blew it. He shouldn't have said anything. He doesn't understand the way the winds are blowing in the country," said one newsman.

What Moore failed to understand was that overnight polls showed 80 percent of the American public approved of George Bush's Iraq invasion. Obviously Moore had missed Colin Powell's speech to the United Nations about Saddam Hussein's stockpiled weapons of mass destruction.

"I think it would be irresponsible of me not to say what I felt," Moore told reporters backstage. "I don't think anyone who voted for me for this award thought they'd get a speech about agents and lawyers or the lawyers of agents."

Moore's performance was cheered by antiwar groups and denounced by film critics like the Washington Post's Tom Shales, who called it the worst Oscar speech he'd ever heard.

"It was so sweet backstage, you should have seen it," said Steve Martin. "The Teamsters are helping Michael Moore into the trunk of his limo."

Hollywood was still debating Moore's performance when he boarded a plane back home to Michigan the next day with his wife Kathleen. There, too, reviews were definitely mixed. Signs had been plastered around the Moore-Glynn property suggesting that he might want to move back to the country where he belonged-France. And it was impossible to get into the garage without a shovel. Someone had blocked his driveway with a four-foot-high pile of horse manure.

Moore's controversial remarks at the Academy of Awards started a run on his *Bowling for Columbine* DVD, not to mention his book *Stupid White Men*. *Library Journal* reported that his latest title, *Dude, Where's My Country*, was among the most requested books in the country. He led Jay Leno's *Tonight Show* audience in a rousing rendition of "America the Beautiful," amazing TV viewers with a singing voice that sounded like it couldn't have come from him. Pop diva Linda Ronstadt was ejected from her own concert at Las Vegas's Aladdin Hotel for dedicating a song ("Desperado") to Moore; the two planned to return and sing a duet there. Personal security also became a major issue. There were threats on his life, and in Fort Lauderdale a Starbucks patron flipped the lip on his scalding fair trade coffee and threw it at the director.

A mere reference to *Fahrenheit 9/11* by Senator John McCain touched off a spontaneous anti-Moore demonstration on the floor of the 2004 Republican National Convention. Fortunately Republican guards were on hand to escort him safely from the hall-whether he wanted to leave or not. The fact that Vietnam prisoner of war McCain had been sacrificed on the GOP altar by George W. Bush during the 2000 Republican primary campaign didn't matter. Moore's reputation had grown to the point where it wasn't necessary for McCain to see his films to know what he was up to and despise him for it. After all, it was a Michael Moore documentary.

Like a *Doonesbury* character, Moore was instantly recognizable, a national hero to his fans but also the recipient of enough death threats to force him to travel with a security team ready to avert martyrdom. *Rolling Stone* ridiculed attempts to pigeonhole the filmmaker as a left-wing Rush Limbaugh. "For one thing," the magazine pointed out, "Moore has never done drugs." (As Jay Leno later explained it, the problem was that the filmmaker couldn't find anyone who knew how to make drugs deep-fried and smothered with cheese.)

From the cover of *Time* magazine to Jon Stewart's The Daily Show, Moore demonstrated that he could outmaneuver his opponents, who were unable to adapt to changing market conditions. While *Bowling for Columbine*, his attack on the National Rifle Association, broke records for a documentary, NRA leader Wayne LaPierre's tome *Guns, Freedom and Terrorism* failed to win any attention in the *Los Angeles Times* or the *Washington Post*. As audiences lined up for Moore's antigun film, LaPierre's badly timed book had a few problems in bookstores around the nation's capital, particularly after a week-long Washington D.C. sniper crisis left 16 dead.

Not one to rest on his Emmy, Moore warned his fans, that his record-breaking documentary was no guarantee that he could go on making movies. "Believe me these media conglomerates would never put me on the screen or TV or whatever because they thought it was a good idea. They are only doing it because people like you actually rent this video or buy my books so it makes them money. Believe me they would like to get me out the door as soon as possible."

Fortunately for Moore, the Bush White House provided an immediate opportunity for a new documentary financed by Disney's Miramax division. His anti-Bush film project, *Fahrenheit 9/11*, evolved into a "date movie" where young couples enjoyed a magic carpet ride to Saudi Arabia to watch their first beheading. The film provided black humor in the form of presidential file footage. Heavy metal rock music complemented combat scenes in Baghdad. A Flint mom told how the death of her Army son in an Iraq war helicopter crash had cost Bush her vote.

The film's most famous sequence reflected the disastrous results of the president's obsession with photo opportunities in public schools. (He was still billing himself as the "education president.") Moore uncovered footage of the president sitting in a tiny kids chair reading *My Pet Goat* on the morning of September 11, 2001, as aides failed to cut his visit short after learning of the terrorist attacks on the World Trade Center and the Pentagon. Audiences wanted to know why key scenes from Operation Iraqi Freedom had never been shown on *60 Minutes* or 20/20. It was Moore who offered Americans their first look at footage that gave network programmers tachycardia—

scenes so horrifying that the film was given an R rating. In solidarity with the filmmaker, theater owners around the country ignored the rating.

In its own way, Moore's film rivaled the dramatic impact of Orson Wells's famed 1938 *War of the Worlds* broadcast, which had convinced panicky radio audiences that New Jersey was being attacked by aliens from Mars. Moore blended the Beat iconoclasm of Jack Kerouac with the largess of *Queen For A Day*, the '50s TV show that lavished new appliances on impoverished moms. Taking his lead from Upton Sinclair and Ralph Nader, Michael Moore saw that it was possible to shift America's political landscape by documenting the malevolence of big business and the military-industrial complex. All he had to do was turn on his cameras and wait for the next celebrity suffering from foot-in-mouth disease.

There was Nike's Phil Knight insisting that he didn't hire 12-year-olds to make shoes in Indonesia. (Actually, explained the foot in his mouth CEO, they were 14.) Bob Eubanks of *The Dating Game* proved he knew how to tell a lewd joke about Jewish women. And *Bowling For Columbine* star Charlton Heston, president of the National Rifle Association, in his final film role proved the difficulty of working without a script. Creating satirical documentaries was fun and rather profitable, even if Moore had to show up in court occasionally to defend the high quality of his work.

In the process, the University of Michigan's most famous dropout made a discovery that virtually guaranteed an audience. Simply announcing a project guaranteed access to precisely the kind of material that his audiences had come to expect. For example work on his new documentary about the American health care industry, *Sicko*, was benefiting from the help of many whistleblowers. Moore denied rumors that he had promised doctors $50,000 apiece to help pinpoint fraud by setting up hidden cameras in their clinics. "I didn't need to," he explained. "So many doctors have offered help for free in an effort to expose the system."

As he said in his pitch for stories to use in *Sicko*, "Maybe you've just been told that your father is going to have to just, well, die because he can't afford the drugs he needs to get better—and it's then that you say, 'Damn, what did I do with Michael Moore's home phone number?'" Moore's "comedy about the 45 million Americans who don't have health care" was based on an *Awful Truth* segment about Chris Donahue, a patient battling his HMO for a pancreas transplant. Moore was finding it difficult to land CEOs willing to be bludgeoned on camera in the manner of his famous interview with Nike's Phil Knight in *The Big One*. This may have had something to do with his filmed *Awful Truth* "die-in" at Humana headquarters. Moore personally invited the HMO's employees to attend Donahue's funeral. After Humana reversed itself and agreed to the lifesaving operation, Donahue appeared on Moore's show to a standing ovation.

"Being screwed by your HMO and ill-served by pharmaceutical companies is the shared American experience," explained the *Sicko* producer, who was making a personal commitment to longevity by embarking on a diet that held the mayo and turned its back on deep fried fare. "The system, inferior to that of much poorer nations, benefits the few at the expense of the many." He even joked that his medical horror film would end with ailing patients abandoning their hopeless vigils in American HMO waiting rooms and sailing to Cuba for free government subsidized treatment.

Moore's determination to color America's central concerns inevitably led to panic attacks in the boardroom. At least half a dozen drug companies warned their employees to avoid being ambushed on film by a scruffy, heavyset guy with a baseball cap. Among the most nervous companies were Pfizer, GlaxoSmithKline, Astra Zeneca and Wyeth. Some employees were warned that loose lips could ultimately lead to government crackdowns and pink slips. This was not the first time major companies had tried to keep Moore off the premises. Manpower, a victim of one of Moore's *Awful Truth* segments, had advised its offices at home and abroad to evict the *Awful Truth* ringleader and his crew if they ever returned. Moore responded by heading off on an international tour of Manpower offices. Several kicked him out on the spot. But he discovered many employees had failed to read the memo and welcomed him in for a chat. With drugs like Vioxx and Celebrex tied to heart attacks, allegations that pharmaceutical industry watchdogs at the FDA had been muzzled, and the battle over importing lower priced drugs from Canada, the HMO story touched the lives of Americans from five to 105.

The timing of Moore's health care exposé was a studio's dream, even though studios were less than thrilled that Moore was still telling fans to pirate his past work off the Internet. His ability to self promote appeared to assure a full house. For example in Utah a real estate developer offered a Brigham Young University student organization $25,000 to simply cancel a Moore appearance. News of this potential censorship brought even more Utah students in the door to hear him speak. While the drug industry couldn't shut *Sicko* down, it was eager to put a few speed bumps on Moore's Hollywood superhighway. "We have an image problem-not only with Michael Moore, but with the general public," admitted drug industry lobbyist M.J. Finland. "We're criticized on the Hill and in the press-put in the category of the tobacco industry, even though we save lives."

Clearly Moore's efforts were not being ignored by the drug industry troops. Nancy Pekarek of GlaxoSmithKline explained that worried employees at all six of the company's American business centers had reported Moore sightings. "It's no fun being targeted. Already people are freaky deaky." The fact that Moore had never actually visited any of GlaxoSmithKline's offices was not reassuring. In the throes of paranoia, industry executives could never be sure when the *Sicko* guy might decide to stage a sneak attack. As AstraZeneca's Rachel Bloom explained the problem: "Michael Moore is becoming an urban legend." For years Moore had been perplexed by this paranoia in the board room. "Why would you be afraid to see me come in the room . . . If you've done something wrong you should be more concerned about your conscience, and if you believe in the hereafter, how hot the fires of hell are going to be for you getting rich at the expense of the poor."

Soon Michael Moore sightings were reaching a fever pitch. On a single October day, three hours apart, two separate reports—one on Gawker.com, the other in a European publication—reported that Moore was seen driving down Manhattan's Second Avenue shooting from the window of a van— and simultaneously shooting a film with

Lance Armstrong in France. (The filmmaker heard of these "sight-ings" while dining at Applebee's in Fort Lauderdale not far from the Pritikin clinic where he was improving his own health care system.)

After the film's fall 2006 release was postponed to June of 2007, Moore broke his own closed-set rule and went public on the delayed project. In September 2006, the director appeared at the Toronto Film Festival where, 17 years earlier, he had arrived as an unknown and left town on a first-class ticket to California compliments of Disney's Michael Eisner and Jeffrey Katzenberg. For Moore, Canada was the ideal venue to explain why his latest project was nine months behind schedule and enjoy being famous alongside other celebrities like Bill Clinton, in town to celebrate his 60th birthday by staging an AIDS benefit.

The filmmaker warmed up on Friday night with director Larry Charles, who was showcasing *Borat,* the story of a politically incor-rect Kazakhstani journalist's innocents abroad tour of America. Star Sacha Baron Cohen of *Da Ali G Show,* arrived at the Ryerson theater in a cart drawn by peasant women.

Unfortunately a projector failure cut the film short after 20 min-utes. Drawing on his projectionist skills, would-be superhero Moore, wearing shorts and a sweatshirt, tried and failed to fix the problem as fans relayed footage of his efforts to YouTube. Cohen took the stage to play reporter Borat Sagdiyev live and promised to fly the entire au-dience home to Kazakhstan where such a thing could never happen.

Turning to festival programmer Colin Geddes, he promised, "We will lynch this man later" and, in the spirit of Mel Gibson chatting with a Los Angeles policeman after a drunk driving arrest, added "I blame this on the Jews."

The following night, *Borat* ticketholders lined up in the rain for a midnight rescreening of the hot film, scheduled to begin at the end of Moore's own sold-out Elgin Theater presentation. Moore took more than half an hour to make his way through the theater lobby, patiently talking with reporters and fans as he signed autographs and posed for photos. *Canadian Bacon* fan Josh Bricker, an air traffic controller in training, who had stood in the Elgin rush line for six hours, was thrilled to get a ticket and enjoy this "once-in-a-lifetime opportunity. He expresses things people are afraid to talk about and he stays on top of what is happening in America where things are getting worse and worse."

Introduced as "the American saint, the American visionary, the American prophet," Moore turned the "Mavericks" program into an off-the-wall, two-hour world premiere for *Sicko* and a heretofore secret work in progress, *The Great '04 Slacker Uprising*. This time Larry Charles, supervising producer of *Seinfeld* and director of *Curb Your Enthusiasm,* was asking the questions during an evening that was funnier than one of his scripts. A clunky DVD soundtrack forced Moore to truncate "the story of a filmmaker's failed 2004 attempt to turn things around . . . to save the Democrats from themselves."

"Is it me?" asked Charles as the projection booth struggled to solve the same problem that had killed his *Borat* screening. Moore quickly accepted responsibility. "It's me—I'm violating one of my rules, which is not to show a work in progress . . . God is spiting me. I knew I should never show a film until it's done."

For the second night in a row, Moore and Charles killed time as some disappointed ticket holders walked out. For Moore, it was a chance to get on the scoreboard the day after George Bush acknowl-edged the existence of secret CIA prisons for interrogating terrorist suspects. Bonding quickly with a festival screening films about the imaginary assassination of George Bush, an Iraqi planning to kill Tony Blair, the political passion of the Dixie Chicks, and *The US vs. John Lennon*, Moore quickly opened fire on the 44th President of the Unit-ed States. Pointing out that Operation Iraqi Freedom had lasted longer than the allied campaign against Hitler, he cried: "We are not able to secure the road from the airport to downtown Baghdad. They don't want to secure the road because it is part of the great distraction."

His solution? Run candidates who can actually defeat the neo-cons. Pointing out that the Republicans "don't have a problem run-ning Ronald Reagan or Arnold Schwarzenegger or Gopher from the *Love Boat,*" he suggested nominating Oprah for the oval office. "It would be great, and at four every afternoon she can still have her show. If they don't behave, turn them over to Dr. Phil."

New leadership was only one part of a solution that required Americans to reexamine their own poorly thought out biases. Far from being prologue, the past can be a booby trap. "I start out with a premise," Moore told his audience, "and have it proved wrong early on." A case in point was *Bowling For Columbine,* where he rejected a pro-gun-control thesis and went with the NRA position that guns don't kill people, people kill people, or to be precise, "Americans kill people."

Moore's problem is that "no one wants to go to a movie on Friday night" to find out "the health care industry sucks. They already know that. I began seriously considering why this audience is different from an American audience. At the core they all believe they are in the same boat together. If one of them is hurt they are all suffering together. In America it's everyone for themselves, sink or swim. You can't take it? You're sick. You've got cancer? Fuck you."

The director's research led to an epiphany at a soccer match in London's Arsenal stadium. He could not grasp why a player taking the ball failed to immediately charge down the field. "In our football we have to wait until there is an opponent in front," a British friend explained. "Otherwise it isn't fair. It's the same with . . . health care. Most of the world has a sense of fair play . . . I decided to explain why the rest of the world is wired the way they are."

In one scene, a bingo-playing senior, feeling chest pain and numbness in her shoulder, drives herself to the hospital, where she is treated for a heart attack and then told that her insurance won't pay because, among other things, she failed to arrive in an ambulance. A victim of a horrifying 45-mile-an-hour car crash is also denied coverage because she forgot to call during her ambulance ride to preapprove her hospital admission. "When was I supposed to call for the approval?" she protests. "While I was unconscious?"

Next a young man is denied coverage because he is too skinny while another woman is turned down because she is too fat. Moore's Canadian relatives offer a hilarious explanation of why they won't set foot in America without their own supplementary health insurance coverage. And in Ghana the director contrasts a new national health care system with far wealthier Americans who are denied medical care.

The new film also examines the medical misadventures of foreign tourists. A Canadian golfing in Florida severs a tendon and learns that the nearest hospital wants $24,000 up front for reattachment. The Canadian health care system flies him home for the same treatment and waives the bill. The patient has a hard time understanding the debate that has stalled national health care in America. In Canada, explains this political conservative, "it is not a matter of which party you are in."

Sicko also adds a new chapter to his eye-for-an-eye theory of American violence. In Norway, a country with one of the lowest murder rates in the world, he shows how chainsaw murderers, child molesters and other heinous criminals are imprisoned on an idyllic island where the guards are unarmed and accommodations could easily be mistaken for a bed and breakfast. Limiting sentences to no more than 17 years, the Norwegians have, he suggested, found a better way to administer criminal justice while reducing capital crimes.

Offering a special welcome to "the drug company salesman and people from the health insurance companies who are here tonight," the director conceded that he underestimated the difficulty of buying exhibitor's insurance for his film. When no company would write a policy for *Sicko*, production was held up for four months. Additional delays took place when Moore decided it would be difficult to credibly attack the medical insurance industry if he wasn't taking care of his own health care system. Interrupting his work to pursue a healthier diet built around fewer freedom fries, more fruits and vegetables and walking four to five miles a day helped him shed 60 pounds, news that prompted the audience to give him a round of applause.

In a career retrospective, Charles pointed out that after *Roger & Me*, there was a 13-year period "during which you are extremely busy and very prolific but you don't capture the zeitgeist" until the release of *Bowling for Columbine*. While acknowledging that the making of his sophomore slump project *Canadian Bacon* derailed his Hollywood career for a time, Moore added that after wrapping up a couple more documentary projects "in my head, I am going back to these (feature) scripts I have been working on."

As more members of the audience drifted away, Moore distracted the impatient crowd with a my leftist foot account of his forced march to a pedicure palace compliments of his wife, Kathleen Glynn. Determined to do something about his sabre-tooth toenails that could inflict bodily harm in the middle of the night, she scheduled an appointment for her husband at a salon catering to women. Horribly embarrassed, the director submitted to cutting, filing, and a foot massage. "When it was over, I thought I had new feet."

Moore's health-kick-driven delays gave the drug companies and health insurance firms more time to block a Moore invasion. One pharmaceutical firm hired a Moore look-alike who, with a film crew, acted out the director's modus operandi for employees. Another put a profiler to work on strategies to disarm the muckraker until security arrived. "The great thing about corporations," the director told his Toronto audience, "is they are full of disgruntled employees." One of them slipped the filmmaker a copy of the profiler's work, and Moore gleefully quoted it to the crowd. "Compliment him on the weight loss and ask him how he has done it. Bring up any Detroit sports team—the Tigers, the Red Wings. That will distract him."

FATHERS DON'T KNOW BEST

Michael Moore's Home Town

MICHAEL MOORE BEGAN HIS LIFE in Flint, Michigan, just like General Motors, the world's largest industrial corporation. In 1908, a buggy-maker named Billy Crapo Durant began making Buick automobiles in Flint. Durant's company started acquiring competitors, launching fledgling lines and calling itself General Motors. Among the small automakers swallowed up by the new supercompany were Lansing-based Oldsmobile, Detroit's Cadillac, the Oakland Motor Company, which became Pontiac, and another Flint company named for race car driver and automotive designer Louis Chevrolet.

By 1927 GM was selling over 1 million Chevy cars a year. In those days, people in Flint never imagined that the phrase "planned obsolescence" might apply to them. Having acquired as many of its competitors as possible, General Motors began buying up its principal suppliers—companies like Fisher Body and AC Spark Plug, which were also located in Flint. "Vertical integration," an economist's term for a business owning its own proprietary suppliers, distributors and retailers, enabled GM to outpace its competitors. Thanks to its significant edge in product lines and dealerships, GM was able to turn competing lines like Kaiser, Hudson and Studebaker into museum pieces.

In 1936, union pioneers like Michael Moore's uncle LaVerne joined the 44-day Flint sit-down strike at General Motors, a battle that made the United Auto Workers a bright star for organized labor. Michigan became the place where labor and industry broke bread over conference tables to create a new middle class. Men like General Motors CEO Charlie Wilson and the UAW's Walter Reuther were determined to chuck Karl Marx into history's dumpster. Lenin's prediction that the capitalists would "sell us the rope with which we will hang them" no longer made sense in a nation where many of the communists were suspected of being on J. Edgar Hoover's payroll.

In 1953, the year before Moore's birth, Charlie Wilson flew to Washington D.C. to face a congressional hearing. Dwight Eisenhower's nominee for Secretary of Defense was asked if there might be a possible conflict between the interests of his employer and the American military. "What is good for the country is good for General Motors and vice versa," Wilson asserted.

The memorable line, which soon morphed into "What is good for General Motors is good for the country," was certainly true for Flint. Among the beneficiaries of this hegemony were the people of Davison, Michigan, a white, middle class suburb just 47 miles north of Detroit and 12 miles east of Flint.

Moore's mother's family had arrived in the region in 1816. In 1820, his great-great-great-grandfather was the first non-Indian baby born in the Elba area east of Davison. Michael was proud of his Irish Catholic ancestry and spoke proudly of the Moores of Dublin and the Walls of Tipperary and the Connors of Cork and the Hogans of Waterford. On his desk he kept a framed copy of the $72 ticket that brought his great-grandmother out of Ireland's dire straits to the United States in 1872. Along with her two sisters and their husbands-to-be, they started at the bottom as maids and low-paid railroad employees laying new lines from Chicago into Michigan. Davison, like many small Michigan farming and lumber communities, grew up around a railroad station. It was on a main train line linking the eastern side of the state with Port Huron and Canada. Its Main Street prospered until 1894, when a fire destroyed most of downtown. Because the community was primarily insured by a company that had recently gone bankrupt, the rebuilding process was slow. By the turn of the 20th century Davison boasted a cheese factory, a creamery, a rolling mill, a bathtub plant, and a grain elevator.

As new residents moved into stately residences and smaller bungalows, Davison began to attract a professional class. Dr. William Wall, the town's first physician, settled in a two-story Main Street Victorian with his wife Elizabeth. Dr. Wall's practice flourished thanks to his reputation for treating pneumonia. He and Elizabeth attended St. John the Evangelist Catholic Church, where their daughter Veronica was baptized in 1921. A beauty and a child prodigy, Veronica graduated valedictorian at Davison High. In 1948 she met Frank Moore at a basketball game and he asked her to a movie at Flint's Capital Theater. After dating for two years the couple married in 1950 and moved into a two-story bungalow on Main Street. It was the kind of neighborhood where no one bothered locking their doors. Eager to give their children a head start, the Moores began educating their children at an early age. Michael and his sisters Anne and Veronica, were all taught to read and write before entering kindergarten. While this eased their transition into the classroom, it also led to boredom for Michael, who proved to be a step ahead of his classmates.

During the '50s Davison continued to prosper as a bedroom community for Flint's auto workers. Employees on GM's "A Plan" lived well. They could buy a new car at cost every three or four years. GM also provided generous health benefits and an attractive retirement plan. Combined with the relatively low cost of living in the Flint area, many employees considered a job in the auto business the sinecure to end all sinecures. Every day Frank Moore, Michael's father, came home from the spark plug factory at 2:30 p.m. in plenty of time to greet his children on their return from school. On a good day it was possible to play golf before dinner. His job included full benefits for the family and four weeks' vacation.

In Davison, a city known for its churches, Catholic families took a lead role in community service. They were inspired by the American Broadcasting Company's *Life Is Worth Living* starring Fulton Sheen. Dressed in full bishop regalia, Sheen would sit before a Madonna and Child statue as he appealed for salvation of the soul, reminding his audience of the church's obligation to the poor and warned of the dangers of Communism. His eyes seemed to follow the viewer around the room. When he spoke of impoverished children in the south who didn't have enough money to buy milk for lunch, viewers across the country showered him with donations. Like Soupy Sales, the famed pie-throwing television comedian who encouraged kids to reach in their parent's wallets, pull out cash and mail it to his office, Sheen knew how to raise money on the boob tube. Sheen was almost the voice of God. One look and you could tell that he knew who'd been naughty or nice.

Sheen's determination to save lost souls was heeded by Davison's sisters of St. John's, the school Moore attended. They began a program to adopt "pagan babies." Each student brought $5 to pay for the baptism of a Third World child. "One year," recalls Moore, "when sister Patricia Marie handed out the baptismal certificates as proof that our pagan babies were now cleansed of Original Sin, it turned out that one of the pagan babies had gone unclaimed. I figured the more pagans I had under my wing, the better my chances were of escaping the eternal fires of Satan's furnace." Moore ponied up another $5.

In 1962, when Moore entered third grade, St. John's began embracing new traditions created by the ongoing Vatican II council. Rome was liberalizing the church liturgy, allowing services to take place in languages other than Latin, condemning anti-Semitism and acknowledging that heaven was not exclusively reserved for Catholics. The Catholic Church no longer had a lock on the hereafter. At pajama parties, where Catholic schoolchildren had burst into tears over the realization that Protestant friends would not be able to join them in heaven, this change of dogma prompted everyone to break out the Vernor's ginger ale.

Equally important, the nuns at St. John's came from the Sisters of St. Joseph, which has a centuries-long tradition of fighting intolerance. Organized in the mid-17th century in LePuy, France, the order is committed to the service of the poor. Under the leadership of Jesuit priest Jean Pierre Medaille, the Sisters of St. Joseph flourished until the French Revolution. Refusing to renounce their vows, many sisters camouflaged themselves as lay women. Others were arrested and five were guillotined in 1807.

The order arrived in America in 1836, initially working with the deaf in St. Louis. By the time Moore enrolled at St. John's, the U.S. Federation of the Sisters of St. Joseph embraced 22 congregations.

Deeply committed to nonviolent social action, they bought shares in corporations like General Motors to fight for diversity and better wages. They organized shelters for battered women, marched for civil rights in Selma, Alabama, went on missions to help the poor in Latin America, fought capital punishment and rejected the notion that any political conflict could be resolved through warfare.

In Davison the nuns also correctly believed they could overcome limited resources. At St. John the Evangelist, Sister John Catherine quickly realized Michael was too smart for first grade and suggested double promotion. When his mother refused, fearing he would become the runt of the second-grade litter, Michael tried to sneak in. Of course, it didn't work. But Moore was inspired by the nun's confidence in his future.

The Sisters of Saint Joseph believed in their God-given ability to accomplish miracles in a packed house. With two grades sharing each overcrowded classroom, the nuns courageously taught as many as 70 children at a time. A book lover, Moore won an award from the Davison library for reading more than any other seven year old. Framed by his parents at the award ceremony Michael felt like a prince. He was an excellent student who could see beyond the superficial. One of the nuns, Sister John Catherine, quickly recognized his potential. "He is a special child," she told friends, "I have never seen anyone quite like this." Moore loved the attention. "She convinced me I was capable of anything."

Like many young boys in Catholic school, Moore was cautioned by the nuns to avoid impure thoughts. In fifth grade the boys were only allowed to head for the bathroom twice a day. One of the sisters marched the children "down a straight line and she'd come in to watch us pee, to make sure we weren't playing with ourselves. I swear it. And if it looked like you were having too much fun peeing, she'd . . . wag her finger. So one day I said, 'Sister when is an impure thought a venial sin and when is it a mortal sin?' You know venial sins you just go to purgatory and mortal sins you go to hell. And she said a venial sin is when you allow a thought to quickly pass through your head. But if you hold that thought for more than five seconds it is a mortal sin. So I spent like most of my adolescence timing my impure thoughts . . . five, four, three, two, one, oh Lucifer, here I come."

Fifth grade also marked Moore's political baptism. A friend, Doug Crim, recruited him to do door-to-door leafleting for his father, a Democrat running for the state house of representatives. On a ride through South Burton Township, Moore asked the candidate, Bobby Crim, to explain the difference between the two parties.

"The Republicans are for the rich man and the Democrats for the rest of us," explained his friend's dad on his way to defeat.

Moore's early interest in politics was coupled with his ability to pose respectful questions in a funny way that brought laughter to the classroom. This knack for providing comic relief in a serious classroom was his playful way of attracting attention. Class clown with an edge, he knew how to make his classmates laugh and even get the nuns to giggle. He also decided to start an underground paper for St. John's. Unfortunately Vatican II did not extend freedom of the press to parochial schools. A second publishing attempt failed in sixth grade. Finally, in eighth grade, Moore decided to launch his dramatic career. He attempted to produce a play about a national rat convention in St. John's Parish Hall. Moore's First-Amendment rights were trampled again and the play never made it to rehearsal. In protest, the producer persuaded some of his classmates to refuse to sing Christmas carols at the school's holiday assembly. Buckling under pressure from their watchful parents, the dissidents began singing, and Moore, who had a good singing voice, finally joined in on "Oh, Holy Night."

Proudly calling itself the "City of Flags," Davison celebrated the Fourth of July with enthusiasm. Michael led his younger sisters in a patriotic parade up and down the sidewalk, waving the flag, blowing a whistle and reciting the Pledge of Allegiance again and again. One year he won a prize at a Fourth-of-July parade for decorating his bicycle with American flags. He also won an essay contest for a piece called "What the Flag Means to Me."

During St. John's faculty meetings, the nuns often discussed the concept that teaching was more than covering the curriculum. "Do you want to leave them hungry?" Sister John Catherine asked her colleagues. Sister Janet Kurtz, who taught Moore along with 50 other students in his eighth grade classroom, believed this approach created a desire to succeed. Clearly it was working with Moore who announced one day that he wanted to become a priest. This was hardly a surprise. Sister Kurtz was convinced that Michael Moore was "the brightest student" she'd ever met in her teaching career.

Moore's eighth grade English teacher, Elsie Sinclair, also recognized the young man's talent. Married to Jack Sinclair, a General Motors lifer who had worked his way up into management, she enjoyed season tickets to the counterculture dramas of the '60s. Her son John (Davison High School Class of '59) had gone to Methodist Albion College for two years before transferring to the University of Michigan's Flint campus. In 1964 he enrolled in a master's program at Wayne State where he wrote a master's thesis on the seminal William Burroughs work, *Naked Lunch*. After completing his course work, he dropped out and formed the Detroit Artists Workshop, which promoted jazz, poetry readings and music ensembles and ran the Artists Workshop Press, a publisher of magazines and books as well as poetry and prose broadsides called free sheets. Columnist and music editor at the Fifth Estate, a local paper that helped found the Underground Press Syndicate, he was an inspiration to younger journalists who wanted to create their own underground newspapers. As a music critic he was in the center of the universe, Motown, the home of musicians like Smokey Robinson, Marvin Gaye, Aretha Franklin, The Supremes, Mary Wells and a Saginaw child star, Stevie Wonder.

While Detroit was famous for its rock scene, Sinclair was also a devotee of the city's jazz musicians such as Yusef Lateef, Donald Byrd, Elvin Jones, Hank Jones and Roland Hannah. The critic was also well known to the Detroit Police narcotics squad, who busted him in 1964 and again in 1965, when he served six months at the Detroit House of Corrections. In January 1967, shortly after moving in to the Trans Love Energies commune, he and 55 other young people were arrested in a police raid. While the case moved forward, he created a booking coop for local rock groups and began managing the legendary MC 5. Back home, old friends and family never knew if they were going to be reading about Sinclair's exploits in the entertainment section or the police blotter. But either way, he was quickly becoming the most important poet and musician to come out of Davison, Michigan.

Some of the neighbors John Sinclair left behind despised his politics. Michael Moore knew a number of these people also believed that a young upstart should not be allowed to publish his own underground newspaper. In Davison, some people did a good job of hiding their biases. But sooner or later the worst of them made it clear they weren't color-blind when it came to human rights.

The idealism of Moore's teachers and his parents was not always shared by others in the St. John's parish. On April 4, 1968, Moore joined his parents for Holy Thursday mass at the church. As he left the service, one of the parents, who had headed out ahead of the crowd to warm up his car, returned with a radio bulletin. "They just shot Martin Luther King." Moore was stunned to hear a cheer go up. "As a 13 year-old I couldn't understand why anyone would cheer the killing of another person."

King's assassination and the June 1968 assassination of Robert F. Kennedy in Los Angeles in the midst of his primary campaign for the Democratic presidential nomination silenced two of the nation's most important progressive voices. Even though Kennedy had agreed to wiretap King at the behest of his nemesis, FBI Director J. Edgar Hoover, these two martyrs inspired young people to further their causes in different ways.

Shortly after the Kennedy assassination, a pair of firebombings prompted John Sinclair to move his Trans Love Energies commune to Ann Arbor, where he cofounded the White Panther Party with Pun Plamondon. Back home in Davison some of Elsie Sinclair's friends asked about her son's new political organization operating on an "everything free for everybody" platform. The party's unofficial publication, the Ann Arbor *Argus,* helped spread the caucasian Panther gospel around Michigan and to sister chapters across the country. "This high-powered LSD-fueled, red-hot rock & roll guerilla fighting unit used dadaist technique, satire, rants . . . and post-modernist terminology in their all-out blast to crush the rancid walls of hypocrisy and the repressive war-mongering authority control," says Sinclair's biographer, Cary Loren. ". . . It soon became a movement too extremist for its own good and lost its support base."

Instead of dabbling in the counterculture, trying drugs or simply sharing beers with his teenage friends, Michael Moore began thinking about religious life. In the fall of 1968 he entered St. Paul's seminary in nearby Saginaw. Although he was inspired by the Berrigan brothers' antiwar activism and the many sacrifices of United Farm Workers organizer Cesar Chavez in California's Central Valley, Moore quickly realized that there were limits to liberation theology.

Another challenge was the young women imported from a nearby Catholic high school to fill vacant chairs in the St. Paul orchestra. The only coeducational program at the seminary, it made Moore feel like he was sitting next to a bag of Tostitos. When financial problems forced the school to close at the end of the school year, a number of Moore's classmates transferred to other seminaries. Not sure he wanted to join them, the young man went to one of the fathers for spiritual advice.

"That's fine," he was told, "because we were going to ask you not to come back . . . You ask too many questions."

Moore decided to pursue a secular education in the Davison Public Schools. Back home he quickly rose in the Boy Scout ranks, receiving his Eagle Scout badge at 15. His community service project focused on pollution in the Davison area, much of it coming from the region's auto industry.

"He gets the point across quicker than anything I know," said Davison City Council member Robert R. Davis after watching a Moore slide show featuring abandoned car wrecks, littered road shoulders, polluted streams, and smoke belching out of Flint factories to drift east over Davison.

Not long after his slide show, Moore traveled to the American Legion-sponsored Wolverine Boys State conference in East Lansing. There he received a plaque for the best speech on Abraham Lincoln's life.

"The Elks sponsored this contest," he said in his acceptance speech to a crowd of over 300, "and don't permit blacks to join their organization. Then they come here to Boys' State and sponsor a speech contest on Abraham Lincoln, a man who was to free the blacks." What about the whites-only policy, asked an Associated Press reporter. After clarifying that the contest was staged by Boys State and not the fraternal organization itself, an Elks spokesperson explained, "The White Caucasian membership policy of the Elks is set by the parent organization, and no change can be made at the state or local level."

The story made the Associated Press wire and Moore received a call from *CBS Evening News*. He turned down an offer for an interview because even an ocean of Clearasil lotion wouldn't take care of his acne. Institutional racism would become a subject of continuing interest at a local Freedom School that Moore helped organize. And at Davison High, he convinced classmates to give up on the idea of homecoming floats in favor of donating money to UNICEF. A related pitch to dump the "sexist" concept of a homecoming queen flopped.

The national media attention to Moore's Elks speech hinted that he was on his way to becoming the second most important counterculture figure in the history of Davison, Michigan. Although he didn't do drugs, Michael Moore reminded local people of John Sinclair, now serving ten years in Jackson State Prison for giving two joints to an undercover agent. Sinclair's prison poetry flowed nonstop as he paid for his legal defense with a series of rock and roll fund raisers. On December 10, 1971 a crowd of 15,000 filled the University of Michigan's Crisler Arena for a "Free John Now" Rally led by John Lennon, Yoko Ono, Stevie Wonder, Allen Ginsberg, Phil Ochs, Archie Shepp, Jerry Rubin and Bob Seger.

Lennon, making his first solo American concert appearance, had been advocating psychedelic drugs and meditation as the mainline to personal liberation. But now he was drifting back into political action. The Ann Arbor rally was a dress rehearsal for a planned series of Lennon-led anti-Vietnam rock and roll rallies that would climax during a political Woodstock at Tricky Dick Nixon's 1972 Republican National Convention.

The highlight of the Crisler Arena evening was Lennon's song, "John Sinclair." Among the rock critics on hand were a matched pair of FBI agents who wrote in a confidential memo to J. Edgar Hoover that Yoko Ono "can't even remain on key." They suggested that the song "probably will become a million seller . . . but it is lacking Lennon's usual standards." Apparently this view was not shared on the Michigan Supreme Court bench in Lansing. Three days after Sinclair's super rally, the justices struck down the state's "unconstitutional" marijuana laws, reversed his conviction and ordered his release.

While Sinclair moved ahead to organize the Rainbow People's Party and promoted alternative music, his mother began sending newspaper clippings about one of her favorite students, Michael Moore. The class clown and debate club veteran decided to take advantage of a new state law that allowed 18-year-olds to run for public office. Eager to channel his frustration with the school board into political action, he decided to nominate himself. He ran a winning campaign on a fire-the-principal platform, capturing young voters as seven other adult candidates split the rest of the electorate. The principal resigned during Moore's first year on the board. After he died of a heart attack, Moore fondly remembered the Davison's educator's many kindnesses to children growing up in the community.

The new board member's tendency to sit on the floor shoeless during meetings rather than take a chair irritated some of his colleagues on the board. But the real problem was a ban on recording devices. After threatening to sue the board over this issue, Moore won permission to tape the meetings.

Another problem was a Michael Moore play that partially financed a Davison High senior class trip. Some members of the audience perceived the play as anti-Christian. For instance, board member Jack Kennedy, a local insurance agent, was troubled by scenes where Christ fell from the cross and was pushed off stage by young actors resembling Davison residents Moore disliked. Kennedy also decried the scenes where Christ was renailed to the cross and the disciples were cussed out. "I can't believe the people of this community would allow something like this in our high school," complained Kennedy.

"I just wanted to make people think," the ambitious playwright told the board. "I wanted people to think if they really are good Christians."

Kennedy and other angry Davison leaders began talking about a recall campaign. Moore agreed to answer questions about his tenure on the school board before a standing room crowd of more than 200 citizens at a local bank. It was the first time he had faced a large hostile audience. Critics peppered him with questions about American Civil Liberties Union backing his lawsuit on recording board meetings, his play, and his informal dress. His Davison High teachers had trained him well. He actually seemed to like being controversial, not to mention the center of attention. Moore dressed in jeans and a sport shirt, his long hair brushing his collar, offered impressive answers that calmed his opponents. Well, some of them.

The recall campaign reflected political divisions within the Davison community. One of his critics, Donald Priehs, taught Moore's government class. Priehs was ultimately fired, and he assigned much of the blame to Moore. "He's always been ugly, fat, and obnoxious, a troubled child with no close friends to speak of."

Moore's performance at the bank temporarily sidelined the recall campaign. But two months later, after the young trustee's lawsuit ended the board's practice of conducting private meetings, the campaign regained momentum. With the support of the Genesee County Democratic Party, Moore fought back against recall leader Kennedy, then campaigning for a seat on the Richfield Township board of trustees.

At a candidate's night meeting, the young school board member called his nemesis a hypocrite. How, he wanted to know, could Kennedy object to four-letter words used in Moore's play when he used the same words himself. Kennedy quickly made a distinction between swearing privately and using the Lord's name in vain during a play for children.

"It may sound corny, but whether it's in front of children or in front of only one other person, the one whose name you took in vain is listening," Moore said, leaving Kennedy with a look on his face as if he'd just swallowed a frog.

It was a perfect example of Moore's ability to target his most articulate opponents. He had learned how to persuade them to defeat their own arguments. At the end of the four-hour meeting, Wilbert Zirnhelt, chairman of the Democratic Club, said he had known Moore since he was nine and suggested that the 20-year-old was "beyond time as far as intelligence goes. He's picked on because he's no yes-man. If I have anything to do with it, this boy's going to be elected again."

In September Moore sued to block the recall election, arguing that some of the signatures on the recall petition were forged. He complained that the recall campaign was actually motivated by his opposition to expensive new athletic facilities, over the top administrative salaries, and the awarding of no-bid contracts. Moore told the voters, "If there is anything I've learned in Davison, it's that ignorance breeds fear, and fear breeds hatred." Predictions of a low vote on special election day shortly before Christmas 1974 were wrong. The citizens of Davison, Michigan lined up for the biggest school board election turnout in city history. Moore's followers gathered in the Central Elementary school gym. (He had lost the battle to rename it after Dr. Martin Luther King, Jr.) Across the court were the recall leaders carefully watching the vote. The young board member's supporters, including a large group of student smokers spared suspension thanks to Moore's efforts, sat for more than two hours until an assistant superintendent announced that the recall had lost.

After the recall campaign was defeated, Moore called a press conference to forgive his opponents. His legal expenses were picked up by the Genesee County Democrats, thanks in part to the support of local chairman Larry Stecco. A key source for this contribution was bingo fundraisers staged by the Democrats. Moore also made it a point to avoid patronizing local shops run by his enemies. "You know in my town the small businesses that everyone wanted to protect? They were the people that supported all the right-wing groups. They were the Republicans in the town, they were in the Kiwanis, the Chamber of Commerce—people that kept the town all white. The small hardware salesman, the small clothing store salespersons, Jesse the Barber who signed his name three different times on three different petitions to recall me from the school board. Fuck all these small businesses—fuck 'em all! Bring in the chains. The small businesspeople are the rednecks that run the town and suppress people."

Determined to serve his hometown in a new way, Moore was busy organizing the Davison Hotline, a Catholic service agency housed at the vacant St. John's Convent where his grade-school teachers had once lived. Furthering the spirit of the nuns who served Davison's Catholic community, Moore trained a team of 15 volunteers, including a social work student named Rachel Haneline. She was impressed by his creativity, work ethic and management skills but noticed that Moore quickly lost patience with people who disagreed with his strategies. "He didn't work well with people who didn't want to do things his way. Michael's ego was a problem."

But another volunteer, Flint high school senior Dan Kildee, saw Michael as a natural leader, someone who knew how to inspire young people and run a nonprofit. "In any dynamic society, someone has to be on that far edge, pushing things so that in some way they become marginalized. If everyone had to play within the boundaries that currently are in effect there wouldn't be any dramatic change."

Moore, living at home when Kildee first met him, was in the midst of one of the political battles that characterized his baptism into local politics. One of his biggest problems was county officials who cut off the Hotline's $30,000 grant for drug counseling. Instead of hiring on at General Motors, he sought alternate funding and encouraged other young people to seek political office. When Kildee decided, at age 18 to run for the Flint school board, Moore came up with $100 for his campaign. "He had no money and I told him this was way too much. But he insisted on giving me that check and also chipped in with graphics for my campaign literature."

The second 18-year-old to win elective office in Genesee County, Kildee wasn't nearly as demonstrative as Moore. "Michael made me look like Winston Churchill. Consequently I was able to be pretty effective on a number of issues. Michael knocked the door down at the Davison School Board. While I was singled out and ostracized, it wasn't anything like what he did. He had this unique ability to color outside the lines."

The Hotline opened at a time when Flint was beginning to experience significant layoffs in the automobile industry. New challenges from Japanese automakers had begun to erode the market share of General Motors and the other US automakers. Japanese cars were more reliable, spent less time in the shop and tended to outlast American vehicles. While GM, Ford and Chrysler slowly copied Japanese innovations like disc brakes, it was hard for these companies to abandon the idea that their customers didn't want to trade in their vehicles every three years.

In 1973 the Organization of Petroleum Exporting Countries (OPEC) embargoed oil exports to the United States to protest American support of Israel in the Yom Kippur War. Long lines at the pump and escalating prices encouraged the sale of smaller, more fuel-efficient imported vehicles at the expense of American nameplates. Michigan's Big Three automakers were gradually beginning to shift production to suppliers in non-union states or foreign countries, at the expense of traditional plants like the GM factories in Flint.

A major source of calls to the Hotline was the community's unemployed population, who needed health care, food and shelter. In 1974, the year sophomore Moore quit the University of Michigan, claiming that a campus parking shortage had pushed him over the edge, the Davison School Board agreed to lease a former school to the Hotline. Walk-in counseling, a shelter for runaways, pregnancy testing, and transactional analysis classes were added to the center, as well as programs on rape prevention, birth control and student rights. With funding from IBM, the Hotline also added a library.

When the Genesee County substance abuse program slashed funding for the controversial Hotline, Moore raised donations from many Davison households as well as a benefit events including a showing of the Vietnam War documentary *Hearts and Minds*. Another fundraiser was a play about American political and moral corruption—written by Michael Moore.

In June 1976, the school board refused to renew the Hotline lease, and the group moved into office space donated by a local physician. The following year, after Moore's lost his bid for reelection to the school board, he decided to move the Hotline to Burton, a suburban community sandwiched between Davison and Flint. But attempts to relocate to a two-story bungalow were initially blocked by the Burton City Council. Community leaders argued that it was a socialist front distributing subversive literature and promoting, among other things, the right of children to divorce their parents and receive alimony benefits. Although the city backed down after Moore threatened a lawsuit, tight zoning conditions quickly put the Hotline in hot water. A Genesee County judge issued a contempt citation after the nonprofit refused to erect a five-foot-high, 213-foot-long concrete masonry wall separating its home office from the surrounding community. Under protest, Moore agreed to build the wall.

"This is not Berlin, it is Burton," protested Moore. "But the concept remains the same—build a wall so that individual expression can be contained and suppressed . . . We are tired of the constant harassment from politicians and self-righteous individuals who wrap themselves in the flag and 'with God on their side' proceed to spew their venom on the Hotline. As I sit and listen to the hostile crowds at the Burton City Council meetings . . . or is it the Davison School Board or the County Commission or . . . as they viciously scream and violently applaud one more member of their pack who has stood up to denounce the Hotline as subversive . . . radical . . . and a menace, it dawns on me that I've seen these people before!

"Despite all attempts to cut off our funds and close us up, we remain open, stronger than ever, with over 800 persons a month making use of our services, thousands of dollars being donated by average citizens. For those who oppose us so passionately, here is the secret of closing the Hotline for good. Start communicating with your children, deal with people on a feeling level, work to improve your self-concept, respect the rights of others, and love your neighbor as yourself. If you would spend one-tenth of the time on this as you do spreading your poison and hatred, our center would be empty. It is time to tear down walls, not build new ones."

Moore added that the Hotline was rethinking the community's approach to charitable giving and employment development. "We're planning to start an alternative to the United Way. It will be called The Other Way and will help people and those agencies that help people without the support of the United Way or other funding. And we're considering an 'alternative' Chamber of Commerce too."

After a long legal skirmish, 1,200 cinder blocks were delivered to the Hotline center and left in the backyard. But just before the masons arrived to construct the wall, the two parties compromised on a less-expensive chain link fence. Moore's critics continued to charge that the center was little more than a front for abortion referrals, political subversion and books promoting anarchy in the schoolyard—and that was before they received their first copy of the Hotline's alternative community newspaper, *Free To Be,* in the fall of 1977. The Hotline home, purchased for less than $20,000, was now a publishing office. Finally Michael Moore was going to be able to write and edit without the burden of prior restraint. Or as peer counselor Kildee explained to friends, "we are discovering that this community is a closed political environment. Rather than only working downstream on behalf of people who are facing individual problems, let's work upstream to create a more civil environment."

Moore's confrontations with the city fathers convinced some of his closest friends that his talents would take him well beyond Genesee County. Among the believers was Dan Kildee: "Davison is a fairly conservative community, and Michael just probably challenged people beyond their ability to be challenged. It's been said that leadership is the ability to disappoint your supporters at a rate they can absorb. Michael wouldn't accept that as the definition of leadership. Some people have to be willing to push people beyond their ability to absorb the message. That is what Michael did. He shook things up where he obviously had an impact, but he ended up being the victim of his own willingness to put himself at risk."

20 YEARS OF SCHOOL AND
THEY DON'T PUT YOU ON THE DAY SHIFT

"The Flint Voice stole their name from a newspaper in New York because of their belief in ripping off anything that looks good and isn't hard to spell."

—Flint Voice *Ad, September 1982*

THE DAVISON HOTLINE gradually became a center of political activism in Flint, sponsoring community forums like a "Student Rights Night" and an appearance by three Flint teachers fired for refusing to cross a picket line. On the print side, the new publication was supported in part by the largess of Harry Chapin, the singer-songwriter known for such songs as "Cat's in the Cradle" and "Dance Band on the Titanic."

Known for his generous support of social activism, Chapin had first met Moore at a 1977 concert in Grand Rapids. Moore sneaked backstage and reached the singer's dressing room before a cop put a hand on his shoulder and asked, "Where do you think you're going?" Hearing the noise outside his dressing room, Chapin opened his door and invited Moore inside for a brief talk. Within minutes the singer agreed to the first of a series of benefits that would raise more than $200,000 for the Hotline center and the new publication that would provide Michael Moore with his first job in journalism since his days as a paperboy for the Davison Index. He was now editor and publisher of the *Flint Voice*. His inspiration for this publication was a San Francisco magazine that always gave him a good feeling when it arrived in the mail, *Mother Jones*. His goal was to make the new publication "the *Mother Jones* of Michigan" a muckraking paper that "took on the powers-that-be."

"We believe the commonly accepted notion of 'objective' journalism is a lie," declared the new paper's statement of purpose. "News isn't objective. Events don't exist in a vacuum. Any publication or electronic news media claiming to be objective is deluding not only itself, but its readers, listeners or viewers as well."

In Flint Moore was up against a formidable competitor, the Newhouse chain that controlled newspapers in eight of the state's largest cities. Starting a weekly with virtually no national advertising and a small retail advertising basis meant donations would be critical to keeping the *Voice* alive. Shoehorned into basement quarters below the Hotline offices, the *Voice* was typically the product of round-the-clock editorial marathons that lasted up to four days. While counselors upstairs persuaded desperate callers to abandon thoughts of suicide, head for help at a battered women's shelter or an Alcoholics Anonymous meeting, the *Voice* staff took a holistic approach to putting the Flint diaspora on the road to better days.

Moore's editorial strategy was simple. Instead of worrying about advertising he focused on creating a unique paper that would draw financial support beyond the local community. Instead of punching in at Buick every morning, he had a desk job with much longer hours, lower pay and worse benefits than his friends on the factory line. The *Voice* exposed teacher assaults on Davison students and published a teenagers' guide to birth control. (Although the author was down on the withdrawal method, he pointed out that "if you find yourself wanting to have intercourse, and you have no birth control, and the drugstores are closed . . . using withdrawal is always better than using nothing at all.")

The publication also took on police brutality, accused Israel of slaughtering Lebanese and Palestinians and denounced Michigan-based Amway and chemical companies that poisoned cattle feed with PCBs. But its number-one target was General Motors. Moore staved off creditors as he struggled to pay for Hotline services, print the *Voice* and work toward the day when "people will feel good enough about themselves to stop all forms of self-destructive behavior."

Al Hirvela, one of the editors who joined the *Voice*'s basement paste-up marathons, recalls that "in the early days we were like a Ramones album—three primitive chords and minimal but somehow listenable melodies. Later we were like, say an R.E.M. record with a cleaner, leaner sound." As the paper grew, Moore took to looping Jackson Browne at a deafening volume. At the end of their sleepless subterranean round-the-clock shifts closing an issue, staffers staggered home unable to get "Running on Empty" or "The Pretender" out of their heads.

This undercapitalized publication benefited from the talents of young writers like Alex Kotlowitz, who would go on to work for the *Wall Street Journal* and publish a classic study of Chicago poverty, *There Are No Children Here*. He took a tough stand against Flint's decision to try to revive local tourism by building a downtown theme park called Auto World.

Victims of the *Voice*'s local coverage quickly sought revenge. A story attacking the Genesee County Board of Commissioners for spending travel money on junkets to Hawaii and Miami Beach and for awarding no-bid contracts to relatives prompted Commissioner Eugene Kovacs to demand that the state's attorney general shut the *Voice* down. How, he asked, could the nonprofit Hotline legally publish such a paper "cutting up good people in public office?"

As the city's double-digit unemployment rose to 24 percent, Moore continued to look for new ways to crusade against the company that employed his father and members of his extended family for decades. A popular target was GM Chairman Roger Smith, who had recently received a $1.5 million bonus in the middle of a serious automotive recession. The paper was also quick to contrast GM's hefty profits with unemployment lines.

By profiling Flint's worst neighborhood, a short stroll from the handsome new Hyatt Regency Hotel on the Flint River, Moore hoped to prod city officials into corrective action. Mainstream media gradually began to take notice of the *Voice*'s work. A Moore story criticizing the Mayor for using CETA employees in his reelection campaign triggered a city-sponsored ombudsman's report. A copy of this document was leaked to the *Voice*, which set the story in type before its official release. This led to a police invasion of the paper's printer and an attempt to stop the presses. Moore claimed the *Voice*'s First Amendment rights had been violated. The story was published by the *New York Times*, *Time* magazine, CBS and the Associated Press wire service. The *Detroit Free Press* also published a favorable feature on the muckraking paper, written by *Voice* contributor Alex Kotlowitz.

For staffers like Kildee who was pressed into service as a copy editor even though he had no concept of what a copy editor actually did, the *Voice* was a happening place. "When I was going to the U of M Flint I would always head over there between classes. It was a fun environment. There were a lot of people who thought like me which was important at a time when I was trying to figure out what I thought." Editing copy with red felt pens, pasting labels on new issues and mailing them off to subscribers, Kildee knew that each issue would spark controversy. "A lot of people related to it and it also made a lot of people mad. But everyone read it. That is where Michael's art has always been effective. Michael holds up a mirror that has a bias, it's slightly distorted. It motivates people to do something. Michael or any other artist or journalist is not someone who should be held responsible for what everyone believes. He is getting people to think about things they would rather not think about. His role is to say what a lot of people have on their mind. The first thing a messenger like Michael has to do is to get people to realize something is wrong.

With pro bono legal assistance, as well as donations from Flint and around the state, the paper continued to make news. Harry Chapin worked overtime for the *Voice*, driving all the way down from an afternoon appearance in the Upper Peninsula to make his evening Flint commitments. Not only did he refuse expenses, but the singer always bought Moore's gas after the editor ran out of fuel while the two were en route to the Detroit Airport. Chapin also tried to mentor Moore in the ways of the business world. When the editor/publisher cut off his shoulder-length hair and discarded it, the singer criticized him. Plenty of people in Davison would have paid for a lock, Chapin suggested.

While Chapin tunes kept the *Voice* alive, the business staff worked hard to attract new subscribers. Readers willing to display *Voice* bumper stickers were eligible to win Windjammer cruises in the Bahamas, membership in a health and racquetball club, or a Honda moped (a vehicle that added fuel to the debate over the paper's loyalty to the local auto industry).

As the paper flourished editorially, generous media celebrities like Gloria Steinem and columnist Murray Kempton donated to his Flint cause. And following Chapin's lead, Peter Yarrow threw a fundraising party for the paper at his New York apartment. His folk trio, the legendary Peter, Paul and Mary, performed a Michigan benefit for the paper that included a special VIP reception aimed at retiring the *Voice*'s debts. When a check for several hundred dollars showed up from folk singer Joan Baez, Moore was so delighted he kept it around the office to impress friends. Baez insisted that he cash the donation and sent along a second check that made a perfect souvenir.

While Joan Baez had declined Moore's request to sing for the *Voice*'s supper, another rock star was on the phone to the editor after he learned in the *New York Times* that the paper's printing plates had been seized by local police. According to Moore, the celebrity "wanted to do the benefit" for the *Voice* and 15-year-old William Taylor, who had been shot by Flint Police. "He suggested the Silverdome in Pontiac or Crisler Arena in Ann Arbor." But on December 8, 1980, plans were cancelled when the star, John Lennon, was shot outside his New York apartment by a crazed fan.

"All We Are Saying Is Give Peace A Chance," sang 800 Flint fans during a candlelight memorial procession down Saginaw Street to Riverbank Park. Cosponsored by the *Voice,* the event was emceed by Moore, who said, "I'm sick and tired of this 'lone nut' scenario. We've remembered what John Lennon said. Don't trust authority. Ask questions. Be an individual. Stand up and fight."

Lennon's death led indirectly to the discovery of star reporter Ben ("Squeezing Rivets Is Fun") Hamper, an auto worker with a self confessed drinking problem and an occasional habit of smoking marijuana at lunch. The editor gave him a call after the writer had taken issue with a Flint Journal columnist who suggested Lennon's murderer had done America a favor by silencing the British pied piper trying to subvert the nation's youth. "I make my living turning bolts in the factory," wrote Hamper. "Being a devoted Lennon fan, I'm suddenly discouraged to realize that, had I avoided this scoundrel's music, I could have been a real success in some lofty vocation."

In his new *Voice* column the auto worker claimed that his ancestors had been "just waiting around for Henry Ford to invent the assembly line." Hamper testified to the physical and mental abuse of workers who actually had to build cars every day at GM. Reading his column made it sound as if auto workers secretly dreamed about being laid off and collecting unemployment. Moore himself had never actually worked on an assembly line. Hamper, now known as Rivethead, demonstrated that the *Voice* wasn't one-sided. Despite Jane Fonda's heroic work for liberal causes, the paper's token working class writer dismissed her as a "pest" who "changes her battle flags as often as most people changes their skivvies." Jane Fonda was not the only liberal icon targeted by the *Voice* team. Moore was delighted to go after the left and the leftover left. "The children of the '80s don't need Bob Dylan," wrote the publisher, who dismissed the singer as a "burned-out folkie" he would never pay to see again. (Years later, in his documentary film *The Big One,* Moore would perform a dead-on impersonation of Dylan singing "The Times They Are A'Changin'" in a duet with Cheap Trick rocker Rick Nielsen.)

Moore even belittled the generation Dylan presumably represented. "When I hear a high school student, say, 'I sure would have liked to grow up in the Sixties,' I tell them that young people then were more apathetic than they are now." To prove his point, Moore published a story on Students for a Democratic Society, created in 1962 at a Port Huron Union Auto Workers camp and shut down seven years later at a "National War Council" in Flint. The group's decision to go underground and stage "complete guerilla warfare" and the backlash it generated meant the left would have a much more difficult time opposing the Vietnam war, the draft, and university investments in South Africa. "Examples of the immense vacuum created by SDS's absence, particularly after the shootings at Kent State and Jackson State universities, are easy to find," the publisher wrote. "One can't help but wonder how different things might be today had SDS not lost control of itself."

Moore's attacks on the left were quickly becoming a warmup act for his new star, rock critic Ben Hamper, who went for the aorta of American popular culture. Rivethead stunned readers with his assault on "hired tongues" like Bruce Springsteen, the would be "construction worker (The River"), garage mechanic ("I'm on Fire"), minor league batting instructor ("Glory Days") . . . Let assembly workers sing about assembly lines . . . no more Bruciemania . . . No more false prophets."

In late 1981 Chapin died in a New York car accident. A tireless advocate for the Flint paper and other worthy causes, the singer was an irreplaceable friend of Moore and his staff. Chapin's sons continued to stage benefits, and Harry's music remained the paper's unofficial anthem. And for Moore personally, Chapin's words and music were a source of inspiration that helped him stay the course as his hometown continued to decline.

The Houston Post, with its hotly sought-after help-wanted section, was showing significant circulation gains in Flint. "Every time the Detroit Tigers play an away game," said Moore in a poignant story about his town's decline, "the failure of our economic system is inadvertently being shown along with the double plays and stolen bases. The thousands of former friends, neighbors and families filling the stands are a not-so-subtle reminder that all of us are expendable and can be traded from the north to the south as easily as a Dave Rosema can be sent from the Tigers to the Rangers."

To compensate for the circulation decline and the loss of Chapin's contributions, the *Voice* began charging 25 cents—a decision that cut circulation by 50 percent. One-third of the paper's subscribers now lived outside the Flint area. The leading donor, Stewart Mott, who even matched some contributions, lived in New York.

Fortunately the *Voice*'s deficit did not diminish the quality of the paper. One memorable piece profiled racial discrimination against a Howard Johnson job applicant. A state investigation led to a $30,000 judgment in favor of the plaintiff. The *Voice* also helped organize protests against Henry Kissinger, published Moore's reportage from Nicaragua and revealed how General Motors collaborated with Hitler's Third Reich. To make sure coverage didn't appear one-sided, the paper also attacked organized labor. Unlike many writers on the left, he believed that union leaders were often guilty of fronting for the special interests of corporate criminals. In his mind labor appeared to be as culpable as management. A Moore column ridiculed United Auto Workers President Owen Bieber for contract givebacks totaling millions in annual worker pay.

THE VOICE OVER ESCANABA

"Michael Moore is the man who hates everything."
> —*Johnny Burke, WTRX, Flint*

IN THE WINTER OF 1983 the *Flint Voice* became the *Michigan Voice*. Suddenly alternative coverage was available monthly in Escanaba, Hell, Climax, Hodunk and Bliss. "The *Michigan Voice* covers the news ignored by the daily media and has made its mark by uncovering wrongdoing and corruption," applauded *Mother Jones* magazine in San Francisco. Unfortunately, advertising revenues failed to cover operating costs for the 25,000 copies given away. Despite the help of over 300 volunteers, the paper went $2,000 deeper in the hole every month. With debts hitting the $15,000 level, Moore justified charging for the paper and selling subscriptions by explaining that "bill collectors have installed their own waiting room at our office."

Moore's decision to go statewide did not make good business sense to one of his role models, John Sinclair. Now the state coordinator of the Michigan chapter of the National Organization for the Reform of Marijuana Laws, Sinclair was hosting a number of jazz shows on stations like Detroit's WDET and Ann Arbor's WCBN. Although the White Panther Party and the Ann Arbor Sun had shut down, he was filled with admiration for younger Flint journalists eager to provide an alternative voice. "By 1977 it was over for underground papers with left wing content. Most of the people of my generation had given up. The *Flint Voice* was great, but I didn't see how they could make it statewide. They were spread so far out. It was going to be hard to get advertising from Lansing or Detroit, where a new paper, the *Metro Times,* was starting up. When Michael came to talk to me about creating the *Michigan Voice,* I told him it probably wasn't going to work even though I admired what he was doing."

By now the *Voice* was benefiting from the artistry of Kathleen Glynn, a fellow Irish Catholic and the eldest of five children. Her father worked in GM management and, like Moore, she was a prodigy. After graduating Flint's Kearsley High School a year early, she enrolled at Western Michigan University, just minutes from the Sisters of St. Joseph Mother House. Glynn left college after a year, returned to Flint and began working as a graphic designer. One evening in the summer of 1977, she went to watch her boss play at a slow pitch softball game. On hand was one of his friends, Wallace Rose, a Vietnam vet working at a local welding company. Rose was impressed by 19-year-old Glynn and her sharp new car. After dating for nearly four years, Glynn and Rose married in early 1981. Glynn gave birth to their daughter, Natalie, in July of that year and then headed back to work at Jiffy Printing. Rose tried and failed to convince his wife to become a stay-at-home mom. Their rift widened when Glynn took on additional work at the *Michigan Voice,* a paper Rose had never read. The couple separated in the fall of 1982, and Kathleen moved to an apartment in East Village near the Flint Cultural Center. As her work load at the *Voice* increased, Glynn considered starting her own graphic design business. And she began going out with the *Voice* publisher.

As Moore's and Glynn's office romance flourished, readers around the state enjoyed the feisty paper, now with its new color covers and added pages. Some were put off by attacks on Michigan right-to-life icons such as Tom Monaghan, who focused his life on "God, family and Domino's Pizza." A number of readers suggested that the paper's focus on human rights and justice for all was really a smokescreen for its hidden mission, turning the publisher into a media deity.

One subscriber wrote, "If the paper becomes successful and takes its rightful place with all its papers in the grocery checkout line, Mike Moore can finally attain his desired status in life, the new Rupert

Murdoch."

The notion that the *Voice*—or Moore, with his $12,000 a year salary—might be going anywhere financially was a standing joke at the newspaper's Lapeer Road office. Jerry Rubin had become a stockbroker. Leftist Jane Fonda was making exercise videos even the right could relate to. How much chance could a leftist publication stand in a media market dominated by a handful of corporations like Newhouse and Knight Ridder. Sure, the *Voice* was allowed to publish Doonesbury abortion strips that had been killed by Gary Trudeau's syndicate. But the *Voice* couldn't publish Doonesbury regularly because the strips appeared in competing papers.

Unlike many editors of similar publications, Moore was reluctant to dumb down his paper. To him weeklies belonging to the Association of Alternative Newspapers were a "hit on the white wine and brie circuit because they run the obligatory story on nuclear freeze between the articles on tanning huts and gourmet cookie shops." Moore was also down on the "well-meaning but boring, predictable left publications. With these magazines if you read the headline, you don't need to read the story. If you do decide to read it, get out the No-Doze. Making it through their polemics is obviously a test of your commitment to the movement."

Moore's editorial influences leaned toward publications like *Mother Jones*, the *Village Voice, Rock-n-Roll Confidential*, Alexander Cockburn in *The Nation* and a few local underground papers. "I like them because they're brash, innovative, irreverent and gutsy. They give me information I can't get elsewhere. And they're just fun to read."

One of the most popular features in Moore's own paper was nostalgic "where are they now" stories about '60s icons, leftists who hadn't sold out. Young readers of the '80s were introduced to '60s geezers like Abbie Hoffman, who told how the FBI hired a psychologist to analyze him. "The government paid him $25,000 to say that I was an exhibitionist. I would've confessed for $200." From time to time the paper's antics did attract new readers with a legal background. Among them was an attorney who filed suit on behalf of the Good Times Lounge, a biker palace. "What this place lacks in ambience it makes up in ambulance," wrote Hamper, who was relieved when the plaintiff dropped his suit, closed up the lounge and headed for Alaska.

The paper also began attracting more national publicity. Alex Kotlowitz, now working for the *Wall Street Journal,* returned home to do a front-page story on blue-collar writers, featuring Rivethead with a sketch Hamper's girlfriend characterized as "a Korean version of Dick Nixon." Soon a *60 Minutes* producer was treating Hamper to lunch at the Hyatt Regency. When asked how he would handle an interview with correspondent Harry Reasoner, Hamper replied: "I'd make sure that I was drunk."

Although the *60 Minutes* piece never ran, visiting journalists were impressed by *Voice* stories on subjects like the return of the draft board, Senator Carl Levin's opposition to automotive air bags, and a Michigan corporate hall of shame featuring Amway's Jay VanAndel, who settled Canadian charges of import duty fraud for $118 million, as well as exploding-Pinto king Henry Ford II. Readers learned how General Motors had torn down Hamtramck's Poletown and evicted several thousands residents to build a Cadillac plant that would ultimately fail to revitalize the community's economy. And they followed travel writer Moore's trip to Bitburg, Germany, with a Flint resident who had survived Auschwitz. While President Reagan laid a wreath on the grave of a German soldier, they unfurled a banner at the cemetery's entrance reading:

> WE CAME FROM MICHIGAN TO REMIND YOU
> THEY MURDERED MY FAMILY

Moore would have been arrested on the spot, were it not for the fact that he had asked ABC's Pierre Salinger to photograph the escapade. Eager not to make themselves look bad on camera, security officials simply escorted Moore from the site.

His story "Bonzo Goes to Bitburg, or How We Spent Sunday in the Graveyard with Ronnie" was characterized as a "one-man act of defiance against an insensitive president." Like other demonstrations—a protest that led to the closing of a nuclear power plant in nearby Midland comes to mind—the Ronald Reagan coverage was part of the *Voice*'s campaign to build its reputation outside Michigan. Moore's iconoclasm demonstrated his gift for taking on the right and the left in the same sentence. Eager to explain why Democrats were not likely to lead America out of the geopolitical wilderness, he told the story of his friend's father, Bobby Crim, who tried to convince fifth grader Moore that Republicans always fronted for the rich. After losing that first campaign, Crim won and moved up to Speaker of the Michigan House of Representatives. Then the Democrat retired to become a lobbyist for the state's leading utility, a Who's Who of big money interests, Consumers Energy.

Like Henry Wallace, Harold Stassen and Ralph Nader, Moore argued that the dominant parties were merely shadowboxing as they spent the nation's democratic inheritance. He frequently took on the left and the Democratic party, arguing that the two-party system was nearly bankrupt. During Reagan's 1984 reelection campaign, Moore argued that "peace candidate" Walter Mondale was more likely to escalate the arms race than his Republican opponent. ". . . We are told once again that we have 'the clearest choice' for president since Roosevelt and Hoover. They do not say since Johnson and Goldwater because, as it turned out, that choice wasn't so clearcut: Johnson, the peace candidate gave us 58,000 body bags."

Crafting an argument against the Democrats that he would paraphrase at critical moments in the years ahead, he argued that it "will be much more difficult organizing against Mondale with his liberal facade than a real villain like Reagan. If you don't believe that, ask yourself when the movement (nuclear freeze, Latin American solidarity, etc.) really grew in this country—under Carter or Reagan . . . The way to beat Reagan, I believe, is to become, the candidate of the Stay At Home Party—the disenfranchised, the disillusioned, the people shut out of the system. Give them a reason to come out and vote! Instead he chose to sit on the fence. The fence may be Mondale's, but the ranch belongs to Reagan."

After Reagan's inauguration, the editor began doing commentary on National Public Radio's *All Things Considered,* his first foray into broadcast journalism since his *Radio Free Flint* adventure. Approaching burnout, Moore, who had been wearing the twin baseball caps of editor and publisher, decided to cut back.

In the fall of 1985 Moore wrote, "I started the *Voice* in 1977 because of my desire to write about issues affecting the people of Flint and other cities in Michigan. Instead I spend my days making sure Bert's Party Store in Wyandotte hasn't run out of papers."

Moore was sick of dodging bill collectors from Chase Manhattan demanding to know why the *Voice* was behind on payments for its typesetting equipment. He didn't want to spend more time trying to break up the romance between star writer Ben Hamper and Jack Daniels. He didn't care if the Tuesday night bingo game brought in enough money to cover the overdue printer bill. He was tired of purist readers picking on the paper because it ran Kool cigarette ads. Then the paper's bookkeeper had a heart attack while trying to sort out the *Voice*'s complicated books—a bad omen.

"You will not see the title of publisher after my name in the staff box because it's the job I can't stand," he told his readers. "If you're looking for a challenge and eventual sainthood, send us a letter. WARNING: This is no 9 to 5 job; if you like to be home to catch *The Jeffersons* at 5:30, stay where you are."

Moore's determination to focus on journalism made sense. For one thing, he had problems with key staffers like *Voice* cofounder Doug Cunningham, who argued that Moore's love affair with himself conflicted with the paper's communal ethic. For instance, Moore spiked a story on one of the paper's most popular subjects, police brutality. Cunningham couldn't understand why.

There was no doubt that publishing interfered with Moore's own writing. He had dabbled in local politics, community organizing, radio and theater. And although he'd made a ripple or two as a journalist, it appeared the *New York Times* was not interested in making him a regional bureau chief like Molly Ivins from the *Texas Observer*.

Determined to focus on editorial matters, Moore began with a self-criticism session. "I will no longer continue to put this paper out with an all-male writing staff," he announced, and the paper scheduled a distaff issue. Kathleen Glynn wrote a story on Tina Lytle, owner of Merlin's Retreat Vegetarian Café. There were pieces about women in film, the women in Ben Hamper's life and adolescent sexuality, as well as a Diane Baum poem, "Words from a Former CIA Station Chief":

>In the last ten minutes
>before the world and I
>end up fried
>I'm going to turn to the person at my side
>and be able to say
>at least
>I tried.

"THEY HAVE PLANTED A MICROPHONE IN MY BRA AND I CAN'T GET IT OUT"

ON JUNE 28, 1971, the American people learned that running the country was more than protecting the common defense, safeguarding the Bill of Rights and making sure that every citizen was free to pursue life, liberty and the pursuit of happiness. On that day the American people learned that President Richard M. Nixon and his White House staff were spending some of their precious time compiling three lists of over 400 political opponents. While celebrities like Jane Fonda, Barbra Streisand, Carol Channing and Teddy Kennedy, as well as organizations like *The New York Times*, made the cut, only three people made all three lists-the original list of 20 names submitted by the office of aide Charles Colson, a second list of political opponents and a third, longer list of enemies.

Two of the these triple threat leftists who appeared on all the lists—actor Paul Newman and CBS newsman Dan Schorr—were well known public figures. The third, Stewart Mott, whom Charles Colson characterized as a man famous for "nothing but big money for radic-lib candidates," was anything but a household name. Ironically this enemy was the son of one of Nixon's key Michigan fund raisers, Charles Stewart Mott.

When he died in 1973 at the age of 97, Mott was at the end of a Horatio Alger path that had taken him from a money-losing bicycle wheel enterprise to a director's seat at General Motors. As one of the company's pioneers and operations managers, Charles Mott had become a multi-millionaire, three-time mayor of Flint and squire of his own estate, Applewood.

One of the most famous photos in *Flint Journal* history shows the generous Republican donor on a Flint podium sitting behind presidential candidate Richard Nixon. The GM legend is holding his nose to avoid unleashing one of his trademark sneezes that could bring down a house faster than the big bad wolf. Charles Mott's son Stewart was hardly a chip off the old motorman's block.

An inconvenient child at times, Stewart complained that he had to make an appointment with his father to discuss his grades. At age 12 he was sent to northern Michigan to attend Leelenau School. He hated it and transferred east to Deerfield Academy, which he also hated. After graduation, Stewart enrolled at another school that was not what he had in mind—MIT. Following a year off for a trip around the world, he enrolled at Columbia, taking a double major in comparative literature and business. From there he took another year off to visit a chain of department stores owned by his father before finding his real calling in the nonprofit sector. After successfully opening a Planned Parenthood office in his home town, Stewart went on to open branches across Michigan, and in Florida and New York.

Unhappy with his son's politics, Charles Mott refused to put Stewart on the board of his vast foundation. When the heir received his $30 million trust fund, one of his first moves was to diversify by selling off most of its principal holding, General Motors stock. The elder Mott protested that General Motors had been very good to the family.

His passion for politics pushed Stewart, who now drove a Volkswagen, to follow his father's lead and run for Congress as a Democrat. But when he raised this possibility, his 92-year-old father scoffed at the idea. "Are you kidding, I'm a Republican."

After giving up on the idea of running on the Lyndon Johnson ticket, the heir donated much of his holdings to the Stewart Mott Foundation, just steps away from the capitol in Washington. He rented out part of the space to the American Civil Liberties Union and referred to his building as the "House of Un-American Activities." Among his causes was the Fund for Constitutional Government, which published a book called *The Impeachable Offenses of Richard Nixon.*

Nixon hated Stewart Mott because he had become a venture capitalist behind Eugene McCarthy's 1968 Presidential run and the 1972 progressive Democratic campaign of George McGovern. Mott's $400,000 preprimary contribution to McGovern was critical to the campaign's startup. At one point the Nixon enemy stood up in the middle of a Madison Square Garden rally for McCarthy and made another big pledge. Although Mott's days as a kingmaker would end with campaign spending limits imposed by passage of the Fair Election Campaign Act in 1973, his foundation was a key player in the progressive movement. Mott supported campaigns against the Vietnam War and nuclear power while donating significant sums to the women's campaign fund and investigative journalism.

Stewart Mott resided in an 800 Park Avenue townhouse in New York, where he tended vegetables on the rooftop and remained a loyal subscriber to the *Flint Voice.* At several crucial moments he gave substantial matching grants to Michael Moore's newspaper. His generosity made him a poster boy for *Voice* fundraising campaigns.

From time to time Stewart tried to honor his crotchety father. A testimonial dinner organized for Charles Mott at the Tavern on The Green in Central Park sounded like a great idea. But when the elder Mott rose to thank his son for that generous introduction, the audience learned the two men had a few unresolved issues: "Stewart has twice the brains and half the common sense I do," said the father regarding his son. To be on the safe side, Charles wrote a codicil in his will that gave Stewart the interest on his inheritance with the actual trust going to his unborn grandson.

Stewart loved Michael Moore's accomplishments and considered him the antidote to much of what was wrong with his father's troubling corporate legacy. One morning in 1984, he woke up and had a crazy idea. He decided to behave like a millionaire. Mott chartered a small plane to ferry himself, his wife Kappy Jo Wells, his foundation director Anne Zill and seven other staff members on an impromptu roots tour of his native Flint. Although the trip was scheduled to coincide with Stewart and Kappy Jo's fifth wedding anniversary, it was also an opportunity to show his wife and colleagues the heartbeat of Mott's America.

Back in 1906, when Buick pioneer William Durant asked Stewart Mott's father to move his factory and 300 employees from Ithaca, New York, to Flint, the city was a minor league town. Stewart pointed out on his tour that his father took great pride in his civic legacy. As a public servant, he fought hard for modern sewers. Flint's largest single benefactor, an important charitable force in the world of arts, education, the environment and health care, the Charles Stewart Mott Foundation had endowed Mott College, the Mott Library, Mott Hospital, Auto World and numerous other cultural landmarks. And as public radio listeners knew, it also donated a lot of money to National Public Radio. By now it was one of the nation's largest philanthropic organizations.

While much of the visit was focused on what the Mott family had done for Flint, Stewart insisted that Michael Moore come along for the ride to offer the group his own unique perspective on Flint's underclass and the decline of General Motors. The low point of the tour came at a dinner where Stewart's half brother Harding, an executive at the Mott Foundation, made it clear that he hated Moore and the *Voice*, an incendiary publication that had done so much damage to the city he loved.

After the Flint visit, Moore asked Zill to host him on a Washington visit. She agreed and began introducing him to friends around town. Zill's idea of a good time was to bring two imaginative people together, sit back and watch the chain reaction. One of the first people on her list for Moore was a close friend, James Ridgeway, Washington correspondent for the *Village Voice*. For this writer, meeting weekly deadlines was more than just getting stories right. In 1964, thanks in part to the Vietnam war, investigative reporting was beginning to give enterprising journalists like the New York Times' David Halberstam the cachet of a rock star. Popular opposition to America's battle to preserve and protect South Vietnam from Ho Chi Minh was spilling over into the streets. Journalists were also getting tougher on big corporations, FBI spymaster J. Edgar Hoover and nuclear power advocates. Inevitably major news organizations could not keep up with all the incipient scandals during a time when reporters ignored presidential peccadillos in favor of corporate corruption and exposing the failure of the American military campaign in Vietnam.

It was a great time to be a muckraker in Washington D.C. where whistle blowing had become a spectator sport. For Ridgeway, a keen student of the many ways that big universities fronted for the interests of corporate America, coming to work felt like walking in to a race track where touts constantly whispered hints into your ear. It wasn't easy to figure out who you could trust.

In the '60s, Ridgeway was a prominent *New Republic* writer who had developed a reputation as a man who listened to people other journalists brushed aside. Alas, he was on the receiving end of sources who had been politely asked to leave numerous newsrooms in town. Aware that his publication, the *New Republic*, was open to breaking stores that had failed to find safe harbor elsewhere, they arrived with shopping bags full of documents highlighted with red felt pens. Some were conspiracy theorists who knew every horrifying frame of the Zapruder film that chronicled the broad daylight assassination of President John F. Kennedy's life. They traded horror stories about the alleged Warren Commission coverups like kids swapping baseball cards. They were American journalism's unwanted, the butt of newsroom jokes often palmed off on cub reporters forced to stand in the lobby politely explaining why the editor couldn't grant them an audience.

On one particularly bad day Ridgeway, struggling to meet multiple deadlines, was confronted by a man who had the inside story on an underground army at the ready in every American zip code. The informer knew exactly how and when these armies would strike. Then a woman showed up and complained that she was the victim of spies: "They have planted a microphone in my bra and I can't get it out."

"Why don't you take off your bra?" asked Ridgeway.

The woman called back later complaining that the FBI microphone was now implanted in one of her teeth.

Ridgeway had finally returned to his deadline story when he was confronted by a tall, skinny young attorney who wanted to talk with him about tires and struts and axles. Who knew anything about tires? Ridgeway began wondering how he was going to get rid of this one who was obviously a little slicker than the others at spewing out a hard to follow tale of engineering disasters.

But Ridgeway, equally at home deconstructing Republicans and Democrats in his well-researched stories, listened to the lawyer who had hitchhiked to Washington and didn't even own a car. He recognized the thread of a story that had eluded the national media. Even that dean of American muckrakers, Drew Pearson, had missed this scoop. The attorney was armed with facts and figures. He believed his exposé was in the grand tradition of Wilfred Burchett who broke the news that America's nuclear bombing of Hiroshima and Nagasaki had created a radiation sickness killing tens of thousands of Japanese civilians who had survived the initial bomb blasts.

The attorney, a Harvard law graduate, freelance writer and Labor Department consultant named Ralph Nader, operated on the premise that every fact had to be documented in the manner of a legal brief. Footnotes were everywhere. Even a skeptic like Ridgeway had to acknowledge there might be a story here.

The writer's New Republic piece on the Corvair disaster, published in the fall of 1964, suggested that General Motors was selling the automotive version of a pineapple upside down cake. Shoppers kicking the tires of the compact Corvair were surprised to find their new cars had an embarassing tendency to flip over.

Death and dismemberment stories are always bad publicity for an auto company. After Ridgeway's report was picked up by newspapers across the country, a publisher named Richard Grossman called to ask if he would like to write a book on the subject. Ridgeway, bogged down with other assignments, turned down the offer and gave him Ralph Nader's phone number at a Washington boarding house. When General Motors learned that Nader was working on the book to be called *Unsafe At Any Speed*, they hired private detectives to trail the critic, shadowing him with gumshoes trying to document the young lawyer's private life.

Among other things, all-work-and-no-play Nader discovered attractive young women suddenly trying to chat him up at Safeway. After the book was published news of GM's surveillance turned Nader into a public figure, pushed his book onto the bestseller list and launched Nader's career as America's nudge, the man who believed that white collar crime was the nation's fastest growing industry.

Nader's book royalties, a $425,000 settlement from General Motors, speaking fees and myriad contributions turned his Corvair story into a public interest juggernaut that would lead to strengthening the pure food and drug act, campaign finance reform, auto recall campaigns, the freedom of information act, compensation for airline bumping and, of course, assisted the death of the Corvair. And while Nader went on to organize a network of public interest law firms in Washington and around the country, he remained at heart a small time operator, working with a staff of just a dozen in the Carnegie Foundation Building on Washington's 16th Street. Although he helped found dozens of public interest groups that took on issues ranging from radiation leaks at nuclear power plants to air and water pollution, his own office, the Center for Study of Responsive Law, was a lean machine that grilled corporations and politicians.

Nader hired hundreds of young college graduates to work on projects like Congress Watch, but only a few were given a desk in his inner sanctum where it was possible to work and travel with the man who was famous for lobbying Senators and Congressmen in the middle of the night. An early morning wakeup call from Ralph Nader in the midst of a critical Senate debate on issues like airbags became as much a Washington tradition as cherry blossoms on the Potomac.

When Jim Musselman graduated at the top of his University of Syracuse Law School class he was in many ways the perfect Nader hire. Like Lee Iacocca he was an Allentown, Pennsylvania native. He discovered Ralph Nader's vision of unstacking the deck in the nation's capital when his parents brought him to a local talk by the consumer advocate. Although Musselman wanted to become a political activist he couldn't see himself sitting behind a desk in Washington D.C. Like Huckleberry Finn, he was eager to light out for the territories.

On his first day working for Ralph Nader, Musselman was handed a folder chock full of internal auto company documents on airbags.

Nader had documented a fascinating private conversation between Chrysler's Iacocca and President Richard Nixon. Iacocca told Nixon he cared more about making money than saving lives with airbags. When Mussleman released the transcript of Iacocca's remarks in the middle of a Draft Iacocca press conference at the National Press Club in Washington, Chrysler's public relations department realized they had a potential Corvair style public relations debacle on their hands.

Iacocca wisely changed course and agreed to add airbags to all his vehicles within six months. The announcement was made public in a Chrysler ad published in the *Wall Street Journal* and the *New York Times*: "Who Says You Can't Teach An Old Dog New Tricks?"

Like a public health official, Musselman realized that education was the best way to protect consumers. Corporate America had the tools to safeguard the public. The trick was to build demand. The air bag campaign, which would save thousands of American lives, was only the beginning of a much broader initiative. Nader's strategy was to bring along young organizers on his speaking tours and, when he found an issue that merited immediate attention, the boss would detach the organizer and leave him behind to build a grassroots campaign.

Typical was Nader's decision to help build an alliance with a group of Michigan taxpayer groups, teachers unions and auto workers who had organized to fight General Motors' program to slash taxes by 70 percent. Offering thousands of jobs for tax breaks, GM threatened to abandon as many as 26 Michigan communities if they didn't acquiesce. Naturally this would force local government to trade the paring knife for the ax as they slashed budgets for schools, health care, welfare programs and emergency services.

For Musselman, now based in Detroit, it was a dream assignment. Borrowing from the playbook of Hormel Union organizer Ray Rogers, he personalized the conflict by going after the enemy's CEO. The idea was to flush the boss out with staged protests at corporate headquarters, signage, flyers, even a visit to his office and home. By spotlighting CEOs they were able to go beyond traditional labor-management confrontations and bring corporate leadership out of their aerie to debate the issues, and in Iacocca's case, to simply admit their mistakes.

Shielded by squadrons of lawyers, publicists and armed security teams, many businesses depended on spokespeople who piled on their favorite euphemisms to sidestep securities analysts, journalists and, of course the public at large. Nader loved Musselman's idea, because it dovetailed with a book he and author William Taylor were writing. It was called *The Big Boys* and targeted corporate leaders such as General Motors' Roger Smith.

As Musselman began working with Michigan community groups fighting the GM tax cuts in April 1985, he learned of another young man in Flint who could help organize a winning coalition. "People started telling me about the great job Michael Moore was doing with the *Michigan Voice*." Moore, had carefully documented GM's tax cut schemes that would slash school budgets, cripple infrastructure and ultimately lead to higher property taxes in factory towns like Flint.

By the time the two men met at the *Voice* office, Moore had clearly become the Rodney Dangerfield of investigative journalism. Powerful people in Flint disrespected his work. A store across the street refused to stock his muckraking paper. And his *Radio Free Flint* show aired during the memorial park of broadcast journalism, 9 a.m. on Sunday morning. Eager to embrace the broadest possible constituency, Moore left the *Voice*'s basement lair to befriend the voiceless. Listeners never knew if they were going to catch a union organizer or a bigot like Bob Miles, the former grand dragon of the Michigan Ku Klux Klan who was jailed for tarring and feathering a black official at a Willow Run school and trying to detonate school buses to put the brakes on integration in the Pontiac schools.

Sparring on air with people like Miles, who according to federal officials had plotted the overthrow of the American government, attracted listeners who knew Moore would always offer a show they couldn't find on any other station.

With Michael at the wheel of his Honda, Musselman surveyed this heartbeat of America auto town that reminded him of his native Allentown. Like Bethlehem Steel back in Pennsylvania, he saw General Motors as an enemy of the people. Even when the biggest of the big three opened a new plant, the Nader critic was skeptical. For example, in Spring Hill, Tennessee, Musselman educated new GM workers about the hidden dangers of working for the world's largest corporation.

For Musselman, Michael Moore was more than a recruitment project. The young lawyer from Washington also had to shift his eating habit toward fast food emporiums that were central to the muckraker's diet, places like McDonald's, Burger King and Angelo's. The Nader Raider would gain 25 pounds during the coming year. As their friendship developed, Moore helped Musselman economize on his paltry per diem by hosting him at his home.

Central to his strategy was creating the kind of visual stories that could land the new campaign against General Motors on the news pages and local television. This approach had worked for Ray Rogers at Hormel and he was confident that it would also work in Michigan.

"I told Michael, 'why don't you flush Roger Smith out and invite him to local meetings in places like Flint and Pontiac, have him face school teachers, and have him say we want to take money out of the school system. He would look horrible.'"

Moore agreed to join Musselman at meetings with unions, school teachers and other activists. The Nader organizer was delighted when a UAW pioneer stood near the end of a Flint meeting and declared: "We fought General Motors in the 30s and won and we can win again. Moore was so moved that he told listeners to his Radio Free Flint show that the Citizens for Tax Justice campaign was the most important thing that has happened in Flint."

Anti-GM tax abatement letters to the editor began showing up in newspapers around the state and Musselman masterminded a showdown at the General Motors Detroit headquarters in September 1985. Armed with a bullhorn he urged Roger Smith to come downstairs and deal with the issue personally as union leaders and teachers explained the controversy to local television reporters. "We wanted GM to either create the thousands of jobs that they had promised under agreements going back to the early 1980s or to deliver the cash on the spot so that it could be returned to the communities that lost millions in revenue."

When Musselman invited Moore to join him for a Ralph Nader Detroit Press Club media event celebrating the release of his new book *The Big Boys,* the editor was delighted. "For Michael this was like going to meet Santa Claus," recalls Musselman. St. Nick Nader returned in July to meet with auto workers, union leaders and taxpayer groups in Flint. His position was simple. A General Motors victory on tax abatements would create a new generation of corporate deserters eager to flee their hometowns if they could not slash taxes. More than 300 people showed up for the protest meeting including Moore.

Nader invited Roger Smith to Flint where he could explain the impact of GM's actions on the city's faltering economy. After the consumer advocate's visit the Flint Journal came around to the *Michigan Voice* position and editorialized against the GM tax cuts.

Moore thought highly of Musselman's ability to confront General Motors shareholders with his coalition of union leaders, teachers, nuns and civic officials worried about losing their tax base. As Citizens for Tax Justice organized more than two dozen Michigan communities to fight GM's proposed 70 percent tax cuts, Musselman escalated his personal attacks on Roger Smith:

"We went to his home in Bloomfied Hills to show people how cold hearted he was, to demonstrate that he wouldn't meet with us. Finding Smith was easy. We knew where he went to church, where he vacationed in the Upper Peninsula."

The *Michigan Voice* editorial campaign against GM tax cuts was a critical organizing tool. Determined to help Moore keep his publication on schedule, Mussleman even loaned the publisher $2,500 to get an issue out. This aid and other emergency cash transfusions from major donors like Stewart Mott did not come close to balancing the paper's books as creditors put the delinquent account's phone number on autodial.

THANK'S (sic) FOR ASKING IF I'M INTERESTED IN BEING EDITOR OF MOTHER JONES

"MUCKRAKING," MOTHER JONES cofounder Paul Jacobs once said, "is like peeing on a rock." Undoubtedly editing a magazine like *Mother Jones* meant you were the rock. Conceived in Jacobs' Pacific Heights living room with Richard Parker and Adam Hochschild in 1974, the magazine became an inspiration for journalists across the country. No one better embodied the spirit of the magazine than Jacobs who had debuted in the charter issue with a frightening story about an Indian nuclear power plant where workers moved dangerous radioactive waste about with long bamboo poles.

Although Jacobs died of lung cancer shortly after the magazine was founded (a film produced by Saul Landau suggested his death was triggered by exposure to atomic test radiation during the 1950s) his spirit was at the heart of the tenth anniversary party held at a club on Columbus Avenue in 1986.

During its first decade *Mother Jones* demonstrated that progressive journalism was about much more than pushing the environment, worker's rights, a feminist agenda or social welfare. Readers understood *Mother Jones* wasn't just about apartheid, Ronald Reagan's patented brand of anti-communism or Ford Motor Company's too hot to handle Pinto. *Mother Jones* was a magazine about important causes other publications sidestepped, pieces of lasting importance that would be photocopied, circulated and quoted in the halls of

Congress, in colleges and even at the news desks of TV networks. The magazine's stories on banned-in-America pesticides and pharmaceuticals being dumped in the third world touched off an international effort to stop the practice. The Pinto exposé prompted a 1.5-million-vehicle recall. And the Reagan administration, a frequent target of the magazine's assault on no-bang-for-buck Pentagon weapons programs, responded with the ultimate compliment, an Internal Revenue Service claim that the money-losing magazine should pay taxes on advertising revenue. After running the magazine deeper into the red with frightening legal bills, the IRS gave up its worthless attempt to take money from the nonprofit.

When the new editor of *Mother Jones*, Michael Moore of Flint, Michigan, rose to address the crowd, there was a feeling that the magazine was about to become a little hipper, in touch with a slightly younger audience that favored R&B over Puccini and Aaron Copland, readers who were slightly more comfortable with *USA Today* than the *New York Times*, people who weren't already reading *The Nation* and were more likely to be found at a U2 concert than a Joan Baez benefit. They were, in short, the petit bourgeois with attitude.

In many ways the anonymity of American magazine journalism, was being replaced by editors who visibly represented the publication's constituency. Seldom seen or heard deities like the *New Yorker*'s William Shawn were being replaced by the likes of Lewis Lapham, the embodiment of *Harper's Magazine*. Like Eros, the Pepsi-swilling Hugh Hefner of *Playboy* cast himself as the god of lovemaking. On the distaff side, *Cosmopolitan*'s Helen Gurley Brown had a pretty good idea of what intelligent young women wanted from their boy toys. Athleticism in the bedroom was a commodity that could sell advertising and give hope to the unwanted who could count on a generous helping of quality fiction and self-help columns.

Some editors of these publications didn't merely practice what they preached, they invited fellow celebrities to pursue an intelligent lifestyle consistent with the publication's table of contents. Like gurus some of them operated in a mi casa, su casa mode. In Hefner's case these stars arrived at the Playboy mansion with jammies perfect for a sleepover.

In a sense Michael Moore was the perfect demographic for *Mother Jones*, a young literate man who liked to publish exposés of cops who harass motorists for driving while black and a thought-provoking review of *The Simpsons* impact on the mass media. He was a great target for advertisers pitching fuel-efficient Japanese cars like the one he owned and study tours to Nicaragua. And if you left out the fact that he didn't do drugs or alcohol, he could jazz up parties like the tenth anniversary celebration of *Mother Jones*. Or to borrow a phrase from that Motown superstar Aretha Franklin, the 150,000 circulation magazine, under his new leadership, was going to deliver the skinny on "Who's Zooming Who."

Michael Moore also had a bond with readers in the market coveted by political strategists, a man from a Middle America swing state where national elections were often decided. He spoke to the hearts and minds of voters who could be persuaded to switch parties. Unlike foregone conclusion states such as New York and Texas, Midwesterners were an unpredictable lot, particularly in battlegrounds such as Ohio, Wisconsin, Minnesota, Missouri, Iowa and, of course, the Great Lakes hotbed, Michigan.

Moore's perfect pitch at the *Mother Jones* birthday gala, his casual attire, stream of one liners and his ability to redefine the magazine made it clear that this publication was ready for an extreme makeover. Like Mort Sahl and Woody Allen, he knew how to throw a punch line. But Moore also understood why phone call centers preferred Midwestern dialects that were ideal for telemarketing. In the same way that NBC's pronunciation guide hewed to a Chicago accent, Moore's voice demonstrated he was more than a coastal comic. A heartland kind of guy who spoke from the heart, Moore knew just how to win friends and influence readers.

There was just one small problem at the *Mother Jones* office on Mission Street. Michael Moore was having a hard time running the "magazine for the rest of us." Some days the staff felt like he was trying to conduct a Sousa march in seven/eight time. Staff meetings turned into self criticism sessions where Moore demonstrated the kind of moxie that endeared him to some of the junior members of the *Mother Jones* office: "You have been publishing a magazine that is a pile of shit."

Michael Moore's journey from the Midwest to San Francisco began in late 1985 when he learned from his Washington friend Anne Zill that *Mother Jones* was looking for a new editor. Half a dozen of the San Francisco publication's founders had written for an antecedent called *Ramparts*. That bright star on the American left exposed the CIA's secret funding of the National Student Association. Heavily focused on the Vietnam war debacle and the cold war, opening the pages of *Ramparts* was a little like stepping on to the Nevada Test Site. You never knew when the next explosion was going to take place. The colorful leftist magazine was a proving ground for many important journalists such Hochschild, Robert Scheer, Warren Hinckle and two writers who made a name for themselves writing dynastic biographies, Peter Collier and David Horowitz. Art director Dugald Stermer and his successor, Louise Kollenbaum gave the slick color publication a look that set it ahead of newsprint based competitors.

Although the publication was generously backed by children of the Rockefeller family, it was chronically undercapitalized, with staff racing to the bank with their paychecks before the payroll account was cleaned out. But *Ramparts* was also an inspiration to young muckrakers who saw it as an antidote to large news organizations underplaying or ignoring stories that needed to be told. From civilian torture in Vietnam to paeans on the students who burned down the Bank of America in Isla Vista, California, *Ramparts* was a box seat to one acts staged by the New Left. Unfortunately, at times, it was also a homeless shelter for conspiracy theories.

As *Ramparts* waned, Hochschild, Jacobs and Parker began a two year Foundation for National Progress fundraising campaign. Their goal was to found an attractive leftwing magazine that would hit a circulation of 100,000. With the help of former *Ramparts* art director Kollenbaum, the San Francisco pioneers wanted to build a magazine "that would uncover critical stories missed by competitors."

"At its best," Hochschild said, *Ramparts* "brought some profoundly important exposés to a large public, and it played a crucial role in the ant-Vietnam War movement. But *Ramparts* had serious flaws; it was not always accurate, its business operations were chaotic, and it often touted and seldom criticized certain sacred cows, such as Cuba, North Vietnam and the Black Panther Party. For most of us *Mother Jones* was a happy second marriage that follows a painful but instructive divorce."

Now after building a reliable base, the *Mother Jones* board was eager to reach a broader audience. When Zill recommended Moore as a candidate for the job, Hochschild was intrigued, particularly by his accomplishments in Flint. It was one thing to sit in San Francisco, New York or Washington and pontificate about the crises of the American working class. It was another matter to go behind enemy lines and fight America's largest industrial corporation, not to mention corrupt officials, nuclear power plant advocates, racist hotel managers and corrupt city officials on a monthly basis.

Moore was flattered by the invitation to apply but worried that the new job would be a bit like standing on a ledge. "Sometimes people are less heard in their hometown," Jim Musselman told him. "They need to move up. Sometimes you have to leap and the net will appear."

But would the net hold for a big guy?

Musselman told Moore that Flint's fate was part of a national story, one that he was in a unique position to tell. Quoting fallen hero Harry Chapin he told Moore:

"'Let your errors be errors of commission, not omission'. He also said, 'it's better to try and fail.' At least you tried. When in doubt do something. Do you want to be 80 years old and wish you tried to do it?" Over the Christmas holiday Moore, with the help of his friend Jim Musselman, wrote an eight-page single-spaced letter of application to *Mother Jones*. It took weeks to come up with words that struck exactly the right note. Except for the fact that they forgot to hire a proofreader, the letter was attractive:

"Dear Adam," Moore wrote *Mother Jones* board chairman Hochschild on the day after Christmas, 1985 "Thank's (sic) for asking if I'm interested in being editor of *Mother Jones*. I am. Here are a few of my thoughts regarding the job, the magazine and the Giants chances this season." After quickly summarizing his own reading preferences he argued that:

"Most left periodicals, unfortunately, don't have a sense of humor. I believe the more wit and irreverence in *Mother Jones*, the more accessible the magazine becomes. And the more effective. When David Letterman blew up a bunch of GE appliances the day after its merger with RCA he probably made a lot more people think about the evils of corporate America than many of us would with a 10,000 word essay.

"*Mother Jones* needs to find its teeth. *Mother Jones* needs to be making some serious waves. *Mother Jones* needs to kick some ass. You can only live on the Pinto/Dalkon Shield exposés for so long. It's time to get back to what made *Mother Jones* so popular—and its circulation so large—in the first place: bold, aggressive, hard-hitting reporting. No sacred cows.

"When I pick up *Mother Jones*, I want to read something very different. I don't want to know what it's going to say before I ever read it. *Mother Jones* should keep taking the risks others won't. One such risk would be to run a cover story sympathetic to the plight of the Palestinians and the "apartheid" they suffer from. Why does the left and its peace groups ignore this issue? *Mother Jones* could take a leadership role here in demanding that this subject be placed on the front burner alongside the concerns of Central America, South Africa, and the Nuclear Freeze."

Moore also believed that "*Mother Jones* needs to reach out to new readers who do not necessarily define themselves as leftists or activists. It needs to report on mass culture and the politics of that culture. Television, sports and other opiates of the masses should be covered with a witty, critical eye by writers who are also participants in that culture. We also need to hear the voices of working people; the most popular item in the *Michigan Voice* is a column by Ben Hamper, an assembly line riveter at Chevy Truck in Flint. I'm sure he's done more to expose the bankrupt morality of General Motors than any analytic piece I've written."

"The success of the Feminist Movement has been in our ability to connect the personal to the political and to let a lot of women join the movement at their own pace. How many women have you heard begin a sentence with 'I'm not a feminist but . . .' and then proceed to describe themselves as a feminist. I caught Ralph Nader on Phil Donahue last week and though he kept wanting to talk about GM and EPA, the most pressing questions from the audience were from women wanting to talk about the safety of cosmetics and high-heel shoes. Nader changed his focus to their concerns, and by the end of the hour he had endeared himself to an audience that saw the 'movement' relating to them. That's what I want to see happen at *Mother Jones*. There are hundreds of thousands of potential readers out there just waiting for the chance to be 'let in.'"

In early February 1986, Moore went public with his anguish over the possibility of closing the *Voice* and the Hotline. The *Voice* had always listed to port and never been self bailing. But now it was starting to look like time for a Mayday call. Moore was particularly alarmed when the bookkeeper, buried in work, had a heart attack. Just days before leaving on a plane for California and a meeting with the *Mother Jones* board, he told the *Detroit Free Press*:

"This is a really hard time for me. I'm worried that if I go, the *Voice* will go, and the people in Flint won't have any kind of alternative to the news they get from the establishment press. This is a company town, where everyone follows what the company does. So it is hard to decide what to do. The *Voice* hasn't been a job. It has been my life."

Several *Mother Jones* editors were dubious about Moore's ability to lead the magazine. Among them was senior editor Bernard Ohanian : "We had an hour with him. When he left, managing editor Bruce Dancis and I were convinced there was no way Adam Hochschild would seriously consider hiring him. He came across like a buffoon. He was full of bravado offering platitude after platitude about how we were going to be harder hitting."

Managing Editor Dancis supported colleague David Talbot "who wanted to make it into a publication like *Salon,* the online magazine Talbot went on to found. Talbot might not have been as serious as other people but it certainly would have been an exciting magazine, a cutting edge periodical as Salon turned out to be. Another candidate was Rick Hertzberg who was leaving the *New Republic* and went to work for the *New Yorker* after turning *Mother Jones* down.

The feeling on the board was that Michael had done a terrific job at the *Michigan Voice* with virtually no resources and that given the resources of *Mother Jones* he would be able to create a new exciting voice for the left on a national scale."

As the negotiations continued, *Voice* readers from Dowagiac to Ishpeming waited for word from California. There was no puff of smoke from the *Mother Jones* offices on San Francisco's Market Street as the board's headhunters announced their decision. But when the news finally moved across the Associated Press wire, the local-bad-boy-makes-good story was irresistible, particularly for Flint folks on Moore's enemies list, who were already humming a few bars of the Hallelujah Chorus.

The *Flint Journal* wrote, "Michael Moore will miss the coneys from Angelo's, the cheeseburgers and greasy battered onion rings that Flint's hash houses seem so adept at preparing. But more than that he'll miss his now infamous role as the prickly thorn in the Flint establishment's rose gardens."

Mother Jones editors began finding their daily routine interrupted by calls from Flint. Total strangers, who claimed to have worked with the *Voice* editor warned how difficult the new hire was to work with. But for board members like Adam Hochschild, who had chosen Moore over distinguished competitors from the New York and California publishing community, these warnings meant nothing. The quality of his work accomplished on a shoe string budget was unmistakable. Never had so few written so much with so little.

Moore, of course, still had a few problems. There was a big jump in salary—to $40,000—but the *Voice* still owed $30,000, including debts to its printers and the Internal Revenue Service. The new job meant closing the *Voice*, even though it had been named one of the eight best alternative newspapers in America. The paper had won its campaign to remove a Mayor from office, lobbied successfully for closing a nuclear plant in Midland, championed a successful campaign to close Flint's Auto World theme park and fought an illegal search and seizure that prompted Congress to pass a news media shield law protecting every journalist in the land. Thanks to the Congressional outcry over seizure of the *Voice* printing plates by the Flint police, Michael Moore's name had become synonymous with freedom of the press.

But the new job at *Mother Jones* meant accepting the reality of infanticide. "I'm drowning my baby . . . I have this terrible sense of abandoning my hometown," said Moore; but in the next breath he praised *Mother Jones* as "one of the best publications in the country, with a strong tradition of hell-raising, muckraking journalism . . . I am taking the job because there are lies being told in places other than Flint."

The final commemorative issue of the *Michigan Voice* was an instant collector's item. Faithful readers across the Midwest passed the crying towel and the beer nuts. "I offer my congratulations and condolences," wrote A.J. Deeds of Milan, Ohio. "Congrats because instead of measly $30,000 debts, you now get to become concerned over $300,000 debts."

"As an agnostic," added Herb Kaufman of West Bloomfield, Michigan, "let me say that if there is a God, may He be with you in your new endeavor." And rising above the letters of thanks and pleas for an occasional intellectual care package from the left coast, was a thoughtful warning from former Ann Arbor resident Bryan Pfeiffer. "Whatever you do," he told Moore, "don't let Ben change the name of the magazine to just 'Mother.'"

While Moore had no intention of renaming the magazine he did have some intriguing ideas for the publication that had plummeted from a circulation peak of 233,000 to just 150,000. He needed to change the way people thought about their government, their employers, their schools, their houses of worship and most of all, themselves. His job was to lead the way in reshaping a political culture that threatened to warp the democratic idealism of the Constitutional Convention at Independence Hall in the same way Joseph Stalin dashed the hopes and dreams of Karl Marx.

One problem for the progressive minority was the fact that a handful of obstructionists had cleverly found ways to outwit the body politic. Thus a few lobbyists in Washington D.C. could bottle up health care reform while defense contractors bribed powerful elected officials with golfing junkets and a side order of prostitutes. Another difficulty was the fact that the liberals kept selling out to the demons of the so-called intelligence community. FBI Director J. Edgar Hoover believed it was his job to persuade his hated boss, Democratic Attorney General Robert F. Kennedy, to wiretap the most important civil rights leader in American history, the Reverend Martin Luther King, Jr. And Moore asked, what was America going to do when a wave of mergers and consolidations morphed the Fortune 500 into the Fortune 5?

A republic in dire straits, America had reached the point where even top muckrakers were willing to plead uncle when confronted by the master builders of capitalism. Who ya gonna call, Michael Moore, wanted to know when Pulitzer Prize winning investigative journalist Seymour Hersh admitted openly that the banks were "beyond investigation" by the media because they were "too big, too complicated, too secretive." And that, Moore explained, was the point. Even if you could get to the bottom of their chicanery, readers would have a hard time understanding how they were being had.

Like Benjamin Franklin, Moore believed that the nation's future depended on the ability of Americans to recognize their shared destiny. "We must hang together or surely we will hang separately," argued Franklin. And now Moore, eager to embrace not just politics but mass culture in the form of *Mother Jones* sports and television criticism added: "We cannot change the world as long as we are separate from it."

BLOOD IN THE FACE

IN MARCH OF 1986, shortly before taking over *Mother Jones* Moore flew to Washington D.C. and checked in at the home of Anne Zill, who had originally tipped him to the *Mother Jones* opening. The Stewart Mott Foundation director wrote about the visit in her journal:

"I have got Michael Moore for the third night upstairs on the third floor, a dear guy whom I hope ought to do some good things as the editor of *Mother Jones* magazine. I like him a lot. He is typically Irish, very slow. He is working class primitive, wonderfully bright, the type I am used to. Ernie Fitzgerald (the famed government whistleblower) was over here today and got into a fight with Moore who had either never heard of Dina Rasor (head of the Project on Military Procurement and now head of the Project on Government Oversight) or more likely thought waste, fraud and abuse didn't matter to the American public . . ."

Shortly after being chosen to lead *Mother Jones*, Moore attended the General Motors annual meeting in Detroit thanks to a proxy arranged by Jim Musselman. At the meeting, Moore sat next to Musselman while hammering Roger Smith with eight questions about GM's tax appeals and the chairman's refusal to visit the troops in Flint, Michigan. Moore's verbal *pas de deux* with the auto company's commander-in-chief, was followed by other critics from the Michigan Education Association. Again Smith refused to meet with this teachers' union leaders and ducked questions about the impact of tax abatements on the schools.

Moore subsequently rendezvoused at a Greenwich Village cafe with fairy godmother Zill and Manhattan Filmmaker Rafferty, who didn't realize he had been double-booked. Rafferty was uncomfortable with the idea of pitching for a grant in front of Moore. But after Zill departed, the two men began talking shop. Both had been self-employed for almost their entire careers. And both loved film. Eight years older, Rafferty was as tall as Moore and had the kind of Nick Nolte looks that could befit a network news anchorman. Like Moore he was also part of the vast left wing conspiracy that rattled Reagan's so-called brain trust.

In his undergraduate years at Harvard, Rafferty studied documentary making in the architecture and design school. After a postgraduate year at California Institute of the Arts, he teamed up with director Richard Cohen and began raising money for *Hurry Tomorrow,* a film on the forced drugging of patients at Metropolitan State Hospital in Norwalk, California.

His partner had a first-class list of organizations who opposed mandatory hospitalization and drug treatments for mental patients, as well as an A-list of celebrities like Jack Lemmon who ponied up. Roy Rogers proved a harder sell, in part because Dale Evans always beat him to the phone and insisted he was out. Thanks to tax laws that made it easy for donors to accelerate depreciation of their gifts, fundraising moved along well. *Hurry Tomorrow* became the first of a series of critically acclaimed Rafferty films, that would later include *The Atomic Café*, the true story of the nuclear weapons and Civil Defense hysteria.

The serendipity of their meeting meant everything to Rafferty's work in progress, *Blood In The Face,* a kind of paramilitary *All in the Family,* based on James Ridgeway's book, which took its title from a hate group that appropriated the brand name of an obscure British sect called Christian Identity. Built around the claim that they were direct descendants of Adam, these supremacists argued that only the white man can blush. Rebels with many causes, the Christian Identity Movement included self-styled freedom fighters determined to blow up blacks, Jews, Communists and government buildings. Ridgeway was astonished that Moore was at home baiting Nazis but clueless when it came to placing a drink order at a bar. "We went out to talk,"

Ridgeway recalls, at a restaurant down the street from the Manhattan headquarters of the *Village Voice,* "and I remember the waitress asking Moore what he'd like to drink. But he wasn't sure what to get. So I looked at him and said, 'I'm having a white Russian.'

"Moore looked at the waitress and said, 'Great, I'll have a white Russian.'"

For Moore, discovering Rafferty and Ridgeway was more than a lucky break. It was a defining moment, like being admitted to seminary. His new friends would provide skills and resources necessary to begin a new career. Soon he would take the oath of poverty central to the life of a documentary filmmaker.

In many ways this Kevin Rafferty, James Ridgeway, Anne Bohlen cinema verité film project was a bit like trolling for piranha. The story told itself. The only problem was finding a reliable guide who knew how to land a big catch without getting hurt. In a New York minute, Moore told Rafferty he personally knew Klan members and other self-styled cross-burners, Jew haters and racists who would be willing to go on camera. Rafferty, Ridgeway and co-producer Bohlen booked tickets to Flint, and Moore drove them to a meeting with Pastor Bob Miles, a repeat guest on his *Radio Free Flint* talk show.

A hospitable Midwesterner, Miles had graciously assembled leadership from the Klan, Nazi hate groups, and paramilitary organizations. Not only did they agree to let Rafferty, Bohlen and Ridgeway film the get-together, they also invited the filmmakers back to Michigan for lengthy interviews at a national convention of America's hate groups featuring a Klan wedding where a couple recited their vows in white KKK robes illuminated by the glow of a burning cross.

True to his word, Miles gave the *Blood in The Face* team full access to the hate weekend, where a bust of Hitler was on display in the "Hall of Heroes" Quonset hut. Moore learned quickly that people would do almost anything to get on camera. A kind of grown up Art Linkletter, he was able to get adults to say the darndest things. He was at his best with a uniformed neo-Nazi woman. "You look like you could be in a Coppertone commercial," said the journalist on camera to the blushing fascist.

I LEFT MY UNLAWFUL TERMINATION LAWSUIT
IN SAN FRANCISCO

ON HIS FINAL NIGHT IN FLINT, Moore did not want a going-away party. It was hard enough saying goodbye to family, colleagues, old friends and Kathleen Glynn, who would remain in Flint for the summer, running her graphic design business and raising her daughter Natalie.

On this night Michael Moore wanted to give himself a special parting gift, he wanted to grab a rivet gun and experience the thrill of life on the line. Ben Hamper provided directions to the North Unit parking lot at the GM Truck and Bus plant, and purchased two quarts of beer to celebrate the sendoff. Moore arrived in his Honda and headed up to the rivet line. Hamper tried to talk the editor out of picking up the gun that delivered up to 17,000 pounds of pressure per square inch by offering him all the beer he could drink. But Moore grabbed his weapon of choice, drove a series of rivets home and then turned to the gathered factory workers. No longer a virgin on the GM Assembly line, Moore flashed a smile at Hamper's applauding colleagues and then headed home to finish packing.

On his flight out to San Francisco the following day, Mikey the Riveter was seated next to one of America's most beloved entertainers, Tony "I Left My Heart in San Francisco" Bennett. Uncertain how to handle the star, Moore decided to let the crooner sleep as the plane crossed the Rockies and began its descent over the Sierras.

Moore disembarked with a long wish list. He wanted to edit a publication that appealed to people who preferred *People* to *Public Affairs*. And he wanted to make news.

He wanted to do an exposé on PBB the fire-retardant chemical used in children's pajamas. "It is also in my and 98 percent of Michigan residents' stomachs. It got accidentally mixed in with cattle feed 12 years ago. No one knows what the effects of this will be (PBB cannot pass out of the body). In 1974 they told us it might be 20 years before we find out what the PBB in us will do. We are human time bombs, ticking away—and only eight years to go before the experts say we begin to find out. Worse case scenario: Around 1992, thousands of Michigan residents begin developing strange cancers or diseases and are dying."

Moore liked the idea of a Michigan story on the decision of Ontanogan County residents to turn their pristine area into a nuclear waste disposal site as well as "A Day in the Life of Reagan's America" featuring the collapse of capitalism with specials on "A Day in the Cheese Line" and "A Day at the Plasma Center."

Determined to give equal time to the "opposition" Moore planned to kick off a series of interviews with headliners such as Jesse Helms, Jerry Falwell and corporate presidents on the theory that "these are far more informative and entertaining than talking to someone who agrees with us."

Another important story was "the secret air war in El Salvador" which has turned "Honduras into one, big U.S. Army Camp." The new editor was also eager to run a "monthly box of names of those individuals in Central America killed by Contras, death squads, government forces, or U.S. soldiers."

Moore was also eager to "forcefully speak out for Palestinian rights without fueling anti-Semitism. One possibility was to profile Israel Shahak, a Bergen-Belsen survivor who headed the Israeli League for Human and Civil Rights. As Moore explained, this article candidate feared that Israel's treatment of Palestinians resembled "what he witnessed in Nazi Germany."

For the new editor the trick was to blend exposés with a witty, literate style that went beyond traditional exposés and gave readers the kind of stories they wanted to share with friends. Moore's first two issues, included hilarious Ben Hamper pieces. The autoworker did a wonderful sendup of General Motors costumed feline mascot "Howie Makem" the productivity cat who wandered the assembly line cheering on the workforce until someone stole his outfit. Hamper also agreed to Moore's request to go off on a national publicity tour for the magazine. The Rivethead always found it hard to say no to Moore's many demands. There was very little hidden about persuader Michael Moore. As Hamper explained: ". . . Michael Moore—a man who could've talked Hitler into hosting a bar mitzvah—was the absolute master of wily persuasion."

Hochschild appeared to love Hamper's grassroots shtick as he celebrated the appointment of a working class hero with his readers: "From six feet under her gravestone in Mount Olive, Illinois, came the muffled voice of Mary Harris Jones (1830-1930), from whom we take our name: 'Hire that young feller!'" Moore returned the compliment, telling friends, "no publication is everything we want it to be, yet I had always had a good feeling the day *Mother Jones* arrived in the mail." And he made a solemn promise to the readers. "There will be no sacred cows at *Mother Jones* on the right or the left. We will challenge our readers to rethink the accepted assumptions and to take action when necessary."

The hypotheses that Moore's talents would benefit the *Mother Jones* community looked good on paper. And when Moore arrived armed with a handful of Detroit Tigers caps for the editors, he was greeted warmly "He had a lot of charm," said Dancis. "I thought he was funny, and sort of sassy. There was a cleverness and a braggadocio about him. The *Michigan Voice* was sharply written, it had a sense of humor." In the office, Moore tried to impress his colleagues with his top down approach to reporting. A discussion about the rise of Federal Express prompted Moore to pick up the phone and put in a call to the company's CEO, Fred Smith. "He didn't get through," said Dancis, "and we never actually did the story but he was saying, let's be audacious, let's be brazen, let's have some chutzpah."

Although Moore did a good job of publicizing the magazine's future prospects, Dancis worried about the day-to-day operation. The new editor's two-guys-from-Michigan national publicity tour with Ben Hamper left a vacuum in day-to-day operations. Editors had deliberately held off on making assignments prior to Moore's arrival on the theory that the new boss would want to bring in new writers of his own choosing. Similarly a key editorial position was left open for Moore to fill. Dancis worried that Moore's ability to put a face to the magazine, his own, just might be a tactical error. "There are different styles of leadership on the left. I was very much influenced by the Student Non Violent Coordinating Committee (like SNCC's Stokeley Carmichael, he had attended New York's Bronx High School of Science). The idea was that a leader is somewhat self-effacing. The point is to get people into motion.

"There is another style of leadership that is personality driven. You have an Abbie Hoffman or a Jerry Rubin, who wants to put himself forward, who wants to be famous. The media is more oriented toward the latter. They like stars, they like people who enjoy being in the public eye. Michael likes to have stuff revolving around him. Most politicians have that drive, that belief in themselves. You could see that in Michael.

"The left does not do a good job of creating personalities. People view the star system as inherently elitist. To me it goes back to the whole thing of the media trying to create a leader. People who did choose to set themselves up as the leaders were self-proclaimed, they were not necessarily chosen by anyone else.

"I was the principal organizer of the first and only anti-Vietnam War mass draft card burning in Central Park's Sheep Meadow on April 15, 1967 (Dancis had attracted the attention of J. Edgar Hoover by tearing up his own draft card shortly before this event.) This was part of a much larger New York mobilization against the war that attracted over 400,000 people. Martin Luther King was part of this event but the leaders of the mobilization didn't want us to be linked with the draft card burning. I was even flown on a private plane from Cornell with half a dozen other organizers to meet with mobilization leaders who wanted to stop the card burning."

Unpersuaded, Dancis was on hand with 175 other draft resisters eager to follow his example. After they set fire to their selective service registration cards in Central Park, the young men marched to the United Nations, where King keynoted a major antiwar rally.

Although reporters from the *New York Times* and other major media sought interviews, Dancis turned them away. Unlike Columbia University, where the media anointed Mark Rudd as a student power figurehead, these draft resisters did not want to have a spokesperson. "Our attitude is we don't have a leader," he explained. "We had no intention of competing with celebrities at the mobilization. We wanted to focus on the act of burning draft cards, to demonstrate that this was a collective decision made by people all over the country. The worst thing we could do would be to show that this was the work of some mastermind orchestrating us like puppets."

Dancis's role model was Bob Moses of the Student Nonviolent Coordinating Committee. "He even changed his name because he was getting too much attention and that had a big influence on me. Of course it's a lot different when you are trying to run for office or become a movie star.

"Think about it. Who were the '60s leaders on the new left? There were SDS leaders like Bernadine Dohrn who went underground. Mark Rudd became a sensation because he was in New York. Abbie Hoffman and Jerry Rubin recognized the power of the mass media in spreading their ideas. They were friends of mine but that is not what I was in to, making myself the center of attention to get my views out."

But the lack of charismatic leaders such as Martin Luther King or César Chávez also meant that it was hard to battle a well organized and politically adroit conservative movement. Ben Hamper knew how to tell a joke. But in the long run, was he really going to give labor the upper hand in its battle with General Motors? When it came to foreign policy, the left failed to recognize that its latest big players made embarrassing and costly mistakes. Like the elected conservatives they despised, these social critics were not always gifted architects of an alternate political universe.

Mother Jones co-founder Adam Hochschild summed up the problem neatly in a tenth anniversary editorial for the magazine. "It is difficult to put out a progressive magazine in a country whose progressive movements are weak and in disarray. One result of this has been that *Mother Jones* has mostly concentrated on muckraking. We've carried far too little material that embodies a vision of what a truly democratic America would look like. On the rare occasions when we've tried to, it has fallen flat, perhaps because it seems so far from possible. It is hard to write convincingly about worker-owned industries and peaceful resolution of disputes when millions of Americans have no work at all and when a president plays with air strikes as if he were directing movie scenes."

"In the ten years of *Mother Jones*'s lifetime, the U.S. military budget (after inflation) has increased 53 percent, our streets have become full of homeless, and our skies full of test beams for Star Wars. And would anybody have ever believed, ten years ago, that a president could laugh at air pollution, dismiss a Soviet nuclear test moratorium, and try to sell the Bonneville Dam to private enterprise? It's a grim picture, and not likely to become brighter during the two and a half remaining years of the Rambo era."

Unfortunately the feisty tenth anniversary keynoter was not the man destined to lead *Mother Jones* and its progressive allies out of the political wilderness. Under his leadership the magazine quickly ran aground in an unfortunate power struggle. Unlike his predecessors, Jeffrey Klein, Deirdre English and Adam Hochschild, Moore did not have previous experience with four-color national magazines. The editors had deliberately let the inventory run low and left him a senior editor position to fill. "We had a lead time of several months," explained Ohanian. "He was assigning very slowly. And, certain that he wanted to fill the open editing position with someone from New York, he ran an ad in the *New York Times*. Hundreds of replies stacked up on his desk, but he wasn't opening them. I suggested that we create a card to thank people for sending in their applications. But he never bothered. He said he was interviewing candidates when he went off with Ben Hamper on his cross-country tour to promote the magazine. But none of these people ever showed up in our offices for an interview. The position was never filled."

While Moore did get some new stories going, particularly for Ben Hamper and Alexander Cockburn, the replenishment rate was dropping rapidly. Ohanian tried to solve the problem by suggesting story ideas. "I had this idea that there were a lot of AIDS conspiracy theories in the black community and the gay community. I told him, 'They are using gays to test new drugs in the gay community. Let's do a story on what it is about this epidemic that makes these conspiracy theories live.'"

"There is only one story I want to do," replied Moore. "I want to find the cause and the cure for AIDS."

Ohanian took a deep breath before explaining the obvious: "I pointed out that many scientists in famous labs were working hard on this question which we were not in a good position to answer authoritatively. It was kind of like publishing a story on what color house you would build on Saturn. He accused me of not thinking big enough."

Moore's outrageous statements were part of a storm pattern that characterized his career. Journalism was more than publishing good stories. You also had to know how to go out beyond the story itself and make yourself controversial. An easy way to do this was to interview someone that virtually everyone hated, such as a neo-Nazi who agreed to go on Radio Free Flint. Another way to attract attention was the theatre of the absurd, i.e., dumping a dog shit pie with a whipped cream copyright C on the news desk at the Flint Journal to protest the appropriation of a *Voice* story without attribution. It was even possible to make news by *not* getting an interview with someone who mattered. This "constant no comment" school of journalism let the writer editorialize without fear of contradiction.

There were so many things about Moore's management style that didn't mesh with the *Mother Jones* brain trust, that some of his colleagues began wondering if they were working for a hatchet man whose sole purpose was to persuade them to quit. Moore turned out to be a poor role model. He failed to show up for editorial meetings. "He didn't call in, and we didn't know where he was for five or six days," says Ohanian. "This was an early warning sign to me and Bruce." During this pre-Blackberry era there was no way to track him down short of calling the State Police. And when he was in the office he would close the door for long phone conversations with the likes of Alexander Cockburn, whom he worshipped. He had this love affair with Cockburn. He worshipped the ground Cockburn walked on.

"Everything he did was based on the idea that number one I am running this show by myself. Number two, you can't count on me. He did stuff that may seem petty in retrospect. He would schedule a meeting with me and Bruce at 10 a.m. and we would sit there for a few minutes, leave a note, and go back to our offices. He would show up at 11:15 p.m. His attitude was, 'I am not going to be where I am supposed to be when I am supposed to be. I am not going to call you and I am not going to deliver my copy on time. And by the way you guys are window dressing.' He had no idea what he was doing. There was this dangerous combination of incompetence and utter ignorance. He was incompetent at running a national magazine. There was a huge vacuum. Adam, who had run the magazine on an interim basis, was detaching himself to give Michael a clean slate. But when he got there we had a vacuum at the top. I ended up spending entire nights in the office editing.

"Bruce and I wanted him to succeed," says Ohanian. "Everyone wanted him to succeed. I went to him on several occasions and said behind closed doors, 'Michael you are really fucking up here. You have to assign stories, you have to involve everyone in the process. You have to get stuff in on time. You have to work with the art department and assign art.' He would respond hopefully by saying, 'You are right, thank you for coming to me with this stuff.'

"He was a nonpresence. You needed a presence there. It wasn't like he was in people's faces. We had to work around him. We had to get the magazine out in spite of him. He wasn't editing anything. He assigned very few stories. A lot of what we ran at that time was inventory stuff. He did one cover on Ben Hamper and a story on Captain Midnight, a guy who was stealing radio signals. He also worked on a story with theoretical physicist Michiko Kaku as well as Russ Plant, a Michigan buddy who was heavily in to conspiracy theories. He was also eager to bring in power hitters like Noam Chomsky and Palestinian Rights expert Edward Said of Columbia."

Ohanian and Dancis lunched with Moore nearly every day at a local sub shop where they presented their own story ideas. Ohanian was intrigued by a piece about the Drug Enforcement Agency's plan to outlaw Ecstasy. "I had a source at Harvard Medical School, a psychiatrist, who said this drug is extremely useful in the medical community. I said 'Let's do a story about this drug that is being outlawed for street use even though some psychiatrists still think they should have access to it for treatment.' This flipped Michael out. He went on a tirade about how everyone in San Francisco liked to smoke pot and he never did drugs or pot in his life. He talked about how the San Francisco vision of changing the world was to get high. He said what you really need to do is 'Get out on the streets with the people.'"

At one point in an editorial meeting he asked, "Am I the only person in this room who has never smoked pot?" Although the new editor did not ask his employees to submit to random drug tests, there was a feeling in the room that he was less than cool on this issue.

One day he was meeting with an editor who was paged by the *Mother Jones* receptionist. A contributor, Laura Fraser, was waiting in the lobby to drop off a story. "She's brought my stash," said the editor. Moore quickly concluded that the editor was trading assignments for drugs, that he had a substance abuse problem which explained why the employee was working long hours. "Of course this wasn't true. The fact is I was staying up because he wasn't doing his job," said the editor.

Unlike a lot of newcomers, Moore did not see San Francisco as the kind of place where God would want to live if he could afford it. The city's Mediterranean climate, marine views, cable cars and sourdough bread did nothing for him. He was not lunching on cracked crab at Jack's with the city's famed *San Francisco Chronicle* columnist Herb Caen. He didn't spend his weekends bird watching and exploring the footpaths of the Golden Gate National Recreation Area. Nor did he hang out at City Lights Book Store, a shrine to the city's literary heritage.

"I remember him not understanding the multicultural aspect of San Francisco," said Dancis. "He sort of didn't fit where he was. He kept asking where the blacks were." The *Mother Jones* office was a block away from a gas station that had instructions in English, Spanish, Cantonese and Tagalog. It's among the most diverse cities in the world with a huge Latino population. He couldn't see this new kind of multiculturalism. He kept seeing a lot of white faces and not so many black faces.

"Michael was very committed to fighting racism but his experience was about the oppression of black people. It was harder for him to grasp that there were other forms of racism in America, beyond the black and white issue.

Looking out his *Mother Jones* window at the welfare office lineup across Mission Street, Moore was reminded of his Michigan friends, the ones who had lost their jobs, their homes, their savings, the ones standing in cheese lines and scanning the help-wanted ads from Texas newspapers. Every day he could see San Francisco's fortunate homeless walking off with overnight vouchers for shelter beds. Those who failed to line up early, were forced to bed down in doorways or underneath freeways. Watching the losers walk away, he wondered if some of them might be fellow Michiganians. Exploring the city, Moore was also stunned by the city's coffee klatch culture. "San Francisco was on the other side of the world from Flint. Everyone had a job yet no one seemed to be working. The cafés were filled with people at three in the afternoon."

At the end of the summer, after closing down her graphic design business in Flint, Kathleen left for San Francisco in time to enroll Natalie at a local kindergarten. Ohanian and other editors took time off from their work to help Moore move his family into their new apartment near the University of California Medical Center in Parnassus Heights, they had a sinking feeling that he was mired in culture shock and not really committed to the magazine. Fellow baseball fan Ohanian invited him to a Giants game at Candlestick Park. He hoped that the ride to the game through the predominantly black Hunters Point neighborhood would help Moore appreciate the city's racial diversity. But the game was a bust. Moore seemed depressed and disinterested. "It seemed like he was in a stupor," said Ohanian. "Then there was the time in mid-August when we had the staff picnic at Tilden Park in Berkeley. He is the editor of the magazine and he spent the whole staff picnic sitting by himself. You have been the editor four months, you should be the life of the party, you should be the leader, you should be leading the group. I kept wondering what is up with Michael. It was very weird."

On the editorial side, Moore, accustomed to paying *Voice* writers as little as $5 to $10 an article, did not find it easy to hire new writers at a considerably higher rate of pay. "The problem," said Dancis, "was that Moore would make a lot of promises and then not do what he had to do to get the pieces. All of my writers were supposed to have contracts. Michael would come back from a New York trip and announce that Edward Said was going to do a piece for us." But when Dancis called the Columbia University comparative literature professor to confirm the piece about Palestinian rights, Said demurred: "No, Michael and I talked about a story, but we never talked about deadlines, or a fee." It was the same story with Noam Chomsky.

"In terms of developing new stories from a writer, he was a failure. Prices weren't set, deals weren't closed, contracts weren't signed and ultimately stories we thought were in the pipeline didn't show up."

Moore did create valuable publicity for the magazine on his cross-country tour with Hamper. When Moore was unable to get away from the office, Hamper was called in to appear on a Chicago television, accompanied by a coworker. And his *Mother Jones* pieces impressed NBC's *Today Show,* which flew a crew out to film Rivethead and his GM party animals. After a four-day shoot, the producer suggested Hamper and friends repair to one of their favorite watering holes, Mark's Lounge, compliments of the network. Just hours before the shoot, Hamper flipped on the news and learned that a berserk, drug crazed auto worker had savagely stabbed two popular Mark's Lounge waitresses. Several days later the attacker was found dead, the victim of an overdose.

While NBC dropped the bar shoot and the waitresses healed, Moore continued to commission stories from Hamper and old *Michigan Voice* colleagues like James Hynes, the TV critic who boasted, "I watch television so you don't have to." And he did enlist James Ridgeway for a look at the fall election campaign. Moore admired the Washington writer who was tough on Democratic candidates buying into Republican chicanery like the Graham-Rudman deficit-reduction bill. Among them was Massachusetts Senator John Kerry who offered the "mind numbing" excuse that the government "should be more honest to the people about the debt."

Moore was also uncomfortable with some pieces that had been bought and were on the schedule. "We sent Paul Berman down to Nicaragua to write a piece about the Sandinistas pro and con," explains Dancis. The editor believes progressives needed to be just as tough on their heroes as they are on their enemies. "We had heard some troubling things about the Sandinistas commitment to free press and civil liberties. On the other hand we certainly supported them for trying to keep a democratic government of the left in Nicaragua, They would certainly be far more responsive to the people than dictator Antonio Somoza or the contras. By picking Berman to write this story we were not going to get a knee jerk support piece. So naturally people who didn't brook any criticism of the Sandinistas were upset.

"We ran the first part in February 1986, and when Moore was hired he was told that we were committed to run Part Two. Part One was positive and negative. It was a no holds barred look at the society and the government. It was anti-Contra, but it looked openly at some of the excesses of the Sandinista regime. When the time came to run the second part Michael said, 'I don't want to run it.' He didn't agree with it. He said 'Bruce I need your support on this,' and I said 'I can't. We've promised to run it.'"

Moore, who had been tough on the United Auto Workers (who represented the Mother Jones staff), Jane Fonda and Students for a Democratic Society at the *Voice,* understood the argument for Part Two of Paul Berman's work. But as he talked the problem over with his friend, Berman critic Alexander Cockburn, Moore also realized that the story, which remained open to further editing, would send a disturbing signal to his new readership. Giving in would make it appear that he lacked the kind of editorial independence that had brought him to the helm. The new editor, who had personally reported in Nicaragua, told his colleagues that Berman's article was so tough on the Sandinistas it sounded like a Reagan speech. When the editors agreed to print a rebuttal by Alexander Cockburn, Moore lightened up. But then Dancis balked on the Cockburn response.

Dancis also believed Moore was starting to sound paranoid: "Our best writer was Barbara Ehrenreich. At that time she was writing a column and she was one of the funniest and most incisive writers we had. Barbara was also our most popular writer, she had authored several books with Moore's predecessor, Deirdre English. Anyone

who paid attention to progressive journalism knew she was one of
the bright lights on the left and we were happy to have her on our
team. She knew how to write for a popular audience and turned in
perfect copy. Barbara was an editor's dream.

"The readers really liked her and she was a wonderful person. But
she was also one of former editor Deirdre English's closest friends.
Moore suggested that her column wasn't very good. Everyone else
thought Barbara was wonderful. Had he axed her, the board would
have thought that he was crazy or that he was so personality driven
that he was making irrational decisions."

Another problem for Moore was art director Louise Kollenbaum.
She was a powerful figure at the magazine who booked the pages
and sent the magazine to the printer. "When Michael fucked around
with the deadlines," says Dancis, "he was fucking around with the
layout."

As always he would bring in his own editorial shortly before the
Fed Ex truck was scheduled to arrive to pick up the final pages for
the printer. "His defense," explains Dancis, "was that he wanted to
keep us topical, to comment on issues of the day. He always thought
our deadlines were phony deadlines. We kept telling him we had to
get more stories.

"The big problem with Michael was that he would talk about
stories he would like to see, ideas we all liked. Unfortunately he was
unable to ever deliver them. Within a short period of time we were
using up all the stories we had in reserve and little was coming in
with the exception of Ben Hamper. He was also missing all of the
deadlines for his own editorial. We explained that if he didn't get his
column in on time we were going to have an empty page in the magazine. I felt he was doing some of these things to upset Kollenbaum."

Moore also had an unexpected problem with the magazine's gate-
keepers, a nearly all-female staff of fact checkers. "He really had
it in for the fact checkers," says Ohanian. "They drove him nuts.
He wanted to know why we needed someone to check our facts.
They may have said to him, 'You know, this may not stand up.' He
felt they were just a bunch of whiners, because they needed stuff
early enough in the process that they could do something with it.

We couldn't change everything at the last minute. He saw them as a bunch of lightweights. They weren't his idea of hard investigative journalist types. He just hated them.

"One of the women asked him to name ten investigative reporters he respected. They were all men. She asked why there were no women on the list and he said he couldn't think of any. I had the impression that he was not interested in assigning a lot of stories to women. When we suggested experienced investigative reporters like Judy Coburn and Kate Coleman he didn't seem interested."

Despite Moore's distaste for Ehrenreich and his run-ins with Kollenbaum, Moore was quick to defend the rights of women at the *Mother Jones* work place—perhaps a little too quick. Acting on a comment from a woman on the staff who read potential harassment into a late evening phone call from publisher Hazen, Moore suddenly picked up the pace. Instead of meeting with the publisher privately to get his side of the story, he raised the possibility of a sexual harassment complaint at an open editors' meeting. Although no charges were ever filed, Moore's public airing of the potential problem set the *Mother Jones* grapevine abuzz. To some it looked like a power grab.

Adam Hochschild, who did not keep an office at *Mother Jones* had been hearing about these problems but was not eager to micromanage the new editor, particularly when he was just one member of the board. But after the founder, who was underwriting the *Mother Jones* deficit with six figure donations, was invited to lunch by Dancis and fellow editor Bernard Ohanian, he began to see the possibility of a staff revolt.

"Moore didn't realize how difficult it was to come into an already existing institution and reshape it," says Ohanian. "If he had been more savvy and patient and knew how to build alliances, it would have totally been his platform in two or three years. He came in with a tremendous amount of goodwill. He got to play in a much bigger sandbox and had more influence for better or worse. He thought he could waltz in like he did at the *Michigan Voice* and just do it. It was so frustrating to him. There were lead time issues and color proofing. We had to plan out the September issue in May. He wanted to know why we couldn't do the September issue in August. Well that is the way magazines work. I don't remember him ever doing anything that approximated editing, sitting down with a writer and helping a writer go through a story. I can't imagine him line by line editing. He didn't seem engaged in the process of designing stories. Other magazine editors are involved in shaping a story, top editing. Most editors have a clear direction on how they want it to read. They read stories a couple of times. They are constantly coming up with ideas that they implement. I remember Bruce and me editing the magazine in terms of actual work.

"He did have his admirers on the staff. He got along well with Richard Reynolds, in part, I think because Richard was from Detroit and also because Richard handled the media and could get him some publicity. The younger people and the staff were wooed by his charisma. But the older more experienced people thought he was full of shit."

By early September Dancis and Ohanian were panicking over the shortage of publishable stories. With the editorial well running dry, they called Hochschild, the most crucial player on the board. "After we told him about the problems, he realized there was a crisis," says Dancis. "Once we met with him, the board moved very quickly and within a week they told Michael it wasn't working out and he had to go."

When Hochschild broke the news to Moore on Labor Day weekend, the editor was stunned and asked the board chairman for a ride home. The publisher offered the editor an all-expense-paid U-Haul for the cross country journey back to Flint.

"I do blame the board in picking Michael," says Dancis. "They didn't pay enough attention to what is involved in putting out a magazine. You have to know how to manage a staff, manage a budget, and manage an office. You can't be a lone wolf and do that unless you are really good at delegating, which he wasn't. Michael was impossible.

"He was someone for whom we all had high hopes," Hochschild said of Moore after the decision was made to let him go. "He ran into increasing difficulties with the job. They had not so much to do with differences of political vision as with more mundane matters that can arise at any workplace: ability to perform a demanding job at the level required, to manage a staff effectively, and to work well with others.

"By September it was clear to almost all of us who had to work with him most closely that there was a real mismatch between Moore and the editorship of *Mother Jones*. It fell upon me, as cofounder of this magazine and president of its foundation, to tell him so. Moore had moved halfway across the country to take the job, so this was not something any of us took lightly."

Dancis agrees: "After Moore was fired, he started a spin campaign and gave a lot of speeches. One of his complaints was that he was fired for trying to put an auto worker on the cover. In fact he actually did succeed in putting auto worker Ben Hamper on the cover. In my case he said that I was too pro Israel, too pro Zionist and not sympathetic enough to the Palestinian cause. I am a secular Jew but I have never been a Zionist. I have always supported peace with the Palestinians and their right for a Homeland. And less than a year before Michael arrived we ran a piece on Israel's huge foreign arms sales called 'Uzi diplomacy.' I felt there was anti-Semitism. I didn't think my position on the Middle East differed with other people.

"He also said that I favored the Berman story in part because I was an anti-Communist. During the '60s many leading radical groups favored open organizations. I was part of the National Mobilization Committee Against the War and we welcomed anyone who wanted to work with us. We were not trying to redo the socialist versus communist versus Trotskyite battles. I didn't define my self as an anticommunist but I was an anti-Stalinist. I considered myself a Democratic socialist.

"As the former president of Cornell Students For A Democratic Society, a draft resister who went to federal prison in Kentucky for two years in the late '60s and a writer/editor who worked for the *Socialist Review* for nine years, this was all slanderous stuff.

"Michael from the moment he got fired from *Mother Jones* conducted a campaign of vilification, lying and slander against the people he used to work with," said Dancis. "Michael can be a very compelling figure, he is clever, he is funny. He knows how to zero in on an issue, playing poor boy versus rich dilettante. It appears in a much milder form in *Roger & Me* where we are there as a bunch of comic relief all sitting around a table with him. Moore said famously, over a scene of people hanging out in coffee houses, that San Francisco is a place where everyone has jobs but no one seems to work. How ironic when you consider the fact that he was chronically late with his own column and couldn't seem to get stories assigned and went AWOL for days at a time. Michael tried to portray his firing as a case of a working class kid from Michigan up against a millionaire from San Francisco whose parents made their money off the black miners of South Africa."

Moore also surprised his former colleagues with the suggestion that the *Mother Jones* editors were working class wannabes. "A lot of people on the left who're wealthy are envious and desirous of being out there with the workers, with the people," said Moore. "They know that the only way we're going to stop the Reagan revolution is to reach out to everyday working people in the Flints and Clevelands of this country. They saw me as that great working-class hope.

"But it was just a fantasy. When the reality sunk in, they got cold feet. They realized they didn't want to be in bed with this kind of person. It's the plantation mentality: The master goes to the shack to put it to the slave, but the slave is never allowed into the master's bedroom."

The rapacious white slavers at *Mother Jones* were astonished by the shortfall left behind by the fired editor. "One of the things we did as soon as Michael left was to see if there were any stories," said Dancis. "I called up a number of writers he met with and asked if they had agreed to do a story and they explained no assignments had been issued. We had to assign a group of new stories on short deadlines to cover our depleted inventory.

"What you see of Michael in his movies is what you saw in the *Mother Jones* office. He was a chubby guy with a sense of humor and the baseball cap. He is funny and clever. Obviously the medium for him all along should have been the visual thing. He created a persona at a time when there aren't a lot of personas out there."

Sadly, Moore would not be leading *Mother Jones* into battle. Instead he and Kathleen Glynn, who had shut down her Flint graphic arts business to join Moore in San Francisco, filed a $2 million civil suit against *Mother Jones* and the Foundation for National Progress for wrongful discharge, breach of contract and two counts of fraud.

"They've destroyed what took me ten years to build," Moore told a press conference on the steps of San Francisco's Beaux Arts City Hall, the same place where police had swept House Un-American Activities Committee protesters down the grand staircase with water hoses in 1960 (45 years later the same location would be back in the spotlight when gays and lesbians across the country flocked to the rotunda to marry). To make his case against the article, Moore, dressed in blue jeans and a work shirt, quoted from a draft copy of Berman's unedited work in progress on Nicaragua. TV cameras recorded the Flint couple explaining how a muckraking magazine had raked them over the smoldering mesquite wood chips. After enrolling Natalie in school, the couple were now being forced to tear her away from California to an uncertain future in another part of the county.

News of the lawsuit was Moore's first taste of media stardom with pieces running in the *New York Times,* on the wire services and in publications like *The Nation*. Some papers, including the *San Francisco Bay Guardian,* where Dancis had worked as arts and entertainment editor, refused to publish an Alexander Cockburn column, calling the *Mother Jones* managing editor a "nonentity." Cockburn defended his friend and trashed Paul Berman's as yet unpublished story on the Sandinistas.

The breakup was nearly as explosive as *Mother Jones'* scoop on fiery Ford Pinto gas tanks. It prompted Berman to charge in the *Village Voice* that Moore's lawsuit was "doing Reagan's work." In his syndicated newspaper column, Cockburn alleged that *Mother Jones* was "the most boring magazine in the world" and accused Hochschild of behaving "like a 19th-century mill owner."

This kind of talk was particularly offensive to the magazine's top seven staffers, who had lived through Moore's counterinsurgency. "Like many people who have not met the expectations of their coworkers," they said in a press release, "Moore apparently tries to find someone else to blame and an evil motive behind his fall from grace."

* * *

As Cockburn's attack was being distributed around the country, Dancis and other editors were putting their finishing touches on the November issue, the final *Mother Jones* created during the reign of Mike from Michigan. Included was Alexander Cockburn's final article for *Mother Jones,* "Pulling the Plug." He was obviously worried about schmucks who abandoned their Underwoods for word processing on computers. The Luddite author worried that the switch was turning writers into "information inputters. The editor's authority is vastly increased. The collective—with obscured lines of individual responsibility—gains power at the expense of the individual writer."

Quoting author Hans Enzensberger, the fired editor's friend explained, "The mind industry's main business and concern is not to sell its product; it is to 'sell' the existing order, to perpetuate the prevailing pattern of man's domination by man, no matter who runs the society and no matter by what means. Its main task is to expand and train our consciousness in order to exploit it."

As lawyers began taking depositions in Moore's lawsuit against the magazine, the former editor suggested that the magazine's drug culture had led to his demise. He alleged that freelancer Laura Fraser was peddling drugs to his fellow editors. Back home in Michigan some of his old friends questioned Moore's conservative approach to drug use. "He was full of shit on that issue," said John Sinclair.

While Fraser said she had submitted a query for a piece "on how the drug MDMA had been banned" she denied Moore's allegation.

"Presumably he said this as a part of a strategy to reveal that *Mother Jones* had fired him because staff members were always so high they couldn't recognize his talent. I have never sold illegal drugs to any editor at *Mother Jones.* But even if I had come by every Thursday . . . it isn't good politics in the age of anti-drug hysteria to accuse of a felony a freelance you've never met, making the accusation part of the permanent public record without any evidence, in order to take some personal revenge. It's more like Nancy Reagan politics."

Mother Jones communications Director Richard Reynolds kept a running lists of Moore's explanations for his firing. The ex-editor told UPI his firing was triggered by his refusal to run the second part of Paul Berman's article critical of the Sandinistas. In a *San Francisco*

Chronicle piece he said "the real reason I was fired was that Adam Hochschild wanted a yes-man, someone to run his magazine the way he wanted it, because he didn't want to go to work." According to the *Village Voice,* Moore's "refusal to participate in management's numerous violations of its contract with the unionized staff" (represented by the UAW) led to regime change. At an Arab-American Anti-Discrimination Committee awards ceremony he reiterated his claim that planned coverage of the Palestinian issue prompted his firing. In the *SF Weekly* he blamed the whole thing on his resistance to running articles on herbal teas. In another paper, *Metro,* he explained "what they really wanted me to do is put movie stars on the cover and make it a *People Magazine* of the left." And readers of the *International Herald Tribune* learned from Moore that "the trouble really began when he interrupted a discussion about hiring more women and minorities to suggest that *Mother Jones* might serve the cause better by hiring a factory worker, a blue-collar person, an actual proletarian."

"The irony," said Reynolds, "is that we actually had published an issue with a blue-collar person, Ben Hamper, on the cover." Back home in Flint, Hamper, who had been chosen for the 1986 *Esquire Register* featuring "the nation's brightest young minds and high achievers under age forty," turned down an invitation to continue writing for the magazine and moved his Riverthead column to the *Detroit Free Press.*

Hamper complained that he "was practically being driven out of my skull by the magazine's crew of fact checkers and researchers. These morons would call me over and over asking the most goddamn insane questions. Particularly frustrating were wake-up calls seeking the name and number of a co-worker who could confirm that "the North Unit parking lot was indeed called 'the North Unit parking lot.'"

While Moore worked on his case, the magazine's editors denied that they were soft on Israel. They pointed out that *Mother Jones* was the first general circulation magazine to publish stories critical of Israel, including a cover story by Ellen Cantarow that questioned Israel's treatment of West Bank settlers. And at the time of the lawsuit the magazine was moving ahead with a piece by Robert I. Friedman on Israel's manipulation of the American press.

This did not discourage Moore from attacking the magazine as a pro-Zionist organization. *San Francisco Examiner* journalist Paul Fahri said Moore attributed his firing to a "proposed series of articles that he wanted to do about Israel that he had planned for, I believe, the June '87 issue of *Mother Jones.* . . . he wanted to send a Palestinian-American writer to Israel to report on Israel 40 years after independence. He wanted to do an interview with a concentration camp survivor who led an Arab-Israeli discussion or rights group in Israel . . . he felt that this did not go over with the prevailing political, cultural bias of the magazine, that these articles would not fit in with the personal philosophies of the people who were his superiors and the people he worked with."

In deposition, Fahri was asked if Moore felt one of his problems was the impressive number of Jews who had worked for the magazine. The list included founding editor Jeffrey Klein and Dancis, as well as Hochschild, Ohanian, and Moore's predecessor Deirdre English who were all half Jewish.

"I believe that came up, yes."

"Did he say that he thought that some of people on the editorial staff had Zionist sympathies, using the word 'Zionist'?"

"Frankly I can't recall," said Fahri. "But I was certainly left with the impression that was what he was saying."

THE NADER EVADER

SHIPWRECKED IN SAN FRANCISCO, Moore considered heading back to Flint and reviving the *Voice*, despite the fact that his old typesetting equipment had found a new home in Nicaragua. "It was a bad time for Michael," said Ralph Nader who had been following the blowup from Washington D.C. and discussing the purge with colleague Jim Musselman.

Shortly after the *Mother Jones* purge, Nader headed out to California for a speaking engagement. Musselman invited himself along to lend a hand. The organizer arrived at Moore's San Francisco apartment to find his friend in a state of shock, parked in front of his television watching *Barney Miller*. "I knew something was really wrong when he told me he didn't even want to go out to eat." Musselman finally convinced Moore to join him for a ride, the fired editor's first step out of his apartment in days.

After crossing the Golden Gate bridge the two men stood on a bluff, looking back at the city of St. Francis. By now Moore was convinced that the only rational decision was to head straight back to Flint, where he could cash his $99 a week unemployment checks and go for the coneys at Angelo's. It was a whole lot better than being stuck in the homeless lineup at the welfare office on Mission Street.

"I belong in Flint," said Moore to the man who had convinced him to apply for the *Mother Jones* position. Referring to "Mr. Tanner," a Harry Chapin song about a baritone who bombs during his Town Hall debut in New York and returns home to resume his day job as a dry cleaner, Moore added, "I am Mr. Tanner."

Musselman insisted it was time to head on across the Bay Bridge and break bread with the Corvair pallbearer. Moore met Ralph Nader at the Berkeley home of the consumer advocate's sister Laura Nader, an anthropology professor at the University of California. Nader was skeptical of adding anyone to his small Washington staff. He also questioned regional editor Moore about his interest in big league Washington politics. But Musselman was an adroit salesman, and Nader agreed to give Moore a job editing a fourth estate newsletter to be called *Moore's Weekly*. It was modeled after the caustic weekly media monitor published by America's self-appointed ombudsman, I.F. Stone.

A media addict, Moore was, in many ways, perfect for the job. Unlike Nader, he was serious about the motion picture industry. "I've always loved movies," he explained, "but after I was fired, I started going every day." He also had a special interest in the Fifth estate, devouring any new book on the media. For example he bought TV pundit Linda Ellerbee's new book *And So It Goes,* on publication day and finished it a day later. "He was always fascinated with the media," said Musselman. " He believed that if you kept saying something enough times, it will become the truth, the media will go along and not question it."

Thanks to Nader, Moore could make a living and collect unemployment. He, Kathleen and young Natalie were headed for the nation's capitol. In January Musselman helped them find an apartment and advanced the security deposit. Nader had allocated $30,000 toward *Moore's Weekly* including printing costs and office space just down the hall from the nation's leading consumer advocate.

Both Moore and Nader built their reputations pursuing the inexact science of investigative reporting. Unlike many journalists and public interest attorneys, both men knew how to make themselves a journalistic commodity. Instead of simply writing stories, they understood how to become the story.

Nader's band of eager young attorneys and political organizers

won a wide range of battles ranging from airline safety, insurance reform and environmental protection to freedom of information. With
the support of key senators, they were able to launch Congressional hearings and lobby successfully to limit air and water pollution.
One of Nader's crusades even had a patriotic name—consumerism. If
Americans couldn't shop with confidence, this country was destined
to end up just like the Roman empire.

"My father warned me that the thing that is harder than success is
to endure," said Nader. "The first thing I realized was that I couldn't
do this by myself. I knew that I had to hire good people right away,
people who had the skills to get laws passed that would protect the
American public from corporate crime.

"The Sixties had given birth to a new generation of moral leadership in America. Martin Luther King, who had the charisma to draw
attention to civil rights—he could command important audiences
and focus national attention on what needed to be done. The same
was true with César Chávez in the labor movement and John Kerry
in the antiwar movement. My idea was to help create new leadership,
spokespeople for important causes, people like Dr. Sidney Wolfe on
medicine and Joan Claybrook on auto safety. To me, Moore seemed
like someone who was effective, who could accomplish great things
because he had a vision. He was also articulate and he knew how to
use humor."

Nader, the picky eater, health fanatic, ascetic, workaholic attorney
who had been named the most distinguished alumnus in the history
of Harvard Law School, had parlayed a muckraking book on auto
safety into an effective public interest lobby. And he had also built
effective alliances with reporters who broke stories that were often
based on shocking information unearthed by Nader's troops.

While Nader commanded speaking fees in the many thousands of
dollars, Moore, for the first time in more than a decade was a captain
without a ship. No longer was he calling up reporters to give them
assignments and tight deadlines. He no longer had his radio show in
Flint and had been let go by National Public Radio, where he had occasionally spoken out. And he definitely was not pulling all-nighters
to get out his new publication as he had done at the *Voice*.

Moore got off to a slow start, putting out memos about the media as he began developing his newsletter. With the help of Nader's second in command, John Richard, he set up a critical network of media and political contacts. Neither man realized that Moore was preoccupied with another project, a movie he had begun shooting in Flint. "He kept it completely secret," says Nader. "We had no idea that he was preoccupied with a film about General Motors."

Moore's performance did not match the pace of an office that had nurtured names like Frank Rich, James Fallows, Mark Green, Robert Fellmeth, David Ignatius and Ron Brownstein. Colleagues like attorney Jim Musselman making $14,000 a year didn't punch a clock. Instead they were expected to approach their jobs like a medical school internship. The political cycle resembled life in the emergency room as Nader's minions fought lobbyists who wined and dined congressmen partial to the lush life. In the Nader organization, a day at the beach was exactly that. When employees said they were headed out to the shore, Nader assumed the holiday was only for a day. "If you said you were going to be gone longer than that," recalls Musselman, "Nader would be mystified. He couldn't understand what there was to do at the beach that took more than one day."

Instead of offering blood, sweat and tears, Moore was a plodding newcomer in the Nader inner sanctum, keeping an erratic schedule as he tried to ferret out "the censored news of the week." Based entirely on subscription revenue, without advertising revenue and a $100 cap on donations, *Moore's Weekly* debuted on December 28, 1987. "I wondered about Michael's name being on the newsletter," says Nader. "I didn't suggest it. His ego was all over it."

Who exactly was the man behind this newsletter determined to reveal "many important events" taking place each day which are ignored by the "29 media corporations which own the majority of the newspapers, magazines, book publishers and radio and TV stations in the United States" primarily concerned with maximizing "profits" and protecting "their various business interests around the world"?

After briefly recapping his journalistic lineage, Moore explained: "I was hired as the editor of *Mother Jones* magazine and was later dismissed for first, refusing to support the firing of an employee who was accused of once belonging to a communist group and secondly for refusing an order by the owner to run a story portraying the Sandinistas as torturers and murderers."

Determined to keep the *Weekly* "entirely independent of any corporation, organization or individual," Moore thanked the media for "opening up" a "new era of public accountability for personal morality . . . I like this new examination of character when it concerns someone who has been given a public trust. The media is also a public trust. It is time to turn the tables on these media entities and investigate their doings behind closed doors."

First up were two reporters who had broken major stories about important political figures. The leadoff hitter was the *New York Times*' Maureen Dowd, who made the front page with shocking news: Senator Joseph Biden had lifted large chunks of a speech by Neil Kinnock, Britain's Labor Party chief, for a TV commercial. The exposé prompted the Delaware Democrat to withdraw from the presidential race.

What readers didn't know was that Dowd herself had been accused of plagiarizing the *Congressional Quarterly* in a story she had written in 1984. The news story, originally broken by the *Village Voice*, was bogus, Dowd told Moore. She politely dismissed the charges as "a bunch of bullshit . . . slime being spread by the Biden people." Her editor, Adam Kleimer, insisted that Dowd had not been taken off the story after writing just two pieces because of her own brush with plagiarism charges.

In the same charter issue, National Public Radio Supreme Court reporter Nina Totenberg, one of the great names in broadcast journalism, was more forthcoming about her own problems. Always on the lookout for a smoking gun, Totenberg had revealed that Supreme Court nominee Doug Ginsburg had toked marijuana in the 1970s. Two days later Ginsburg decided to pull his name from consideration by President Reagan. Moore rang up Totenberg to chart her own drug use. She flatly denied smoking marijuana. Moore asked if anyone else at NPR bogarted joints. "Probably," she said, "but we're not up for Supreme Court." Then she added, "I've never heard of someone wanting to write an investigative piece on the personal lives of Ted Koppel or Nina Totenberg."

Two days later Totenberg conceded to a *Los Angeles Times* writer that she had taken a single puff." Moore was miffed.

"You were the first person to ask me such a question," Totenberg said. "I didn't think the question was the least bit relevant. I was busy, I was crazed, and to be honest, I just wanted to get rid of you. Yes, I had one puff once in my life and I almost died coughing. I had waited until it was decriminalized in D.C. before trying it. I had always made it a great policy to not use any drugs because of the damage it could do to my reputation."

Moore remained "curious about Totenberg's initially less-than-honest response to me, and considering how reporters like Totenberg have made this the year of the character test, I decided to investigate further. What I discovered was that Totenberg was fired from her job as a staff writer at the *National Observer* in 1973 for plagiarizing a story from the *Washington Post*."

The NPR legal affairs correspondent chalked the problem up to youthful indiscretion. "I was young, I was in my twenties," she told Moore. "I don't want to have to go back and talk about something that happened twenty years ago." When Moore suggested that sounded similar to Ginsburg's explanation of his marijuana use, she replied, "He was in his thirties. Besides, I don't think it's the least bit relevant."

And what about the firing at the *National Observer?* Moore wrote, "Totenberg said she lifted the sections from the *Post* article because the week she had to write the story on O'Neill, her sister had a terrible headache 'and I thought it might be a brain tumor.' She took her to the doctor who told her it was just a migraine headache.

"The fact that she once committed plagiarism, she said, 'has had no bearing on my work, no bearing on my reportage. I just rewrote an article and I did a lousy job. It is the single thing—that, plus an affair I once had—that I am most ashamed of in my life. Nobody's perfect.'

"That, I suppose is the point," suggested Moore. "Nobody is perfect, but how many of these reporters could pass their own 'morals' investigation?

"Totenberg pointed out that there were 'commentators' who were writing negative columns about Gary Hart who were also carrying on affairs behind their wives' backs (she didn't want to mention any names). She also said that it has not been uncommon for male reporters to sleep with secretaries of government officials in order to get a story. The Totenbergs and Dowds say they as reporters should not be asked personal questions because they're not running for anything. The media though, in many ways, is as powerful as any of the three branches of government; it is our fourth estate." When Totenberg took umbrage and called to complain about the newsletter story, Nader noticed that Moore actually enjoyed "arguing with her on the phone. That's the kind of thing he likes. A good fight with someone in power is his oxygen. That's what he lives for."

Of course the media could also be muzzled. As a former school board member, Moore was intrigued by a Supreme Court ruling that reporters working for school sponsored student newspapers are not covered by the First Amendment. "We stay away from all that controversial stuff," exclaimed a proud Debby Fink, the current editor of the Missouri paper that was the subject of the ruling. Determined to undo rampant censorship of student papers across the country, Moore wrote, "it is little wonder that young people, upon leaving high school, bother to get involved politically, read a daily newspaper or even register to vote. To expect them to become sudden participants in the democratic process after spending their "formative' years under the boot of an educational system which won't allow their participation in even the simplest of decisions is absurd. When schools censor student papers, the real lesson they're teaching is that a free press is not a good idea."

Self-censorship was certainly not a problem for Moore who took on liberals just as eagerly as he flailed conservatives. He was outraged when just four of the 200 progressive organizations that fought the Supreme Court nomination of Robert Bork agreed to battle another abortion rights opponent, Judge Anthony Kennedy. After the Reagan appointee took his seat, Moore criticized groups like the American Civil Liberties Union, the National Abortion Right League, the Women's Legal Defense, even Stewart Mott's beloved Planned Parenthood for refusing to "Bork" Kennedy. "Desirous of appearing fair minded and even-tempered, afraid to take on Ronald Reagan twice in a single decade, or too busy making bank deposits—whatever the reasons, these organizations decided to take a walk on the Kennedy nomination. That decision could prove to be very costly."

Moore's attack on the progressive left mirrored his complaint against *Mother Jones* and the Foundation for National Progress. These would be heirs to the legacy of freedom fighters like Mary Harris Jones were actually self-absorbed bigots who ran their empires like 17th-century French aristocrats. All too often the left sided with the conservative political and business interests who sold out women's rights and so many other important causes like the environment and, of course, the working class.

For the first time since he lost reelection to the Davison School Board, Moore was no longer part of a larger team. He had been running organizations since he started the Davison Hotline. Now he didn't even belong to a collective. There really wasn't anyone around to argue with because the *Weekly* was a solo act. Like a distant thunderstorm that could be heard but not seen, Moore had trouble being taken seriously. Lightning never struck. Unlike I.F. Stone or Ben Bagdikian, he had become a media gadfly no one seemed to know. People didn't seem to care what he thought. They weren't even sure what *Moore's Weekly* was about or where you could buy it.

"Who are you? Who are you with?" asked a CBS vice-president when Moore tried to make the point that the network was short on black journalists and managers in a piece called "The Thighs of CBS." Eager to show the hypocrisy of a network that had fired Jimmy "The Greek" Snyder for suggesting that blacks were superior athletes because of their thigh size, Moore argued that CBS had a hopeless affirmative action policy.

Backed up by designer Kathleen Glynn and assistant editor Andrew Morehouse, Moore found that many of his subscribers came from far beyond the beltway. A mailing to former Flint and *Michigan Voice* regulars produced a heartening response. But the new publication had difficulty gaining a foothold in the media top-heavy District of Columbia. Bates College graduate Morehouse, who had worked on Latin policy issues at the Council on Hemispheric Affairs, focused heavily on Nicaragua related coverage. Moore zeroed in on a region that had fascinated him for many years, the Middle East. "The Occupation: Day 7,532" headline focused on Yassar Arafat, the man who ordered the 1972 Munich Olympic kidnappings that led to the murder of 11 Israeli athletes. Moore's piece focused on a disagreement between Arafat and ABC *Nightline* anchor Ted Koppel, who tried to argue that the ongoing battles between the Israelis and Palestinians had led to the killing of innocent Arabs and Jews. "On both sides?" asked Arafat. "Who? Where? It seems that you are insisting on speaking some jokes . . . Women have been killed on both sides? Only our people are suffering." Moore followed up with a long list of recent Palestinian victims of Israeli security forces. No Israeli deaths were mentioned, nor was there any discussion of the fact that Arafat's participation in the Munich Olympics murders had probably killed his chances of winning the Nobel Peace Prize.

On an eight day trip, foreign correspondent Moore described the "collective punishment" used by Israel to harass Palestinians whose 'lives are a dead end, a miserable, slave-like existence, contained by the brute force of the Israeli system."

"It is a method of terror which blames an entire racial or national group—in this case, the Palestinians for the activities of a few of its members. Herod used it against his own people when he ordered the slaughter of all first-born Jewish boys. The Nazis later perfected it to insanity. Today those same victims of 2,000 years of collective punishment have become true-blue believers."

Moore's two part series argued that the American media was simply refusing to cover Israeli roundups of thousands of Palestinian boys and men who were systematically harassed, beaten and tortured. Israel's Palestinian camps in the Gaza and West Bank were becoming the scene of brutal subjugation, not unlike the Warsaw Ghetto. Shortly before his visit to the Jalazon Camp, soldiers "broke into homes and dragged dozens of boys out into the streets. At the home of Khadiegh Hassan Abu-Sharif, the soldiers were removing her five-year-old son when she tried to stop them. She grabbed her son in a tug of war with a soldier who drew his pistol and shot her twice at point blank range.

"We are now in her home where she is laying on the cement floor recovering from her wounds. She is glad to see us and commences the long and eloquent discourse on life. She has had 15 children; she is only 32 years-old. 'I have children for Palestine,' she tells us. 'For each one the Israelis deport or kill, we replace them with ten more.'

"On her wall are two shrines to Bruce Springsteen, tattered photos of The Boss encased in the kind of wooden frame usually reserved for Our Lady of Fatima. It is a strange sight. She says her son loves him. Another Palestinian tells me that Bruce 'won't play Tel Aviv,' won't play the Promised Land in this broken promise land."

Confronting an Israeli soldier at the nearby Al-amari camp, Moore pointed out that peacenik Yasir Arafat offered to recognize Israel if the nation would agree to an international peace conference."

"Look, I'm not a politician. I'm a soldier. I don't like doing this. But I have orders."

"That's what the Germans said at Nurnburg."

Leaving the camp, Moore suggested another Israeli assault on this Palestinian camp was inevitable. "We all know, though no one says it out loud, that within a short time hands will be broken and skulls will be cracked open."

After more than a week on Israeli soil, Moore was convinced that "if Israel continues to insist that it is a democracy, the Jews will be in a minority and Israel will no longer be a 'Jewish state.'

"So what are the alternatives to insure that Israel remains racially pure? Forced sterilization? Forced deportation? Annihilation? Or continue the status quo of apartheid . . ?"

Moore's solution to this complicated problem was to cut off American aid to Israel. To wit: "The two Israeli soldiers who supervised the burying alive of three Palestinians last month pled guilty on Thursday to the charge of disgraceful behavior. Farting is disgraceful behavior, Placing the spoon and the knife on the wrong side of the plate is disgraceful behavior. Burying alive human beings is attempted murder and terrorism. Cut the $3 billion (in aid)."

Assistant Editor Morehouse never felt "for a minute that Moore could be portrayed as being anti-Jew or anti-Semitic. He just felt very strongly about the plight of the Palestinians in the occupied territories. I remember Michael very clearly distinguishing between Jews and Zionists. There was a clear distinction between the average Jewish person and a person who is strident about the nature of the existence of Israel. It's a sensitive topic. The minute you try to criticize U.S. foreign policy in Israel, you are immediately labeled an anti-Semite."

Was it possible that Arafat was correct when he tried to tell Ted Koppel that the only victims in the conflict were Palestinian?

"Obviously that is ludicrous," said Morehouse. "From his perspective the mainstream media focusing on the issue was more slanted to the position of Israel. His talent is to dramatize hypocrisy and a double standard with humor, to attract attention to the issue."

This approach was applied to many issues such as the way the white media wrote off the presidential candidacy of Jesse Jackson. "What does it take to convince the media that Jesse Jackson is 'electable?'" asked Moore. "I'll tell you what. White shoe polish, hair straightener and a concerted effort on Jackson's part to sound as stupid and superficial as the other candidates.

". . . Beyond the racism lies the contempt the press has for anyone with a populist message which offers hope to the disenfranchised. Pat Robertson, a right-wing populist, faces a similar lack of respect and scrutiny in the media. Jackson and Robertson have brought millions of people, who long ago gave up on becoming participants in this democracy, back into the electoral process . . ."

In his eagerness to find linkage between Jackson and Robertson, Moore's space limitations prevented him from sharing details on the conservative preacher's unique brand of populism.

Missing from Moore's analysis was Robertson's notion "that termites don't build things, and the great builders of our nation almost to a man have been Christians, because Christians have the desire to build something. He is motivated by love of man and God, so he builds. The people who have come into (our) institutions (today) are primarily termites. They are into destroying institutions that have been built by Christians, whether it is universities, governments, our own traditions, that we have . . . The termites are in charge now, and that is not the way it ought to be, and the time has arrived for a godly fumigation."

The media's indifference to God's exterminator underscored the key message of every issue of *Moore's Weekly*. Like Adam Hochschild, America's media barons on the right and the left simply didn't know how to find the pulse of the American public. And even when they got the story right, they often killed it.

Citing his perceptive boss Ralph Nader, Moore pointed out that when the *New York Times* finally got around to covering a trial against America's tobacco companies, the story wound up on page 44. No surprise here, pointed out Nader who calculated that the cigarette merchants invested $250,000 an hour year around to flog Joe Camel's deadly wares. "The trial continues," Moore wrote. "The coverage does not."

The first Washington couple officially skewered by *Moore's Weekly* was columnist George Will and his wife Madeline, an Assistant Secretary of Education. George Will, who informally coached Reagan for the Presidential debates, won the 1988 Lester Maddox Journalism Award after summing up Jesse Jackson's foreign policy this way: "Don't want no Midgetman missile for Christmas. They don't want no Star Wars for Christmas." And, Will added, "What Jesse Jackson has is presence. He is a naturally endowed leader."

Moore also published a Washington television station's assertion that Madeline Will collected $12,000 in pay for a staff member who never showed up for work and was reimbursed for trips she never took. Although the columnist's wife paid the money back, her husband's employers, the Washington Post, and *Newsweek* did not cover the story. Neither did ABC, where George Will was a paid commentator.

Another grand prize winner in the Moore's Weekly sweepstakes was Gannett/*USA Today* chairman Al Neuharth who took the "McNews Happy Meal Award." After wrapping up an around the world "Jetcapade" tour, Neuharth complained that American journalists were insensitive to leaders in countries such as South Africa and Chile. Among the victims were South African Peter Botha who had "been mistreated by the press." He argued that "attempts to curtail or suppress freedom are, of course, very unfortunate, but they go with the territory." For example the Singapore government was not "entirely wrong" when it decided to limit distribution of the *Far Eastern Economic Review* and the Asian *Wall Street Journal* because the paper wouldn't publish a letter from the Singapore government. "If I had an argument with a foreign head of state, certainly I would give them that extra five inches."

" An 'extra five inches' in *USA Today*," wrote Moore, "that would make it a three-part series."

Every issue of the *Weekly*, which ran I.F. Stone's mantra, "All governments are run by liars and nothing they say should be believed," served up Moore on wry. When Former Miss America Bess Meyerson was arrested in a Harrisburg, Pennsylvania department store for stealing six bottles of nail polish, five pairs of earrings, a pair of shoes and several six-packs of D batteries, Moore challenged readers to explain why she needed the batteries and offered to print the best responses.

Facing a readership that made the late lamented *Michigan Voice* look like a mass circulation journal, Moore did not get the bounce he had hoped for in Washington. His pitch letter to former Voice subscribers explaining that he had been fired by Mother Jones after "a number of women employees at the magazine approached me about the sexist treatment they were receiving from the publisher" received pass-along readers. But he simply didn't have the drawing power of an I.F. Stone. And unlike the *New Yorker*'s famed media swordsman A.J. Leibling, he went into battle with a dull blade.

"It was mainly reaching out to his previous readership at the *Michigan Voice*," said assistant editor Morehouse. "I never felt his heart was in it." As Moore's uncertain performance reinforced Nader's skepticism, the editor realized he could no longer operate in the small space allotted to him. He needed more room for a new project that had become his passion.

"We moved to a new Washington office," recalls Morehouse. "Suddenly there was a woman [Wendey Stanzler, a former *Voice* colleague] working on a film project." The assistant editor felt uncertain about his own job as work on *Moore's Weekly* took a back seat to the nascent film on Flint and General Motors.

"He was obviously distracted. He was doing research putting to-

gether a story line. All his shots were on index cards. I remember
one time he needed to get me a piece. It was either late or we were
getting close to deadline. It was a personal story of him sitting in a
sixth floor office on a hot Washington D.C. night. It was off the cuff
kind of thoughts on what was going on in his head that hot summer
evening. It is always political at some level, very sardonic and humorous. When he finally did it I thought he was very creative."

Underfunded, understaffed and operating on a shoestring, *Moore's
Weekly* began reading more and more like a message in a bottle that
had washed up on the banks of the Potomac. "I remember I was very
inexperienced at finding stories," says Morehouse. "I was looking
for direction from Michael. One afternoon I was not doing much
and Michael was pretty alarmed. I was hanging out and didn't know
what my responsibilities were. I said provide me with some direction,
tell me what stories you would like me to research. I told him I could
write about Latin America, a region I knew, and he said continue
doing that. But I sensed there was a need to broaden our coverage of
other issues.

"My take was that he felt the same way that I did about the Con-
tra War in Nicaragua. It was a gross injustice of international law.
There is a legacy of U.S. support for dictators and human rights abuses that quite frankly make any human rights abuses the Sandinistas
committed miniscule by comparison. He was trying to balance the
media coverage.

"His readership and his followers are believers so he is not really
converting anyone to his position. I think he is preaching to the con-
verted. That would be my one criticism of Michael Moore. If you are
trying to change society, what is the most strategic way to do that.
His approach isn't going to win over converts who are more conservative because they have strongly held beliefs. If you want to appeal
to their greater sense of humanity you have to be able to get them to
let their blinders down and appreciate different points of view in a
nonthreatening way so they are not defensive. The minute you portray issues in black and white, in the way the mainstream media does
you are not providing an opportunity for people to think fairly about
issues and beliefs you might hold.

"As people discover they can't maintain the same standard of living they and their parents had, we are confronting a new reality in American society," says Morehouse who now directs the Food Bank of Western Massachusetts. "We need to really question whether our actions are really in our best interests. As more and more people are personally affected by the actions of our government, people will start to see that prior beliefs and opinions have been unfounded. We see it all around us, the erosion of the strong support for war in Iraq that is not in our nation's interest and not in our national security interest. As a society and country we are learning that."

By the spring of 1988, when Morehouse tendered his resignation, Moore's film project had become his top priority. The newsletter editor tried to persuade his assistant to stay on.

"We can make this really happen. I am going to need you to do it," said Moore.

"I don't want to solo this alone," replied the assistant editor who explained afterwards, "I felt I had a lot to learn and he realized he couldn't give it the attention that it needed. I wasn't prepared to do it."

Moore's failure as a media critic may have had something to do with his own lack of interest in his *Weekly*. Unable to attract attention from the people he was covering, his attention shifted to his film project. As Jim Musselman points out, "the mass media was not interested because every time he critiqued one of them he was critiquing their whole profession. If you are breaking a story on the media it is like they are a little club. They are not going to turn on one of their own.

"He was writing stories that needed to be written and showing the corporate influence of the media but he was getting less coverage than the time he took on the Elks Club for refusing to admit blacks while handing him an award for an essay on Abraham Lincoln."

Nader agrees: "He couldn't get the kind of outraged response he was looking for. He was jabbing but his subjects weren't jabbing back. Mike wanted his stories talked about in the *Washington Post* and the *New York Times*. It was all part of the overall media situation as Reagan and later Bush pushed back the Democrats. The media just wasn't interested in someone like Michael Moore."

YOU CAN TAKE MIKE OUT OF FLINT BUT
YOU CAN'T TAKE FLINT OUT OF MIKE

ANDREW MOREHOUSE'S DECISION to quit *Moore's Weekly*—he was never replaced—may have surprised the publisher but it did not come as a shock to people in the Nader organization. At a time when his newsletter circulation was stagnant, he was not focusing on attracting new readers. There were no globetrotting assignments, Q-and-A interviews with Al Neuharth or additional shellings of the National Public Radio office down the road with juicy scoops on correspondents' personal drug use. Sitting in the back of Nader's office playing media critic was dull. For one thing he wasn't getting any hate mail or angry calls from people who were angered by *Moore's Weekly*. In fact no one seemed to be paying much attention to his efforts. He had plenty of causes but none of his writing was rousing the rabble.

"It was not a position he wanted to be in," says Musselman. "The premise of *Moore's Weekly* was that the media was not doing its job and the reporters were a bunch of incompetent lap dogs. This was the Reagan era when the media was becoming cheerleaders. And corporations were saying if you cover us badly we will pull our advertising. GM pulled its ads from publications that ran exposés on them. Ralph wanted to show how major media outlets would cave in for fear of an advertising backlash. Obviously, Michael was covering stories that the media did not want to promote because it made them look bad."

In the Nader organization, Moore discovered the devil was in the political details, searching through the fine print of Congressional legislation that would fatten corporate profits at the expense of minimum-wage workers or give tax breaks to developers at the expense of the middle class and the poor. Drafting new legislative proposals, selling their ideas to political leadership, lobbying the press for favorable coverage and politicians for their votes, stumping legislative districts, pressuring voters to email or write their elected representatives in support of antipollution legislation and against tax cuts for the plutocrats—this was progressive politics Nader style.

Moore's career change was triggered, in part by a bit of serendipity within the Nader office. Mike Westfall, a third generation GM worker who drove a truck for the Flint plant, sent in a proposal for a movie on Moore's hometown and General Motors. Concerned about the impact of automation, Westfall chaired the UAW's "25 and out" committee designed to create early-retirement packages for furloughed auto workers. Several years earlier, Moore had met with Westfall after Musselman had shown him the film proposal at the *Michigan Voice*. The editor felt project proposal was a little dry in the manner of PBS—"Pretty Boring Stuff."

But the Nader office remained enthusiastic and developed a proposal with Westfall, and producer Nina Rosenblum of Daedalus Productions. The 90-minute television feature, to be introduced by Nader and Mike Westfall, included a lengthy panel discussion with an emphasis on global sourcing, automation, downsizing, restructuring and relocation of suppliers to the vicinity of assembly plants, thereby wiping out vendors and their labor force. Bruce Springsteen was being recruited to write the film's score while Waldo Salt, one of the "Hollywood Ten" writers blacklisted in the 1950s by anti-Communist witch hunters, was mentioned as a potential writer. "Characters based on careful research into the lives of assembly line workers from General Motors in Flint will be interwoven into a powerful, emotional and compelling story," suggested the working draft.

Westfall was gratified by a letter from producer Rosenblum demonstrating her commitment to the project. "As Ralph Nader was saying you are one of the truly greats of our time, among the ranks of Martin

Luther King and Franklin Delano Roosevelt. You will be the greatest on camera because all you have to be is yourself, and your true genius and profound humanism comes through without any effort."

Although Moore had a chance to join the Westfall project in the Nader office, he decided that this approach would not be memorable. Indeed, as his camera team began shooting scenes it was clear that political protest would merely be a historical footnote, not a motif for the film. The heroism exhibited by the famed Flint sitdown strikers in 1936-37, a group that included his uncle LaVerne, had been subverted by the very United Auto Workers union they had brought to power at the Saginaw Avenue Plant. Moore's own 1987 footage of heroic anti-tax abatement rallies led by Westfall and his UAW colleagues looked weak in the Washington editing room. So did footage of Moore's own appearances with Westfall at Flint rallies against GM. While Moore spoke with Westfall more than once, the union organizer was never a part of the project. The relationship between the two men deteriorated as Westfall realized that the newsletter editor did not want to use the film to directly benefit the UAW and its membership. In fact, Westfall sensed correctly, the UAW was on its way to becoming one of Moore's targets in the film.

For homeschooled documentary maker Moore, the trick was to personalize the film, to become the story in much the same way Ralph Nader had become a hero thanks to the bumbling GM gumshoes eager to malign his Corvair exposé by trying to uncover a scandal in his private life. Moore's vision, if you could call it that, was to play Curious Michael, going after the man in the yellow hat, Roger Smith. He even had a working title for the project, based on an old Harry Chapin song, "Dance Band on the Titanic."

While the Westfall inspired film project withered and died in Nader's office, Moore pursued his own documentary on his own terms. The storyline did not have room for the modern day protest movement taking on General Motors across the state. Instead the film was created to demonstrate that Flint was as doomed as Pompeii on the eve of the eruption of Mt. Vesuvius. A subtext was Ronald Reagan's voodoo economics that was paralyzing so many towns like Flint. Unemployment checks, evictions, laid-off workers fleeing their hometowns-in its immensity, the human tragedy rivaled Steinbeck's *The Grapes of Wrath*. The film would be told as a personal narrative along the lines of the recently released *Sherman's March*.

In that groundbreaking documentary Ross McElwee visited old girlfriends along the General's route. His failure to find a paramour was the film's comic premise and delighted audiences, who enjoyed watching his playful struggle. Now Moore was going to offer a cook's tour of another American battleground lacing it with his brand of humor and compassion. Moore's work in progress, inspired in part by his *Blood In The Face* apprenticeship, would tell America why *Money* magazine had declared Flint "the least desirable place to live in America." At the heart of his story was General Motors' decision to shut down 11 plants, including two in the Flint area. Moore would become Flint's Bob Cratchit. General Motors CEO Roger Smith was cast as Scrooge, and thanks to deputy sheriff Fred Ross, Flint's peripatetic eviction expert, astonishing newcomers turned the Tiny Tim role into an ensemble part.

Moore proved to be an ideal on-camera interviewer. He understood the importance of working with people who were best at playing themselves. His ability to cast unknowns and blend them with celebrity cameos was an art form. There were no film studios to interfere with his vision or argue with him about whether or not the Sandinistas were closet Leninists. Now he was the writer, producer, editor, on-camera talent and marketing director. Because there was no union to deal with, much less any job security, all positions on the poorly paid film team were work for hire. With his *Moore's Weekly* money and an advance from Doubleday for a book on the Flint/GM story—a book he would never deliver—the producer had the startup capital to begin bankrolling the project. He also landed an impressive group of foundation grants including one from the Michigan Arts Council and another from the MacArthur Foundation.

After Andrew Morehouse left the newsletter, Moore was able to spend more time working with editor Wendey Stanzler. Moore also received checks from personal heroes like Ed Asner who was happy to support the work of an unknown filmmaker. As the Washingtonian spent more time back home in Flint in preproduction, Nader decided that it was time to let the newsletter editor go. He explained, "You can take Michael out of Flint, but you can't take Flint out of Michael."

Moore began focusing full time on his film, convinced that he could reach a broader constituency as an entertainer. His timing was excellent. No longer did the American public share the view of legendary Hollywood studio chief Jack Warner who defined a screenwriter as a "shmuck with an Underwood." Robert Redford and Dustin Hoffman huddled over a typewriter in *All The President's Men* demonstrated that Americans still lived in a country based on a true story.

Although Flint was a long way from America's political and entertainment power centers—New York, Washington and Hollywood—it had the potential of becoming a place that just might resonate as America's ultimate hit and run, the victim of a corporate superpower never held accountable for what it had done wrong.

When Kevin Rafferty and another top independent documentary filmmaker, Anne Bohlen, agreed to fly back to Flint in February 1987 and begin shooting a 20-minute trailer for Moore's movie at their own expense, Moore began to realize what the Sisters of St. Joseph were talking about when they referred to the milk of human kindness. By extending a helping hand to the fascist tracking nonfiction *Blood In the Face* team, he now had the critical talent he needed to make the trailer of all trailers.

WHO IS MIKE WESTFALL AND WHY IS HE SAYING THESE TERRIBLE THINGS ABOUT ME?

"Give a lie a 24-hour head start, and the truth will never catch up with it. In other words, always confront dishonesty immediately and without equivocation."

—*Michael Moore*

FLINT, MICHIGAN, IS HOME to America's third-fastest-growing airport, a handsome University of Michigan campus, an admirable cultural center, a great library, a fascinating planetarium, and the romantic Charles Stewart Mott estate. It is also a city without a movie theater. And theatres in the city's suburbs seldom show documentaries.

This can be tough on Ed Bradley, the film critic for the Flint Journal. "I enjoy documentaries," he says overlooking the city's downtown from his vantage point in the paper's cafeteria. "I really do. It's just that most documentaries don't come to Flint."

Flint is not what Michigan Governor Jennifer Granholm calls a "cool city" like Saugatuck, Traverse City, East Lansing or Ann Arbor, where presidents, All-Americans and Diana Krall delight cheering crowds. Although Michigan has more than 1,500 miles of shoreline, landlocked Flint has no "cool" beaches. There aren't a lot of "cool" brewpubs or nightclubs. And sadly for Ed Bradley, there aren't any "cool" movie theaters either.

In the spring of 1989, Bradley received a call from Michael Moore, who told him about his work in progress under the ponderous working title, *A Humorous Look at How General Motors Destroyed Flint, Michigan*. Watching people get laid off in the Wolverine State did not sound laughable, much less bankable. It was hardly a new story to people in downtown Flint, which was beginning to look like America's doormat. But Ed Bradley liked Moore's synopsis, and he made reservations to see the little movie with the terrible name at the Toronto Film Festival.

Unlike many brand new directors, Moore, who had cancelled the Flint Voice Cinema in 1981 after poor box office put the film series $4,000 in debt, understood the difficulties faced by first-time film-makers. He turned to experienced professionals to shoot the fundraising trailer and key footage central to the film. Kevin Rafferty was an all-star cameraman, and as a producer Anne Bohlen knew a good deal about Flint's General Motors heritage. She had been nominated for an Academy Award for her first film, *With Babies and Banners*. This documentary told the story of the Women's Emergency Brigade who provided crucial support to the GM Sit Down strikers marooned for 44 days at the Flint automobile plant. In addition to providing their husbands, sons and brothers food and warm clothing, they broke windows when the National Guard tried to tear gas them.

Moore's initial shot list, a picture-perfect delineation of his Flint world view, made it easy to get the project moving. "His story sense was amazing," said Rafferty. "He knew what he wanted to do. It was the film." For *cinéma verité* directors like Rafferty, a Bauhaus trained minimalist who never put himself in his films, there was just one problem. While documentary filmmakers like Ross McElwee were successfully putting themselves into the story line of diary-style projects like *Sherman's March,* this approach was obviously a misstep for Michael Moore. Not just another pretty face, he was a lumbering presence destined to put audiences, even union hall audiences, to sleep.

"I told him that it was absolutely a mistake to put himself in the film, that it wouldn't work," says Rafferty in his basement Greenwich Village office, a veritable museum of classic film editing equipment. "It was the worst piece of advice any filmmaker has ever given to another filmmaker. Thank God he didn't listen to me."

Similar advice was offered by Conrad Martin, Anne Zill's colleague at the Stewart Mott Foundation. When Moore, clad in his traditional working man's garb and baseball cap, came for a grant, Martin instantly turned him down. "I read his proposal and said, 'Who is going to watch this? Maybe you'll get an audience at some union hall.'"

The director understood the problem. He hated watching documentaries in school. "They felt like castor oil, and Flint was the last major city in the U.S. to get PBS. I didn't have all these documentaries in my head. I didn't call them documentaries." As the project grew, some people on the Moore team complained that he was difficult to work with. Others disagreed; they said he was impossible.

There were also technical difficulties. Moore was so inexperienced that Jesse Jackson had to pause during an interview to show him how to work a microphone. This kind of problem was easily offset by Moore's gifted interviewing style. He had a natural feel for his potential audience. He wanted antiheroes like deputy sheriff and Flint eviction expert Fred Ross to tell their life stories with the kind of seriocomic realism missing from the evening news. He wanted to offer a satiric twist akin to the best of British television. "For most people," Moore liked to say, "the American dream is just a dream." It was a typical Mooreism, the kind of one liner that reminded you many Americans are just one step ahead of the posse, living paycheck to paycheck, hoping one of their taller children just might become a first-round NBA draft pick.

The Rafferty/Bohlen shoot took place at venues well known to Moore. They recorded Rhonda Britton, the Bunny Lady skinning a rabbit, Tom Kaye of the Michigan Manufacturers Association and numerous scenes of Moore trying to track down Roger Smith at the GM Building, the Detroit Athletic Club and a Grosse Pointe Yacht Club. On the third day of the shoot, Rafferty mentioned to Moore that his mother was first lady Barbara Bush's older sister. The shooter had also played football at Andover, where his cousin, George W. Bush, was a cheerleader. Temporarily speechless, Moore looked at Rafferty and finally said, "You're kidding." When he realized that his friend really was President Bush's cousin, the shocked director shook his head.

After Rafferty reassured Moore that he was not a Republican, the project continued to move ahead quickly. "Michael didn't know much about filmmaking," says Bohlen. Nor did one of his loyal *Flint Voice* employees Wendey Stanzler, who was available to shoot and edit. "But he did know how to engage people. He relied on us to tell him how to do it."

This coming of age story relied heavily on Moore's ability "to bring people together. He's very entertaining and has the right kind of humor. He had become quite a character in the town with his newspaper and radio show." Back in New York, Rafferty pulled the initial footage into a great 20 minute trailer, perfect for fund raising. It became a lasting contribution to the project and a big thank you present for his work on *Blood In The Face*. That film, ultimately screened by George and Barbara Bush at the White House, gave the president and first lady their first look at journalist Michael Moore as well as possibly the most famous wedding scene in cinema-verite history, Michigan Klan nuptials in front of a burning cross.

Unlike Bohlen and Rafferty, Moore was able to bring a narrative voice to his film, now proceeding under the working title *Hometown*. Instead of simply letting the characters tell their own stories, his personal approach offered a coming-of-age slant for himself and his hometown. Predictably, a string of creative roadblocks meant that Moore spoke regularly to filmmaker Anne Bohlen. "It was kind of film school by phone," said the Antioch professor who was still editing those Klan wedding scenes shot for *Blood In The Face*. The calls were an inventory of the sorts of problems film students often run into lack of money, lack of sleep and lack of time. When he ran out of film, Moore turned to his fellow Irish Catholic Dan Kildee who threw a $50 a head fundraiser with county commissioner Art Busch. Although the director was able to raise money from friends, families, nonprofits, and the coffers of *Mother Jones* thanks to a $58,000 out of court settlement, his creative team was not well known. Newcomer Wendey Stanzler, soon emerged as his principal editor. And Moore's vision, that he had just landed in Flint like an alien, appeared to depart from the story others in Flint wanted him to tell.

Left out was the fact that many organizations in Flint and across the state had fought long and hard against the wretched excesses of Roger Smith and General Motors. In May 1987, Citizens for Tax Justice, union leaders, school teachers, Catholic social activists and other community activists took to the microphones at the General Motors annual meeting for what CNN called "the roughest day of Roger Smith's life." At the same time General Motors was asking for huge tax cuts to preserve Michigan jobs, the company was off on a downsizing binge. What was the point of cutting taxes if promised jobs were going to evaporate.

Unlike his confrontation with the GM chairman at the 1986 annual meeting, Moore wasn't about to let this performance be forgotten. The filmmaker was able to attend a General Motors annual meeting thanks to a proxy provided by Mike Westfall, the UAW organizer who originally proposed a movie on Flint and General Motors with the Nader office where Moore worked. His film crew adroitly shot a Q-and-A session with Roger Smith. You just never knew when this footage might prove useful.

"Roger," he told the GM president, "I attended a Flint City Council meeting, and a representative of General Motors was there to ask the city council for a 50 percent tax break on new property and equipment at Flint Truck & Bus. He made a contract with the city, and the city council agreed to this. They agreed to give GM that 50 percent tax break. It amounted to $130 million in tax savings for General Motors over the last four years.

"A part of the agreement according to state law is that GM has to create or retain jobs. I have a printout here from the Flint City Tax Assessor's office that says GM would retain 7,000 jobs at Flint Truck & Bus in return for getting this 50 percent tax abatement. Next week, at Flint Truck & Bus, you will eliminate 3,500 jobs. My question to you is: Are you going to return the money to the city of Flint that you saved as a result of this tax break, or are you going to return the jobs? Which is it?"

The night before the annual meeting Moore's crew recorded critics calling for Smith to deal with GM tax issues in Flint and other Michigan cities. Speakers included Musselman who called for Smith's resignation. Shooters also zoomed in on Musselman's call for

Smith to return the money or the jobs to Flint. In the event he chose the former, an ersatz Brinks truck was standing by to guarantee safe passage for the millions at stake. This vehicle was actually a dolled up Ryder truck. Moore was originally assigned to pick up the vehicle. But when he fell behind schedule it was rented by Musselman with the backing of Nader's right hand man John Richard who was also on the scene.

Musselman explained the importance of using a humorous visual to attract attention: "Our 15-page report on Roger Smith's incompetence got press coverage the day before the annual meeting. I told Moore the reports are great but you are not going to get the TV coverage without a visual. They need to see something to make the nightly news.

"Michael's eyes lit up when the TV cameras were out there shooting the truck. It was the way to get TV on board. His crew shot the whole scene for his film. It was perfect. The Brinks truck made the whole thing look like a heist. Our protest made PBS, the CNN nightly business report and the national networks. We had people out there demonstrating against GM with signs, bullhorns and the trucks. A CNN correspondent said the people of Michigan were rebelling against GM. He called it the worst seven hours of the chairman's life."

The high point of the Smith roast was the CEO's self congratulatory explanation for the raise he was pocketing in the midst of widespread layoffs. As the lily white GM men on the dais nodded approval, the multimillionaire got a laugh out of his critics when he explained that his pay boost was merely an adjustment for inflation.

Moore's film crew got a lucky break as community resistance to the auto maker began to unite taxpayers all over Flint. General Motors demand for property tax breaks as high as 82 percent while it was earning profits of $5 billion a year, frightened community leaders. But even if the communities defeated this proposal, UAW activist Mike Westfall pointed out, the auto company was not going to have any difficulty slashing its costs. Already the company was operating 14 plants in Mexico where workers were earning just 72 cents an hour. Of course there were a few unexpected problems here for the GM human resources department.

It wasn't easy finding employees who could afford transportation, adequate work clothes and the kind of sustenance necessary to live up to a demanding auto production job. But GM, facing south-of-the-border turnover of up to 100 percent a year, was quick to demonstrate that success in business was more than just satisfying the shareholders with ever larger profits. CEO Roger Smith was proud to announce that he had launched a free breakfast program to make sure that his new Latino workers did not go hungry. Unfortunately, there was no such thing as a free lunch at the bargain basement plant.

This showdown echoed a 1995 Flint community meeting on GM's tax break scheme where the editor spoke alongside Jim Musselman, Flint's City Attorney and other invited speakers. Michael Moore offered the kind of succinct analysis that had his audience laughing and cheering. As the camera rolled, he suggested that the citizens of Flint were on the verge of a showdown that was every bit as historic as the 1937 sitdown strike:

"You always know there is a problem when town leaders start putting up billboards and the ministers of propaganda at First and Howard (the home of the *Flint Journal*) start running ads in the paper that 'Flint is Alive and Well.' Remember that was the first billboard a couple of years ago when there was 27 percent unemployment. The next billboard was 'Tough Times Don't Last, Tough People Do.' That one was supposed to make us look guilty if we didn't last, if we started running out of cheese and butter in the cheese lines and the unemployment had run out and we are asking for $50 a month welfare, somehow it was our problem. They moved into television, 'Flint, it means so much to be here.' They have this woman who talks about how she went out to California and it was just so terrible out there and she couldn't wait to get back here to Flint.

"Then last year to top it all off it was 'Visit Auto World and Leave The Real World Behind.' Now what was the real world they wanted us to leave behind, using $10 million of our money to build the place and another $10 million in bonds they expect us to pay off and the real world of Flint is 25,000 families in the cheese line each month and 20 percent unemployment and 80 percent of black and Hispanic youth are unemployed. A world where if you are in high school you can forget about finding a job.

"If you talk to anyone 15, 16, 17 years of age that is a scary feeling. That's the world they don't want us to think about. What they want to do is divert our attention with . . . 'Flint is coming back, we have Auto World, we have the new Hyatt,' and for ten years now we have been told this. If we put tax dollars into Flint we'll come alive. If we put in a downtown campus of the University of Michigan and spend $12 million in tax money to build a Hyatt Regency, then the stores will come back on Saginaw Street. We have to say we are a town that is going down the drain. We have to admit it and we have to realize GM is doing this to us, to get past that. It's a scary thing to say, it's a scary thing to feel that this could be a ghost town by year 2000. No more giveaways. The law that created this tax abatement in 1975 has to be repealed . . . The candy store is closed.

"There has to be a federal law passed that prevents companies from packing up and leaving the country, a uniform property tax and utility tax across the country. No more of this pitting Michigan against Tennessee and Alabama. For all Americans this is crazy. No more Phil Donahue shows where seven governors sit on stage while Roger Smith sits on his new car and leaders of the government come begging to him. This isn't a game show where behind door #1 we have a new auto plant and behind door #2 we have a steel plant. The UAW has to be supported in fighting back.

"My dad has been a UAW member for 46 years. This is the first time that so many different kinds of groups have come together to fight the #1 manufacturing company in the world in its birthplace, Flint Michigan. This is very, very significant that all these people, teamsters, United Auto Workers, black groups, women's group, peace groups, all come together for the first time. Sometimes in history you don't recognize the significance of events when you are living them. But years from now, if we are successful in this fight they'll look back at this time period when all these people got together to take on GM and eventually won."

* * *

In January 1988, Moore was credentialed for GM's Teamwork and Technology for Today and Tomorrow gala welcoming 14,000 of the company's closest friends and stockholders. The company also hosted mayors from 100 GM factory towns including Michigan communities facing the company's demand for a 70 percent tax abatement. In addition to a special meeting for top shareholders, the biggest of the Big Three hosted a champagne press luncheon. After finishing his scripted remarks, Roger Smith moved from table to table for one on one interviews with the press. Moore was one of the lucky reporters who scored a 15-minute interview with Roger Smith. Because the sound man the filmmaker scheduled for the event was unable to work, Jim Musselman stood in on audio. This was perfect for Michael. Here General Motors was ignoring Flint and claiming it needed these huge tax breaks and then it was treating key stockholders and mayors and the press to this elaborate and expensive dog and pony show at the Waldorf in New York. It fit perfectly into his thesis.

"During this 15-minute session Moore did a good job of interviewing the GM chief about Flint and job losses," says Musselman. "Smith answered every question in an evasive and at times whiny and irritated manner. "

Like his interview with the "Coppertone" neo-Nazi in *Blood In The Face,* this meeting was a coup for Moore demonstrating his Q-and-A artistry under fire. And unlike a print reporter, he didn't have to worry about Smith trying to claim he was misquoted. After all, thanks to his camera crew, the whole world was watching the GM chairman.

"I had talked to Ralph about this potential interview and he and I suggested questions to Michael who of course had a good list of his own," said Musselman who had handed over hundreds of pages of GM documents and research notes backing up Nader's co-authored book, *The Big Boys.* "Smith answered at least a dozen key questions. We got in there, we got to Smith and we got to ask what we wanted. The working title was now *Dance Band on the Titanic* and the film was about what Smith and GM were doing to Flint. It was some good footage about the destruction of the rust belt. Moore was incredibly on target, so on target that Smith was literally struck dumb by some of his questions. Roger Smith was his own worst enemy. It was the kind of footage guaranteed to upset the average middle American family because he looked so callous and insensitive. Michael was perfect.

"Moore asked Smith how could he do this to the birthplace of General Motors. He wanted the GM Chairman to come to Flint to address problems created by the huge layoffs and export of jobs to Mexico. Smith replied that the company 'had representatives up there meeting with the people. I have to do my best for the shareholders. We will not abandon Flint. We care about all the communities including Flint and Mexico.'

"Michael felt he had hit gold because he had fifteen minutes with Roger Smith one on one. He had gotten an opportunity to pose questions to the head of GM and get answers. Michael was elated. We both called Ralph and said 'You won't believe it, we just had fifteen minutes with Smith.'"

In Washington, Nader was astonished by the good news. "I was completely surprised that Michael got the interview, he said, "particularly when GM had just thrown one of my associates, Russell Mokhiber, out of the meeting."

Not one word about Moore's big interview with Roger Smith made it into the January 18, 1988 issue of *Moore's Weekly*. The editor's scoop, an exclusive interview with the Chairman of GM, was killed. Instead the lead story focused on the fact that Russell Mokhiber, a fellow editor working in Ralph Nader's office, had been hauled out of the Teamwork and Technology conference by GM security. "It was a shocking sight to see a member of the press hauled away and arrested. What was more shocking, though, was how two hundred other members of the press stood by and watched this event unfold without any of them reporting it to their viewers or readers. Instead, what I heard was a number of reporters mumbling about 'some kook.'

"Imagine the same scene, except that the press conference had been held in Moscow or Warsaw. A writer who is critical of the government shows up and, before he can take his coat off, is physically carted off by plainclothes security police. I can guarantee you that the incident would receive major play in the U.S. on all three network newscasts and photos would appear in nearly every daily newspaper across America. If it had happened in Managua, you can bet that Congress would stay up 'til the dawn's early light to vote another $200 million in Contra aid.

"But if the world's largest corporation, in collusion with the local police, silences a reporter in the middle of New York City, you can count on exactly what you got the next day in the media: huge photos of a smiling Roger Smith standing in front of his 'car of the future.'

"Headline in the *Washington Post*: 'GM Seeking edge on Japanese Cuts Prices.' *New York Times*: 'GM's High-Tech Vision of Sales.' Not one single uncomfortable question asked of the Chairman; not one single mention of the arrest of Russell Mokhiber. . . . It was the best press money could buy."

While Musselman headed to California to join a protest over a leukemia spike among young people living near GM's Van Nuys plant, Moore was busy editing his film. Months later, on his return from another Nader organizing project in California, Musselman visited Moore at his new Washington office to discover the documentary's direction had shifted. Moore's own filmed confrontation with Smith at the annual meeting was out. The Brinks truck scene was gone. The rookie filmmaker's remarkable one on one interview with Roger Smith at the Waldorf-Astoria was also eliminated. Mike Westfall, the auto worker who had courageously led the fight against GM's tax abatements and layoff with the help of the Michigan Education Association, women's groups, black groups, peace groups, Ralph Nader, Flint government leaders and the *Flint Journal*'s editorial page, were also missing from the shot list.

To Musselman Moore's decision undermined the very cause the filmmaker espoused. For example, one of the most poignant scenes in the film was a call for a rally at the historic Saginaw Avenue Plant on the day it was scheduled to be torn down. The scene of the famous 1936-1937 sitdown strike, a focal point in the documentary's opening, this plant was a centerpiece in American labor history. Moore's point, that only four people showed up for this rally, suggested that no one in Flint was willing to stand up for the proud tradition of the United Auto Workers and the American labor movement.

But this approach sidestepped the fact that Flint in particular and the state of Michigan in general were doing an impressive job of taking on GM, its lobbyists, lawyers and adept public relations team. Leaving out the many well organized protests that spilled over into every community where GM was a presence felt like trying to tell the story of the American revolution without mentioning the Boston Tea Party. Ignoring the heroism of grassroots organizer Mike Westfall was unthinkable. For decades courageous men like him had stood up in the tradition of UAW founder Walter Reuther who was bashed in by Henry Ford's security goons at the historic 1936 Battle of the Overpass outside Dearborn's Rouge Plant. Not playing favorites, Moore had also dumped footage of Westfall's fiery Patrick Henry style speech to the coalition courageously fighting General Motor's battle for emergency tax relief.

In the midst of that historic battle, Moore had pointed out that "sometimes in history you don't recognize the significance of events when you are living them." Now, said Musselman, Moore himself was hitting the delete button and failing to recognize the significance of the coalition.

Instead Moore had created an irresistible story built around his own personal failure to track down Roger Smith and hold him accountable for bringing down the economy of Flint, Michigan. Cutting back and forth between discussion of GM's enormous profits and his hometown's financial collapse, Moore made it clear that one man was ultimately responsible. Laid off workers were evicted from their homes and struggled to find minimum wage jobs at fast food centers. The poor lined up to give blood at local plasma centers as their community was terrorized by overzealous police. And no one—not the Governor, the head of the United Autoworkers, the surviving work force, the Chamber of Commerce or business leaders—had any idea how to stop the city's decline. Clearly only Michael Moore could articulate what was wrong with Flint and only Roger Smith could put the city back to work.

Musselman felt this approach might fill theater seats but it was not going to solve the city's economic problem. "I supported the film because I thought it was going to chronicle the broad opposition to General Motors downsizing and tax abatement program. When citizen activism succeeds it can motivate people in Michigan and elsewhere. All movements in this country come when middle class people in Ohio get angry.

"The civil rights movement inspired other movements and made others realize they can fight back. He was neglecting what had been accomplished in this campaign. He was making it look like he was the only person in Flint who really understood what General Motors was doing to the community. It was as if the sit-down strike in Flint was the last time that anyone in town had really put the screws to GM. He was mocking the citizens of Flint who were fighting back. He made them look indifferent. Even though he filmed scenes of union rank and file effectively taking on GM over tax abatements, not wages, this footage had disappeared.

"When Michael told me he was leaving out his own interview with Smith in New York and the GM annual meeting scene that he had loved in Detroit, I couldn't believe it. I asked him what had happened to that footage and he looked down and said: 'Cutting room floor, you're there too.'

"I didn't care about myself but I did care deeply about the deletion of scenes showing the well orchestrated Citizens for Tax Justice protests.

"I said: 'Michael it is important to show the anger of the average American, to prove that this isn't just coming from some liberal.' The film was going to reflect the anger of middle American school teachers and union members. We wanted to know why the head of GM was willing to meet with the Republic of Ireland, the government of South Africa, but not the school boards in his company's hometowns.

"The key thing was including ordinary citizens. What mattered was scenes showing the average school teacher from Grand Blanc blasting GM for hurting kids with tax cuts. This is your typical American, not a radical, not a liberal. He had footage of all these average citizens, teachers, nuns from his church's Mother House, business people, police and fire officials and political leaders protesting GM's plant closings, outsourcing to Mexico and outrageous tax abatement schemes that shifted some costs of vital public services to families losing their jobs.

"Doesn't it look worse if some guy in a suit, such as the leader of the Michigan Education Association, asks to meet with Roger Smith and he says no?"

When Moore refused to back down, Musselman told him, "There is a transcript of the General Motors annual meeting. It's going to be out there. You have to be factual. I can't lie at a press conference to a reporter."

Musselman realized he couldn't win this argument with a director who was a master at publicity. It was the end of a beautiful friendship. By now Moore's commitment to his Flint film and his frequent absences persuaded Nader to let him go. Musselman was summoned to Nader's upstairs office for an explanation. "Here I was working for $14,000 a year and it didn't look right that Moore had failed to fulfill his contract. His performance was erratic, I agreed that Michael could never work with other people."

After Moore was asked to leave Nader's inner sanctum, he invited Musselman over to his new Washington, D.C., office to look at rough cuts. At one point Moore mentioned that he was considering using Bruce Springsteen's song, 'My Home Town.'

"'But Michael, you have to get permission.' 'But if I don't and he sues me, it will bring attention to the film and I'll look like the little guy.'

"That was his mindset at the time," said Musselman. "Anything to get attention for the film. Because he knew that attention to the film was key. He did eventually get permission from Springsteen.

"That is when I realized it wasn't about the issues it was about him. He's got to be the underdog, the victim. It's always the world against Michael. In effect he was creating what didn't happen in his film and ignoring what did happen in Flint. By ignoring the efforts of a large number of people who were doing a good job fighting General Motors' tax abatements and downsizing, he was telling his audience that there was no hope, that no one cared except him. He came off as a Don Quixote figure unable to change anything.

"When he talked to Smith it was like the Holy Grail. He asked these very poignant questions not being asked by the media. And now he was leaving them out of the film.

"The whole film was predicated on Roger Smith's personality, personalizing Smith and getting him to meet with people. This was all stuff we had discussed from the beginning of the movie. I had personally picketed Smith's house, and now Moore was claiming he couldn't find the same place. Of course he knew how to find him. When he switched gears I was in a state of shock. I was walking the streets of Washington wondering what to do. In summary he had talked to Smith three times. He asked him questions at the GM annual meeting in 1986, filmed an interview with the GM Chairman at the 1987 annual meeting with credentials I helped arrange and again at the Waldorf in January 1988. All three interviews were missing. I felt like Dr. Frankenstein. I had helped create a monster.

"A documentary filmmaker documents. You don't make changes to a story line. But it became a fictionalized movie. Things happened in the movie that never took place. And things that actually took place in Flint didn't happen in the movie. When the film was done, it didn't look like anyone was mad at Roger Smith except Michael Moore."

By May of 1989, with the cutting room floor beginning to look like the Grand Canyon, Moore's film was near completion. His private tutor, *Blood In The Face* filmmaker and Antioch professor Anne Bohlen felt the rough cut came up short: "It was very sprawling, all over the place. The elements were there, it was tremendous achievement but it was not put together exactly right. The focus wasn't quite there." Good, but not good enough, the film needed another pair of editing hands. Bohlen recommended New Yorker Gini Reticker, then seven months pregnant and not looking for work, particularly in Washington, D.C., with someone paying César Chávez wages.

A fellow Irish Catholic from Chicago, Reticker began her career with virtuoso Haskell Wexler on a film about Nicaragua. She went on to edit a Deborah Shafer documentary on the Sandinistas/Contra war called *Fire From the Mountain*.

Like a lot of people who enlisted with Michael Moore, Reticker quickly offered remarkable loyalty and commitment. "The last thing I wanted to do was go down to Washington in the heat and sit there in a dark editing room. If it had been anyone else I would have said no. But Michael is just a force of nature," she explains at a Yonkers Burger King, speaking over the dinner hour din. "I wanted to be part of this.

"When I saw the rough cut it was really rough. He was still finding his voice as a filmmaker. Michael wanted to get it into the New York Film Festival and I was one of three editors working on the project. He just loved working in a crisis situation. The only catch was that I couldn't work Michael's long hours. My doctor limited me to eight hour shifts."

Telling the story from his point of view meant significant cuts of scenes that worked well. For example, auto workers filmed at a bar featuring exotic dancers were cut. So were additional scenes of amiable sheriff's deputy Fred Ross who never met a person he didn't feel comfortable evicting.

As the editors cut the film to the music of artists like Pat Boone, blended in archival footage and juxtaposed the city's cheerleaders with the dispossessed, he moved closer and closer to creating a tragedy that was also a comedy. "Michael had such a sense of humor," says Reticker. "And he had no pretense about being objective."

By the time Reticker returned to New York to give birth to her daughter, the editing team had smoothed out transitions, stepped up the pacing and most of all, created a film that had the feel of a rust belt *Sherman's March*. Where McElwee went looking for women in all the wrong places, Moore's prey was a 64 year-old auto czar. "By now," says his mentor, "the film had been smoothed out. Ginny Redeker made it sing. She got a good rhythm going."

Bohlen saw Moore had mastered many of the key elements of documentary filmmaking, using the right music for emotional impact, juxtaposing Flint eviction scenes with self congratulatory shots of GM's Roger Smith and artfully sprinkling in archival footage to document how big business sells people products they don't need at prices they can't afford. "The process of making a film" she explains at a café in Yellow Springs, Ohio, "is looking through a lens and making choices based on aesthetics. In *Roger & Me*, Michael was the quintessential American character. The semiautobiographical film was so close to his personal life in the town where he grew up. He had been quite well known in Flint, with his newspaper and radio show.

"You wouldn't look at Michael and think he's a charismatic. Performing yourself is different than being yourself. Michael can pump up, he can project on screen. Performing is about timing and Michael has very good timing. His movie was also one of the best films on capitalism I've ever seen, very funny, very entertaining. I could see that it would be a crowd pleaser. The film had been smoothed out. It was ready for the festivals."

DRIVING A STAKE THROUGH
THE HEART OF REAGAN'S AMERICA

*"In filmmaking you can start either with fiction or documentary. But which-
ever you start with, you inevitably find the other."*

—Jean-Luc Goddard

By LATE SUMMER, Moore was ready to show a rough cut to judges
screening entries for the late September New York Film Festival.
"You didn't have to be the brightest bulb in the room," to see how
good it was," says Reticker. After the movie was accepted, Michael
called John Pierson, a New York independent film maven who had
parlayed his passion for low budget projects into a remarkable cottage industry. A film student who learned the industry by managing a small theater on New York's 42nd Street, he had broken in
to the agency side of the business by selling *Parting Glances,* the
first theatrical release of an AIDS-themed film treating gay characters
as ordinary people rather than deviants. When an unknown Brooklyn filmmaker named Spike Lee showed him dailies from a work in
progress named *She's Gotta Have It,* Pierson wrote him a $10,000
check to complete the project. With his successful gay film and black
film behind him, Pierson was soon on the receiving end of calls from
directors like Lizzie Borden, who wanted him to take on *Working
Girls,* the story of upmarket Manhattan prostitutes making a living
with their Johns on the spot. Soon the producer's representative was
sitting on the Sundance Festival screening committee trying to figure

out why so many aspiring filmmakers were using friends and family money to create films that echoed recent successes.

Pierson's passion for independent filmmaking is best summed up by his wedding ceremony which took place at a theater where the guests were treated to a movie. Inevitably his reputation as a king-maker for unknowns made him a magnet for a wide array of cin-ematic wannabes. "Every single low-budget film seemed to have a story behind it—a story that was often more compelling than the film itself. I'll never forget the director who offered my dentist a point in her film in return for some fillings and a crown. Leading the pack in the Most Misconceived Movie of the Year Sweepstakes was Yaphet Kotto who waived his normal fees to direct a "sexorcism film featur-ing a possessed basketball."

Pierson was appalled by the lack of breakthrough films. "Being hopelessly out-of-touch was no worse than being a clone." Far from being the sincerest form of flattery, imitation was an embarrassment. Of the 57 films and works-in progress shown at the 1988 Indepen-dent Feature Film Market in New York, none received a significant American distribution deal for aspiring filmmakers. Without this kind of marketing backup, self-distributors had to rent art houses in major cities and college towns, hoping the gate would cover the cost of "four walling" their films. This event was the first step in the long festival march that would launch breakout independent films. Like a NAS-CAR race, the film market was also the scene of numerous wipeouts. Or as Pierson put it, the IFFM was in danger of becoming a "toxic dump" filled with unreleaseable dreck. At times it seemed like every self-proclaimed writer in America had a screenplay in the drawer and, unfortunately, that was where most of them should have stayed.

Pierson's track record brought him a steady stream of strays who confused enthusiasm with talent. Pitch packages began piling up on his desk including one from a Chicago filmmaker who had turned a good public access cable TV show into a bad feature. "You may have noticed another little item included in the package," said one director. "This particular item once belonged to the last producer's rep I showed my film to . . . he didn't like it." Pierson reached inside and found a bloody tissue with " a very lifelike severed ring finger- with the ring."

Referred to Pierson by Karol Martesko, head of the non-profit Independent Feature Project, Moore showed Pierson a rough cut of his work at tiny DuArt Film Lab room on an old Bell and Howell projector. "It was completely, absolutely done," said the producer's agent. There was only one problem. "If you watch the film alone, as I did the first time, you don't quite understand how funny it is."

"Michael was very good at knowing how to start with a bang and keep it up and not pad it. His message was powerful. General Motors made $5 billion that year. How can they treat people like that? How can they send their jobs away? That is so wrong. The movie weaves it's magic."

One of the best scenes in the film cuts back and forth between Roger Smith reading Dickens at a General Motors Christmas party in Detroit while Deputy Fred Ross was evicting tenants in Flint who lost their jobs on the same day. Moore modeled the idea on a *Godfather* scene that intercut a series of murders with a baptism.

Out of money, Moore completed the audio mixing at New York's Sound One lab. In a photo finish he wrapped up the work at 3 a.m. Instead of demanding payment, the lab owners extended him $13,000 in credit and wished him well as he headed for LaGuardia Airport and a 7 a.m. flight to Colorado, compliments of the Telluride Film Festival. There Moore's colleagues surrounded Roger Ebert and persuaded him to skip a Peter Greenaway tribute in favor of the unknown Michigan filmmaker's newly retitled feature, *Roger & Me*. The debut screening at Mason's Cinema was also the first time the director saw his finished work.

Proving that there is no substitute for inexperience, *Roger & Me* brought standing ovations and a major award at the Toronto Film Festival. It's amazing," he told Kevin Rafferty, "People are offering $70,000 for distribution rights." Moore also proved to be no piker when it came to tchotchkes. Critics like Sheila Benson of the *Los Angeles Times* loved the lint rollers handed out by Moore's team in honor of lobbyist Tom Kay, the film's de facto stand in for Roger Smith. Kay claimed that this kind of made-in-Flint product was one way the city could rebound from the decline of the auto industry.

By the time the film was accepted for the October New York Film

Festival, Moore was the nation's newest celebrity. Even embarrassing mistakes helped his cause. When the Detroit Free Press film critic visited Moore's Toronto hotel room to use a phone jack for her computer modem, his staff worried that she had lifted a videotape of *Roger & Me*, possibly on behalf of GM's Roger Smith. Perhaps mindful of the way General Motors had harassed and intimidated Ralph Nader over his early exposé, the critic volunteered for a strip search to prove her innocence. The Moore team backed off, and she went on to give the film her highest rating.

Another rave came in from Miramax's Harvey Weinstein who asked for a private screening which took place in a small room where the projector was realigned by propping it up on a book. While the producer considered his options, Disney vice-president Andrew Hersh sprung for lunch. After peppering the executive with questions about the studio's links with General Motors, Moore accompanied by Pierson, agreed to fly to Los Angeles on first-class tickets arranged by Disney's second in command, Jeffrey Katzenberg. On this, the filmmaker's first trip to Los Angeles, it was clear that the buzz in Toronto was resonating in Burbank. Moore walked in to a Disney screening room as Katzenberg and CEO Michael Eisner were watching the end of *Roger & Me*.

When the lights came up, Eisner gave the director a warm California greeting: "General Motors is going to have you killed." The mid-September journey, which included a side trip to Universal Studios, was followed by a quick trip back to New York.

Setting up a command post in Stewart Mott's guest townhouse just off Fifth Avenue, Moore's team focused on film promotion while corporate suitors continued in hot pursuit of the documentary. This was a surprise to Conrad Martin, the Mott Foundation man who refused to give Moore a grant because he thought the film would never work. In town on foundation business he was downgraded to a foldout couch in the first floor office. Walking upstairs, he found Moore and his brain trust working overtime amidst a sea of dirty laundry, takeout pizza and Chinese food boxes.

On September 22, the night of the New York Film Festival press screening, an unrecognized man walked on stage uninvited, grabbed a microphone and began introducing himself as festival organizers debated calling security. "I'm from Flint, Michigan, and my dad was one of the cofounders of General Motors. I want to commend Michael for this film."

During his unprepared remarks Stuart Mott forgot to mention that his mother had banned Moore's film team from covering the crucial Great Gatsby party at the Mott estate, Applewood. It was Stewart who had helped Moore's crew sneak in to Applewood under the auspices of the Michigan Historical Society to capture stunning shots of black models entertaining the Caucasian crowd as human statues. Like another scene featuring a jailhouse rock benefit at Flint's new Genesee County prison, the Applewood scene was the movie's society page, a tribute to movers and shakers boogeying in the slammer. Shortly before the film's release, Moore, with typical understatement, signed his contract with Warner Bros. in front of this showcase jail "full of casualties of General Motors."

Moore's team was standing in the lobby of the *New York Times* as the first trucks rolled with the early edition. The Grey Lady was tossing a welcome bouquet in their direction. One of the largest thumbs in the movie business, Vincent Canby's, was now officially up: "America has an irrepressible new humorist in the tradition of Mark Twain and Artemus Ward. He is Michael Moore, the writer, producer and director of the rude and rollicking new documentary feature, *Roger & Me.*"

Moore invited Rafferty and Bohlen to his box for the festival's opening night, September 27. At Lincoln Center's Alice Tulley Hall, for the first public New York film festival screening, agent John Pierson felt he was an eyewitness to independent filmmaking history: "The seven minute standing ovation felt like forever. People didn't want to stop."

Finally, Moore himself took the stage to ask his mother and aunt Lois to take a bow. "It was as if Michael had been waiting all his life for this platform in front of people," said Pierson. "The movie had woven its magic and now he was entertaining and charming. People didn't want to leave."

Celebrating at a restaurant near Lincoln Center, Kevin Rafferty and Anne Bohlen watched as well-wishers came to their table to congratulate Moore. The irony of George Bush's cousin being feted for his unpaid contribution to this attack on American capitalism was lost on no one in the room, least of all Rafferty. And in the spirit of the evening, Miramax's Harvey Weinstein, always on hand when there was money or publicity to be made, promised the Michigan filmmaker a $1.5 million advance for rights to the film. Standing in front of the dinner party, he promised that *Roger & Me* audiences would fill out petitions refusing to buy General Motors cars unless company chairman Roger Smith came to see the movie. Another fan of the movie, Susan Dalsimer of Warner Bros., phoned her boss Lucy Fisher in Los Angeles. "I've just seen the film that drives a stake through the heart of Reagan's America and we should find a way to be involved."

Like a lot of old friends who had lost touch with Moore, former *Mother Jones* editor Bruce Dancis was surprised by the film's reception. Now the *Oakland Tribune*'s entertainment editor, Dancis hadn't seen the filmmaker since his deposition in the *Mother Jones* wrongful termination suit. "I hadn't kept up with Michael since he left *Mother Jones*. I was shocked: one, to see that he was making a movie and two, that he was getting such an amazing response. One of the most prominent film critics in the country was calling him the next Mark Twain."

Back at his guest townhouse, Stewart Mott and his foundation colleague Conrad Martin were up for hours taking phone messages from callers in Hollywood, Telluride, Amsterdam and dozens of other cities. The following day film festival patrons organized an impromptu party for Moore on the upper east side. "I like films that threaten to destroy my way of life," said one of the sponsors as the Midwestern winner charmed his hosts with funny stories about the quaint folks of America's heartland. Producers weren't merely bidding for the rights to his debut work. They were begging.

"We're trying to decide which multimillion-dollar offer to accept," Moore told the *Flint Journal*'s Ed Bradley on the phone from New York. After securing a verbal $1.5 million guarantee from Miramax's Weinstein brothers, he put these suitors on hold with a deal memo that represented a fallback of sorts. Of course if enthusiasm for the film cooled and there were no other Hollywood studio buyers, the price could drop dramatically.

At the same time Pierson, pressured by independent production companies out of the running "felt the need to make a gesture that would strongly signal that I had internalized the spirit of the movie and had no greedy motivation for pushing the return to Hollywood." On a walk down 65th Street, he told Moore that he would limit his fee to 5 percent of the $1.5 million deal with the Weinsteins, even if a Hollywood studio agreed to their demand for a $3 million advance.

"I wanted to give him back the money ($75,000) to use for something good in Flint. Michael seemed moved. I felt proud although in reality we needed the money. It also eliminated the sting of any of my independent friends calling me a sellout. They had already begun doing this in Toronto."

On October 6 it was time for another trip to Los Angeles, this one paid for by Universal. At the end of the meeting, chairman Tom Pollock walked Moore and Pierson to their cars and made a remarkably accurate forecast of the film's ultimate American gross, $7 million. The number was a friendly way of letting the two men know that the Hollywood studio was not going to top Miramax's $1.5 million advance. They drove on to Warner Bros. for another round of meetings with Lucy Fisher, Susan Dalsimer and their team.

On October 15, the two men returned to Los Angeles and checked in to a suite at the Chateau Marmont, where another comic genius, John Belushi spent the last tragic hours of his short life on the cocaine superhighway. After a second session at Warner Bros. on the afternoon of October 17, Moore insisted that they make one last pass at Universal. Although the agent didn't see the point of another meeting, Moore was relentless. When designated driver Pierson lost his way, he suggested they return to the hotel. "I had tired out and begged off," recalls Pierson, "and he said, 'You don't want to go back to Universal right now, then get out of the car.'"

The two men arrived at Universal City to discover the Universal executives tuned in to the first game of the San Francisco Giants/Oakland Athletics World Series. Tom Pollock explained that the San Andreas Fault had rocked the Bay Area at 5:02 p.m. A major freeway had collapsed along with, a portion of the Bay Bridge. On the big screen TV, rescue crews and good samaritans on step ladders were digging through the rubble desperately trying to pull victims out of the Oakland's Nimitz Freeway wreckage as the coroner's office began counting the dead.

"Michael understood what was happening," said Pierson, "but he couldn't quite understand why Pollock and his Universal executives weren't able to focus on us." Back at the Chateau Marmont the men sat in their suite watching a flock of diverted Northern California jets descending over Hollywood like blinking stars. The next morning they returned to Warner Bros., where the studio decided to agree to Pierson's astonishing asking price, $3 million.

Moore's film demonstrated that there was a serious audience for a film that told the truth about big business and big poverty. The lifestyles of Flint's poor and infamous resonated as powerfully as the American civil rights movement. A nation built on social justice had turned its back on the same autoworkers instrumental in creating the nation's middle class. It couldn't happen here, but it did.

Even Ralph Nader, who hadn't seen the film, conceded that he understood "it's a pretty good satire of GM and I've got no problem with that." Moore received a $3 million advance for a film that showed live footage of a rabbit being skinned by a welfare recipient, a movie that focused on poverty, racism and, worst of all, the evictions of five Flint families who couldn't pay their mortgages in the richest country on earth. Among them were Sabrina Thompson and her son, evicted along with their Christmas tree on December 23.

If there was a simple explanation for the audience reaction and the frantic competition for the rights to Moore's film, it was the scene where President Reagan came to Flint to throw a pizza party for seven unemployed workers at the Italia Gardens. The event, which played like a Marx Brothers routine, ran into technical difficulties. While the commander-in-chief's Secret Service team secured the building in advance of the Flint event, they didn't realize that a thief had walked out the door with the restaurant's cash register. And then there was Ronald Reagan the actor, giving his out-of work dining companions free job counseling. He suggested they saddle up and head for the robust employment market in Texas. Flint's reality was funnier than Mel Brooks and Bill Cosby combined.

But at the Warner Brothers legal offices in Burbank, not everyone working on the Moore deal was smiling. Unlike movie stars who demanded a Pilates trainer on the set or a 24/7 sitter for their schnauzer, Moore's wish list read like a Tom Hayden speech. Invoking his own foreign policy, Moore insisted on the right to block distribution of the film in Israel unless Palestinians could see it at any time, even during curfews. Similar restrictions applied in South Africa. Eager to keep five members of his team employed, Moore insisted on setting them up in a grassroots publicity office.

In their contract, Warner Brothers agreed to do "whatever it takes" in terms of advertising and publicity to secure the Academy Award nomination and win. In a rare concession to a new filmmaker, the studio promised to release the documentary even if it failed to obtain insurance against litigation from General Motors, the world's largest manufacturing company, or anyone else who sued Moore. And, if a lawsuit was filed, the studio agreed to pay for a Moore defense team that included some of New York's most expensive publishing attorneys. Warner Brothers also complied with Moore's demand that they not book him on any flights operated by union-busting Continental Airlines. In return Moore promised to only fly first class on red-eye trips.

With the fine print carefully vetted, all Moore needed to do to break the hearts of all the independent production companies that lost out to Warner Brothers was to sign. Mocked for selling his anti-big-business film to Hollywood, Moore decided to press one last demand. During the making of the film, the crew had all dipped in to their pockets and offered to give sheriff's deputy Fred Ross the money necessary to halt the Christmas Eve eviction of Sabrina Thompson and her family. Ross declined the offer. Now Moore decided to focus on the problem again with a potential deal breaker. The director insisted Warner Brothers set aside the first $25,000 in distributor profits to buy homes for the five families evicted in the film. After wavering slightly, the film studio agreed.

Davison native James Bond was one of the five *Roger & Me* evictees who received a $5,000 check from Warner Brothers. Another beneficiary was Sabrina Thompson. But Stephanie Alison, who also lost a Flint home, was less enthusiastic about her gift. She was disturbed that the money was coming from Warner Bros.' coffers, not from Moore's own checking account. After all, his ability to merchandise the "Flintstones" had put him on the road to becoming a millionaire. "If these evictions helped make his movie, why can't he help us out with a little change?"

By the time *Roger & Me* premiered in late 1989, Flint had become part of the most extraordinary promotion campaign in Warner Bros. history. Not since David O. Selznick, Vivian Leigh and Clark Gable had debuted MGM's *Gone With The Wind* in Atlanta had there been a local opening quite like it. If fans would pay money to see the burning of Atlanta, they would certainly be willing to watch Flint flop, especially if Moore was handing out free tickets by the thousands.

In town for the Warner Bros. gala, an event that spread across all 14 screens at the Showcase multiplex in suburban Burton, Moore argued that the film might liberate Flint and turn it into a cool city. To insure that the *Roger & Me* premiere did not mirror the movie's Great Gatsby party scene contrasting the community's affluent society with Flint's less fortunate, Warner Bros. agreed to give away thousands of tickets to the unemployed, who would be admitted on the honor system. They had to enter via side doors while Moore and other VIPs stepped out of a Cadillac stretch limo and paraded down a red carpet in front of TV cameras and photographers.

Not far behind the producer, in long red gowns, were leading ladies like Rhonda Britton, the self-employed widow surviving as the bunny bashing "Pets or Meat" lady, and Sabrina Thompson and the man who evicted her from her humble home, Sheriff's deputy Fred Ross.

In a perfect display of Midwestern graciousness, there were no hard feelings shown by the five families Ross put out on the street in *Roger & Me*. The deputy described the documentary as an educational film perfect for classroom use. "I think it would be good for young people to see it. They've got to know they just can't move in to a house and not pay the mortgage." After the premiere, Warner Bros. literally let Flint's poor eat cake at a gala party staged downtown at Flint's 14-story Hyatt Regency, which had just declared bankruptcy.

Junketing critics flown to Flint from all over the United States, as well as Europe and Asia, were generous in their reviews. Moore's handling of chronology led to criticism from Harlan Jacobson of *Film Comment* and the *New Yorker*'s Pauline Kael who suggested the film was "a piece of gonzo demagoguery that made me feel cheap for laughing." Kael, who also lobbied hard and unsuccessfully to block the film from winning a New York Film Critics Circle Award, had asked to view a video of the movie at her home in Massachusetts. Moore refused, insisting that she travel 150 miles to watch it on a movie screen at a theater in Manhattan.

Kael's criticisms did not hurt the film's gate. Unfortunately, Moore found that some viewers were offended by his story line. Among them was his stepdaughter Natalie Rose's father, Wallace Rose, a Flint lifer who felt the movie was way too hard on his home town. "It made Flint look awful." And much to Moore's disappointment, the film did better in the bookend states on the east and west coast than it did in other industrial Michigan cities like Battle Creek and Muskegon where, unlike the big Flint benefit, people had to pay to get in.

Moore was proud that a team of Flint residents was heading out to 30 poverty stricken American cities, at Warner Bros.' expense, to show his film as a political organizing tool. But back home not everyone saw the movie as a hopeful beacon. The tide of threatened legal actions against Michael Moore looked like it could exhaust the supply of available courtrooms in Flint. First at bat was Moore's old buddy, Larry Stecco, an attorney who had provided pro bono legal advice for the *Flint Voice* and the *Michigan Voice*, not to mention significant donations to the muckraking newspaper. After attorney Glen Lenhoff filed for Stecco, he represented three more *Roger & Me* plaintiffs. Another plantiff who ultimately settled out of court was sheriff's deputy Fred Ross, who appeared in the film's publicity stills.

Reporters covering the controversy found themselves on the receiving end of the same hostile Pauline Kael review from the UAW and the General Motors public relations departments.

"The bottom line is we think it sort of says to people it's all right to buy Toyotas because GM is shown to be a repugnant organization," said the UAW's Frank Joyce.

Also hurting was Bob Eubanks who was trying to find a way to get Moore to cut out his anti-Semitic joke, which many critics ridiculed in their reviews. According to Musselman, Eubanks had asked Moore for assurance that the cameras were off before he told this offensive joke. "Michael promised him they weren't shooting," says the attorney.

On the Hollywood scene, Moore was feted in Beverly Hills by the L.A. Film Critics for best documentary. At the same function was Spike Lee who won best film honors for *Do The Right Thing*.

For Moore, who decided to embark on *Roger & Me* a week after seeing Lee's breakthrough film, *She's Gotta Have It*, the event was a fortunate pairing. The filmmaker explained that he had read Lee's books, "hired his lawyer and producer's rep, used the lab he used—and spent $10,000 less!" Following the lunch Lee suggested getting together for a talk. But Moore's Warner Bros. publicist barged in between the two filmmakers and told Moore "You can't do that. You have a full afternoon of interviews and there is no time for anything else."

As the publicist pointed to the door, Lee smiled: "Just who's in charge here, Mike?"

Back home in Flint, Moore, who had originally planned to show his film at union halls if he couldn't find distribution, was surprised to receive a $10,000 bill from the UAW. Union executives decided to charge a steep rental fee after Moore took to the dais at a UAW hall and accused union leaders of selling out to the automakers. Naturally his attack on both the union and General Motors helped keep his controversial film alive.

Perhaps the loneliest figure of all was Mike Westfall, National Chair of the UAW committee focused on early retirement for a downsized GM workforce. Gathering dust at his Chesaning, Michigan, home was the seven page treatment he had drafted with Nader and filmmaker Nina Rosenblum. Moore had never responded to a draft that raised the possibility of a Bruce Springsteen score for a Waldo Salt script. Only when talk show host Phil Donahue came to Flint in late January 1990 for a Moore interview, did Westfall finally emerge from obscurity as the working class muse who allegedly inspired the project. Like a reporter for *Moore's Weekly*, the famed television host tried to assign credit where credit was due.

"You got a lot of help . . . here in Flint," said Donahue. "Among others, Mike Westfall, a proud UAW member, Jim Musselman, an attorney drew up the idea for the film about what was happening here."

"Oh, that's not true. Oh, they lied," said Moore.

"They worked hard—they fought General Motors."

"No, no."

"Please let me finish, Mike. You do get to speak . . . back in 1985; Ralph Nader and a few of his people who work for him were challenging General Motors publicly on their attempt to get tax rebates. The idea for a film came up . . . Interviews were made with people in the union, and others—real solid citizen types doing in-the-trench work. And those people suddenly disappeared from the film. The film suddenly became *Roger & Me*. ME . . . Michael Moore . . . Michael, this is not classy, Mike."

"Our movie was not to be a malicious comedy farce promoting Michael Moore at Roger Smith's, General Motors and the UAW's expense," Westfall said later. "It was to be a serious movie, intelligently sounding an alarm and targeting the many problems by thoughtfully telling the honest story of the suffering of America's workers and their families due to the horrific price of Middle American job loss due to corporate restructuring . . . The story never got told."

"Unlike Moore, we were blue-collar activists who worked for these companies. We cared and were not out to destroy the companies that supported us or the unions that represented us. Our mission was to change the direction of bargaining, which we did, and raise major societal questions as to how these companies were being directed, which we also did.

"The money made from our film was not going into our pockets like the millions of dollars from Moore's film went into his. Our films profits were going back to our suffering communities and the families of workers who were losing their jobs because that was where it belonged and that was the right thing to do."

Soon Moore was channeling Mike Westfall into an impossible dream riff on late night talk shows. Asked by talk hosts to explain the genesis of *Roger & Me*, Moore claimed he was sitting in Flint, Michigan unemployed and raising money with bingo fundraisers when he hit on the idea of a film about General Motors.

"It was like he dropped out of the sky," said Jim Musselman who was upset by Moore's revisionism. "There was no mention of the fact that Nader had given him $30,000 to produce the newsletter, that he had raised money from the MacArthur Foundation in Washington or that he had a big book contract with Doubleday. He never mentioned that he had been living in Washington where he was editing the film at his own office."

While Jim Musselman did not appear in *Roger & Me* he remained important to Moore in a new way. "It never occurred to Michael that his film would be such a huge success," said the Nader organizer. "Now he was getting nervous about critics challenging the credibility of the film." Eager to control damage, Moore responded with cranky late night calls. He was particularly worried because some of the critics were asking Musselman about questions raised on the Donahue show and repeated in papers such as the *Flint Journal*. They wanted to know more about the accuracy of the film.

"It really scared my wife to be woken up at 3 a.m.," recalls Musselman. "She was with me when he called to ask me to say the conversation with Smith never existed."

Like George Washington, the bleary-eyed attorney couldn't tell a lie. "Michael, there are transcripts of the GM annual meeting. I am not going to put my credibility out there. Other members of the camera crew were there. And we called Ralph after your Waldorf-Astoria interview with Smith."

Although Moore insisted this conversation never happened, Musselman recalls receiving calls from mutual friends about the Roger Smith scenes left out of the film. As the attorney listened to their arguments, he felt none of them were worried about the consequences of sidestepping the truth. Their problem, protecting Michael Moore, had nothing to do with his battle against GM. Sitting in a coffee shop at Philadelphia's 30th Street Station years later, he plows through a stack of clippings and transcripts central to his debate with Moore.

"I had a lot of people calling me up saying you have to fall on your sword and lie for the cause. But if I say that Michael never talked to Roger Smith, how does my credibility look the next time?

"Michael is never going to lead a true social movement in this country because it is always going to be about him. You can't build movements that way. The left wing puts too much faith in Michael. The fact that he is on every book cover and every DVD jacket says its about the me, not the we. The only way social change is going to happen in America is when it's about the we, not the me. A lot of energy is misdirected toward him when it should be directed toward the issues."

Ralph Nader demanded a $30,000 reimbursement for direct and in kind support of the film project. He also attacked the film in the *New York Times*. Moore denied moonlighting while exposing journalistic malfeasance and insisted he never two-timed Nader. He denied cashing Nader's checks and pumping the money into his documentary, although he did credit Musselman, Nader, John Richard and Nader's Essential Information project.

"Ralph is very upset now," Moore told his friend Ed Bradley at the Flint Journal, "because when Cable News Network or the *New York Times* wants a quote about GM they call Michael Moore, not Ralph Nader. More people have seen the movie in three weeks than have ever read a book about GM by Ralph Nader. Naturally he's a little jealous. The torch has been passed to a new generation."

Nader insisted on a refund that he would hand over to Essential Information, a nonprofit journalism foundation destined to further the mission of the late, unlamented *Moore's Weekly*. The filmmaker dismissed the complaint and related criticism from Musselman as a "lie by somebody who wants to cash in on the profits of the movie. He's a Nader Raider—they want money and they are trying to extort it from me."

"Here is Ralph lending him money and helping him and he is telling Ralph to go out to pasture," said Musselman. "It is so surrealistic. I trusted him. What would you think if someone did a movie about looking for someone they talked to three times, twice on film. He never once said thank you. He never recognized that so much of what he did was the result of people who helped and influenced him, people who taught and assisted him in so many ways. He turned against people who helped him and empowered him and taught him a lot. Personally I think it is more about Michael than the cause. I feel Michael has abandoned so many things he once stood for. Our conversations show the Michael Moore of 1985 should be criticizing the Michael Moore of today.

"I don't think Ralph objects to not getting credit. But the whole *Roger & Me* thing would have never happened without Ralph Nader. I really liked Mike and respected him. It was 100 percent to my benefit to say no transcript of the Smith interviews existed. He didn't reference anyone who helped. Michael Moore would not have happened were it not for people that reached out and helped him in a personal way. I was shocked at what he took from everybody. I never imagined he would exploit this tragic situation."

On a more personal note, Miss America, Michigan's Kaye Lani Raye Rafko, was also hurt by the way her comments about the unemployment situation ("I'm all for employment") were used in the film. Her scene appeared in a Miss USA Pageant "orientation" film created to teach contestants how to handle the press. And the head of the Genesee County Medical Society reported that the film had hurt the community's ability to recruit new physicians.

Moore's suggestion that Flint was in danger of becoming a "ghost town" may have been one of the reasons that Standard and Poor's decided to lower the city's bond rating. With residents suffering from low self-esteem, psychologists and sociologists who specialized in depression (clinical, not economic) tried to put a positive spin on the film's impact. This was a great opportunity for Flint to bond (socially, not fiscally). "People really need each other around something like this," said New York University psychologist Ellen McGrath.

At GM headquarters in Detroit, Roger Smith did not appear to be suffering from low self-esteem. Mindful of the public relations debacle over Ralph Nader's *Unsafe At Any Speed,* the CEO did not go on the attack. "The film doesn't help GM, and I don't like it personally," said Smith, "but I've got a thick skin." After pointing out that a scene showing the demolition of a GM water tower failed to mention that this landmark was razed to make room for a new plant, Moore's target added: "He didn't let any facts get in the way of his humor . . . So should we sue or take out ads in the paper telling our side? Our public relations staff said not to do anything, not to make something bigger out of this than it already is."

John Pierson, Moore's agent on the project preferred to take the long view of his client's 15-year journey from college dropout to overnight success and the Warner Bros. Wall of Fame: "The film was a classic, one that people will be watching 100 years from now." While he was sensitive to some of the criticisms leveled at *Roger & Me*, the indie guru was certain that Moore had one of the best shit detectors in this business. He knew where to cut.

"There are times when you want someone to achieve their goal. The film would not be nearly as satisfying for people if it contained an interview with Roger Smith. The Don Quixote hopelessness of the film was so appealing. It is funny that Roger Smith didn't immediately get out the word that, 'Hey, I talked to this guy.' It would have really changed things, carrying through into the release and promotion of the film. Where is Roger Smith? The guy wouldn't talk to me and now he won't see the movie. There is a through line that holds his story together. Michael is constantly trying to bait him. It would have ruined the movie. I don't think it would have gone as far as it did."

Although many underestimated Moore's potential as a filmmaker, Pierson was perhaps the only person rash enough to actually quantify his view. He had predicted *Roger & Me* would sell for $200,000, a number Moore would never let him forget. One reason for the $3 million sale was the filmmaker's ability to win the hearts and minds of the critics. There was something irresistible about Moore's salesmanship, when he told everyone that the film, which grossed $7 million in America, had actually done $25 million.

"I'm still looking for that other $18 million," said Pierson who gave up half of his $150,000 commission to Flint charity at Moore's behest. When the filmmaker began asking the agent to give back part of the remaining $75,000 fee, Pierson resisted. "You made more than anyone else," Moore told his agent, "even [editor] Wendey Stanzler."

"Then why don't you give Wendey more money?"

NOT BRINGING HOME THE BACON

Michael Moore on Television

THE FAILURE OF *ROGER & ME*'S BID for an Academy Award nomination the following spring did not diminish the film's lasting impact. Even suits against Moore in Genesee County courtrooms, including old friend Larry Stecco's case, which brought a $6,700 judgment against the filmmaker, failed to damage *Roger & Me*. Moore laughed at Stecco's suggestion that he'd promised the movie would be favorable to Flint. "Anyone who knows me understands that's not true. It would be like Jesse Jackson making a favorable movie about the Ku Klux Klan."

The legal actions were settled out of court or dismissed as Moore made the first of a series of charitable contributions to the community and gave away a thousand turkeys to needy Flint families a few days before Christmas. He set up a foundation to support promising filmmakers, donated to scholarship funds, the Blind Bowlers League and a UAW reform group while promising college tuition for "bunny lady" Rhonda Britton, who wanted to pursue her dream of becoming a veterinarian's assistant. He was also heartened when a local politician proposed that the city put an end to holiday evictions, a good idea that went nowhere, to the relief of another litigant against Moore and *Roger & Me*, Deputy Sheriff Fred Ross. Moore also began showing up on filmmaker panels where he delighted promising talent by simply whipping out his checkbook and handing out instant grants. One night, on the way back from an award ceremony in New York he asked editor Gini Reticker: "Everyone else has been hitting me up for money, why haven't you."

Recognizing a clear signal she asked Moore for help with her next film project and he graciously obliged. She was touched and flattered by this kind thank you for her eleventh hour work in that stifling Washington editing room.

Moore decided to follow up *Roger & Me* with a 28-minute PBS show called *Pets Or Meat, The Return To Flint*. This time he didn't have Roger Smith to kick around. The GM chairman stepped down in July 1990 with a $1.2 million a year golden parachute. Moore was not invited to the retirement party. But there was no doubt he had hastened the CEO's departure. Moore's dismal appraisal of the man who wouldn't give him an interview was seconded by the *Wall Street Journal*. "It was clear that Smith's nine years at the top had been a Reign of Error of historic proportions," wrote Pulitzer Prize-winning Journal reporters Paul Ingrassia and Joseph B. White in their book *Comeback*.

Now that the General Motors story was behind him, Moore began working on a feature film, *Canadian Bacon*, a satire of the Gulf War. In his script a faltering president decides to boost his plummeting polls by going to war with Canada. This concept gave Moore an opportunity to be greenlighted by every major studio in Hollywood. Moore began thinking about the project in 1991 at Sundance. The film festival's opening day coincided with American bombs bursting in air over Saddam Hussein's Baghdad. Moore asked John Sayles to introduce a resolution against the assault. When this motion flopped, Moore began thinking about Bush's 90 percent approval rating with the American public.

"I understand why people got wrapped up in it because Sadaam Hussein is a very bad guy who invaded Kuwait, so it's not like the situation with the Sandinistas, where our government was up to no good. But I felt at the time, this world is filled with really evil leaders, and we don't go and bomb the civilian population of those countries. So why this one? Well, economics, of course, I just feel that when we talk about human lives—especially civilian—that it better be for the right fucking reasons."

Moore's effort to persuade his film industry colleagues of the error of their ways via a screenplay fared no better than Sayles' pitch at Sundance. The script was dismissed as "too political." And the word around town was that every day on the job with Moore was Friday the 13th.

Undeterred by 38 consecutive turndowns, the college dropout returned to Hollywood in November 1992 to give his script another try. Moore was sitting in his Hollywood hotel room keeping one eye on *The Price is Right* and the other on the mini-bar when he received a call from the Burbank office of NBC entertainment president Warren Littlefield. Would he like to stop by for a chat about ideas for network television?

"Uh, sure!" said Moore, who, at that moment, was pitchless on ideas for television.

NOT TAKING YES FOR AN ANSWER

"There is nothing wrong with your television. Do not attempt to adjust the picture. We are now in control of the transmission. We control the horizontal and the vertical. We can deluge you with a thousand channels, or expand one single image to crystal clarity and beyond. We can shape your vision to anything our imagination can conceive. For the next hour, we will control all that you see and hear."
—Control Voice, The Outer Limits

BACK IN THE DAYS when he was working his way through college piloting 52-foot bobtail rigs on New Jersey highways, Warren Littlefield, aka "Big Red," was determined to move beyond his Teamster background and take a degree in psychology. But after graduation he began rethinking his destiny and took the first step toward a career that would lead him in an unexpected direction. A friend working on a remake of *The Little Rascals* for the Hearst Company gave Littlefield a series of gopher assignments on a television pilot. Alas Hearst hated it, the pilot bombed and the project ended up in the ashcan of broadcast history.

It was a perfect introduction to the world of network television where millions of dollars are invested in pilots leading to audience tests that read like a coroner's report. Littlefield worked as a junior development guy on sitcoms like *Cheers* and *Hill Street Blues*, learning that slow-starting shows could develop into surprise hits. As he moved up the ranks, he began trying out pilots that would not have

had a chance at other networks. During his nine-year career in the
'90s as president of NBC Entertainment, Littlefield had the pleasure
of reading many such test reports. One of his favorites is framed on
the wall behind his desk. Here are choice excerpts from this market
research report created by NBC's entertainment/prime time division:

Pilot Performance: Weak

. . . Portions were very popular. But the more typical sit-com
scenes of Jerry and his friends at common day locations were
negatively received—as one viewer put it, 'You can't get too
excited about going to the laundromat (sic).' No segment of the
audience was eager to watch the show again . . .

Jerry . . . created on balance lukewarm reactions among
adults and teens and very low reactions among kids . . . In his
'boring' ordinary, everyday life, he appeared sensitive but pow-
erless, dense and naïve. Jerry's "loser" friend George, who was
not a particularly forceful character, actually appeared somewhat more in charge and viewers found it annoying that Jerry
needed things to be explained to him. There was a loose connection between Jerry's on-stage material and his outside life—
viewers were unclear whether Jerry worked as a comedian or
if his routines took place outside of the show as commentaries.
The movement back and forth was also considered abrupt and
somewhat disorienting, especially to elder viewers . . . People
familiar with Jerry particularly enjoyed his stand-up routines,
but they resented its being interrupted by the storyline . . .

None of the supports were particularly liked and viewers felt
that Jerry needed a better backup ensemble. George was negatively viewed as a "wimp" who was only mildly amusing—viewers said he whined and did not like his relationship with Jerry.
Kessler had low scores . . . Claire the waitress, did not stand out in
a small part . . . Laura was disliked for leading Jerry on, and viewers found it unbelievable that a newly engaged woman would be
sleeping over . . . Despite the slice-of -life approach, the program
was considered only mildly realistic and believable, and many did
not identify with the things with which Jerry was involved.

* * *

Ignoring the experts in his own company, Littlefield commissioned four episodes of *Seinfeld,* a record low in a business that normally launches a show by ordering six to 13 segments. "We borrowed money from the specials department, to finance them," says Littlefield. "I think the network may have had to settle for one less Bob Hope Christmas special." One person who shared the dismal view of the NBC marketing analysts was the show's would-be star, Jerry Seinfeld. He was convinced that the program carrying his name would never go on the air and believed that at some point in the future, he and writer Larry David would end up showing all four episodes at a dinner party/wake for friends.

"In hindsight," says Littlefield, "the incredibly short order kept the idea alive. It kept a hold on the property and helped seal the creativity they had on the show." Just a few steps away in the waiting room was a trade magazine confirming that this television classic, remained, in syndication, one of the top-rated sitcom reruns in America.

"I was told not to develop *Friends, Frasier, Mad About You* and, of course, *Seinfeld.* These shows and other programs like *Grey's Anatomy* and *Will and Grace* all overcame poorly received pilots and lukewarm initial receptions to become hits that commanded a premium from advertisers due to exceptional demographics."

Unlike the writers, stars and agents in the holding pattern outside the NBC chief's audience, Moore was not focusing on trying to break in to prime time television. When Warner Bros. suggested he work on a TV show building on the success of *Roger & Me,* Moore said no. Television was a medium poorly suited to Moore's love for film projects that took years to execute. There was all that network bureaucracy, standards and practices departments to satisfy and, worst of all, sponsors who would, of course, want to actually see his material before they would commit to advertising. There was something else wrong with television for Michael Moore. Unlike *Canadian Bacon,* television would force him to go through a rite of passage. He would have to actually make a pilot and get it approved *before* he could actually take a program on the air. And he would have to hire a large production team that would have to blend traditional journalism with comedy writers and actors. The result, subject to censorship, could be frustration, humiliation and ultimately a step backward for a one-hit wonder.

When Warren Littlefield called for Michael Moore it was, in many ways, the longest shot of his career. Moore had no track record in network television except for his minor PBS followup to *Roger & Me* called *Pets and Meat*. The filmmaker worked entirely outside the studio system. He was not an established actor. And his shtick was built around the notion that journalism, particularly broadcast journalism, spared corporate America and political leaders on the altar of capitalism. After all what could you expect from networks who were financed by the kinds of companies they had to cover and regulated by politicians who advertised heavily during campaign season. The idea of bringing Michael Moore on board at NBC felt like turning a pyromaniac loose at a fireworks stand.

"One of the privileges of power," says Warren Littlefield at his office where guests are shown a refrigerator stocked with Perrier, soft drinks, beer and champagne, "is that you get infinite choices. When you sit in the network president's chair, you are exposed to a massive number of unbelievably successful people. Lets face it, it's the world of entertainment and they are larger than life. And you are in a power role in entertainment. There are many obligations, many black tie dinners. You have long days and long nights. The worst thing you can do is go off to a boring evening. If you ask me to name five people I would really like to have dinner with, Michael Moore would be on that list. Before I had even met Michael I was intrigued by *Roger & Me*, his background and his biography. I was really interested in meeting him.

"When you are in those top network jobs, you might as well take an egg timer. You are in there for a limited period of time. I ran NBC Entertainment, for nine years and was at the network twenty years. When you are in those jobs, time is very precious, and time spent with Michael, was incredibly stimulating, emotionally and intellectually."

Littlefield's preferred way of creating shows was building a link with coveted audiences, well-educated, relatively upscale, literate part-time evangelists unable to curb their enthusiasm for promising new talent: "Their passion for these shows helped build audiences through sheer word of mouth. In television you need viewers who say, 'Get out of the way, don't cut me off on the freeway, I must get home and see the show.' You need that if you are going to break through.

"In the early '90s, NBC sucked. We had a great run in the '80s and then our program got old, it got safe, it got predictable. When I started we were in a creative hole. It was clear that our future was going to be taking risks, shows that scared us. Shows I developed like *Seinfeld, Homicide* and *Life On The Street* were, by all research criteria, fool's errands, but they worked and became a successful broadcast business. We were getting our mojo back with intelligent adult entertainment.

"We were less concerned with the size of the audience than the quality. We wanted the urban, adult, college educated, upscale audience, a treasured audience in danger of leaving us for cable and pay TV. We found that if something turned them on and made them think we were off the charts. In a world of infinite choices you need that kind of audience.

"Today there are many more shows like *Seinfeld* that began with disastrous research. I was a junior in comedy development, when *Cheers* went on. It was the lowest rated show in its first year. You have to believe in shows that are different, you have to think differently.

"I loved *Roger & Me*. Here was an original voice, I loved his roots, I loved his story. I identified with him and where he came from as an individual. I grew up in New Jersey in an upper middle class neighborhood. But we didn't have a lot of money, I worked in a plastics factory in high school, a dirty job. Then I put myself through American University's international school of government and Hobart and William Smith where I got a degree in psychology. I worked as a Teamster trucking freight out of Paterson, New Jersey. I had the Catskills and Poconos and Brooklyn, Queens, Bronx, Harlem, the Jersey Shore. I was Big Red, a guy with an enormous beard. I was able to make enough money to pay for my education at a private school.

"There was this whole zen of Michael Moore, this guy from Flint, this guy who was in touch with real people and really was so proud of his roots. There was Michael calling over Thanksgiving from his

family home in Flint. It seemed like he was always back there. I think
I just identified with where he came from. I loved that he was a rebel.
It seemed to me that it could be a train wreck if we turned Michael
Moore loose and it was with that kind of a mindset that I invited Mi-
chael to come and sit down. We needed that kind of renegade in TV.
When we had taken risks before, we had found success."

Moore arrived at NBC for the meeting with Littlefield and his
subordinates with nothing in hand. With only a few hours to prepare
for the meeting, he launched into a pitch for a show that "would be a
cross between *60 Minutes* and Fidel Castro on laughing gas. The correspondents would look like shit. I mean, they'd look as if they were
either on their way to Betty Ford or had just spent a year working at
Taco Bell—or both."

Moore described his plan to pay homage to one of his advertisers
each week by going "after them like a barracuda. They won't know
what hit them. Then we'll go after organized religion, starting with our
fellow Catholics. I've got one idea where I'll go to confession in twenty
different churches and confess the same exact sin to see who gives out
the harshest penances. We'll run the results and call it 'A Consumers
Guide to the Confessional.'"

"That's the funniest idea I ever heard," said the NBC Entertainment chieftain.

"He just took over the room," recalls Littlefield. "He talked about
the things that he wanted to rail against, the things that irritated him.
I sat there and I laughed. I found him really entertaining I found myself leaning forward because I was interested, intellectually. Whenever I was in the room with a creator and a producer, I tried to imagine
myself being surgically sliced opened, and let all the other crises and
financial burdens that go with being a network president fall by the
wayside. My day job was kind of like being a fireman. But in these
pitch sessions I tried to forget about the rest of my work and let myself be exposed to everything coming at me. There were times when
my posture receded when I was not intellectually stimulated, when
my body just wanted to shut down and go to sleep and take a nap. I
learned to pay attention to that.

"I was always sleep deprived, my body was back into an infant state of being polymorphously perverse. All my synapses were snapping. My job was president of NBC Entertainment and I was entertained by Michael's vision. I was intellectually stimulated by what he wanted to attack and what he wanted to do, That made me look at him and say I want to be in business with you, I want you to do a show for us.

"I had no idea if jumping into the water with Michael Moore might lead us to say, 'My God, were we drunk.' I knew that, yet I was excited to work with Michael and see what he would do and where he would go."

Working in association with Columbia TriStar Television, NBC approved the pilot while Moore was walking out of the network office to his car. By the time he reached his hotel room, The *TV Nation* pilot had been greenlighted to the tune of one million dollars. "We were stunned," Moore and his wife and co-producer Glynn wrote. "Two years of trying to get a movie made with no luck, and in less than fifteen minutes in Burbank, we get a million bucks to produce a prime-time TV show. This is a very strange business, indeed."

For Littlefield, there was no question that Moore offered precisely what his network needed: "Michael attracts a lot of attention and as we were now developing a show with him in late 1993 and 1994 the television universe was changing. When I started in television in the late '70s the average household had less than ten channel choices. In the '80s, the average household had twenty-five to fifty choices. In the '90s they had a hundred choices.

"Michael was both a personality and filmmaker who could break through that clutter, who could draw attention to himself and his product, attention to television. With his little documentary, which cost nothing, Michael had broken through into the public consciousness. You had to pay attention. You were compelled to check it out, sitting there watching the world change, each and every day. The average household had infinite choices and having someone like Michael break through the clutter of those choices was very intriguing.

"*TV Nation* wasn't going to be terribly expensive. That was one thing that helped us jump into the sandbox with Michael and play. It wasn't high price scripted dramatic TV. It was probably $500,000 an episode. I was getting an hour show that would be relatively low cost and that helps jumping into the water.

"Remember the opening of *Outer Limits*. 'Do not attempt to adjust your television. . .' The brilliance of the idea was that we've taken over your TV, that's how powerful we are. As a kid I was captivated by *Outer Limits*. I loved the idea that a bunch of men and women turned over the airwaves to a brilliant madman. Hey, it's time for guerilla TV. He came in with guns blazing and he is taking over. I was completely turned on to that."

Littlefield pauses, smiles and adds, "And I knew we would have problems. I knew that sales had concerns about what the content would be. Broadcast standards also had concerns. It is a business, it's network TV and in network TV the only source of revenue is advertisers. I knew there would be advertisers that would be skittish, I just felt that it would be worth it. My feeling was we needed to try and let Michael go do his show. The best thing we could do, was not have the system grind him down, I think TV can take the bumps out of any creative idea, just plane them down, and flatten them out.

"It was my philosophy to allow producers to make mistakes and go places we couldn't immediately envision. If you had pitched me that we were going to be on a street corner in New York timing how much longer it takes black actor Yaphet Kotto to get a cab versus a convicted white felon, I wouldn't have seen it as breakthrough television. My point here is everything wasn't outlined , submitted and scrutinized before the fact. We took an incredibly talented visionary filmmaker and we said 'Go do the stuff you do.'"

And he did.

In New York, Moore warned his new *TV Nation* staff that this could be their last chance to work in television. "All of us need to behave as if we'll never work in television again. Because if we do this show right, nobody will ever want us. It will be too dangerous to have us around . . . This is not the place to build a resumé."

Unlike *Roger & Me*, *TV Nation*, which went on the air in the summer of 1994, did not divide the critics. Publications as far apart politically as the North and South Pole, did handstands for the new show. "Three Cheers for Michael Moore and his snappy satire," said

The Nation. "*TV Nation* may be that rarest of species, a television program both funny and important," said the *Wall Street Journal.* Just as Warren Littlefield predicted, loyal viewers cut short their other commitments to rush home for this show of shows. They were well rewarded.

One of the show's cleverest moments took place at the suburban New York home of Audiovox's CEO. A dozen cars pulled into the driveway of the man running America's largest car alarm company. When every vehicle's alarm triggered at 6 AM, the CEO came storming out in his pajamas and immediately called the police. The executive tried to block the segment with a lawsuit and failed.

Moore understood that satire works best when it exploits stereotypes. This view led to hiring a real pollster from Flint who discovered that 65 percent of all Americans believe that "frozen pizza will never be any good and there's nothing science can do about it." Another survey showed that 88 percent of all Bush voters "have no idea what rappers are talking about."

Eager to cool off during the long hot summer, the *TV Nation* staff rounded up a racially mixed busload of Brooklyn residents and took them to the residents only waterfront of lily white Greenwich, Connecticut. Backing a legal challenge to the city's "closed to the public" waterfront, the *TV Nation* invasion force came aboard a boat, transferred to dinghy landing craft and were halted by police and Coast Guard officials. Twelve members of the party, including reporter Janeane Garofalo decided to make a splash. They jumped off and swam the final half mile to Greenwich. Michael Moore was not one of the swimmers. Filmed to the strains of "The Girl From Ipanema," the Greenwich beach crowd was outraged by the televised invasion. "Buy some property in Greenwich," suggested one resident eager to see the city unload some of its pricey unsold inventory.

While the *TV Nation* extras did get a chance to cool off in Long Island Sound, their visit was anything but a day at the beach. Although they were evicted on the day of the shoot, the Connecticut Supreme Court, acting on a complaint filed by a young law student, ultimately ruled in favor of opening the Greenwich beaches to the public. A major victory for the show, this decision was celebrated by the staff, not to mention law-abiding beachcombers who believed the state's waterfront should be open to the public. It also showed Moore and his colleagues how to design a segment that has a direct impact on the political process.

Another outrageous *TV Nation* episode was "Love Night for the Ku Klux Klan" in Georgia. The segment began with the show's Love Night Mariachi Band strolling in to the rally to the strains of "Amor." The Klansmen had barely finished shouting down these intruders when Love Night Cheerleaders from African-American Spelman College leapt on stage and shouted:

> "Be really cool! Be really neat!
> Put away that tired old sheet!"

TV Nation invited the KKK men to kiss the black cheerleaders. There were no takers, even when the women walked the Grand Knights to their cars (with police protection) and handed out red balloons.

A *TV Nation* chorus line also drew a crowd at an Idaho get-together of the Aryan Nation. The event was remarkably peaceful, with the love, sweet love, performers. Determined not to let the spirit of brotherly love slip by, one of the Aryans declared: "We are motivated by love, we love our race very much, so much we are willing to fight and die for it."

"It is amazing how much Michael got past the censors," says David Wald, who broke his contract at NBC to become a senior producer at *TV Nation*. "He didn't want to make concessions. It was kind of like *The Simpsons*. He was very subversive and able to get away with it. I've never seen anything like that before."

"He was incredibly focused. What he did at the school board (in Davison) he did with the show." For Wald, a veteran producer who had developed shows with Katie Couric and Tom Brokaw, the experience was a sharp contrast to the typical news feature program where producers worked on segments independent of one another.

"The thing that he did that was different was that he ran the program like an entertainment show. A group of writers sat around the table every day throwing out ideas. There was no limit as to what anyone could do. It worked. I felt this is what I had come into television for."

With Michael's raw talent and Jerry Kupfer's organizing skills there was a very good team. There was no limit to what anyone could do. Wald's assignment was improving segments produced by talented young independent filmmakers without a TV background. "My job was to be a calming influence, because no one (including Michael) had much TV experience.

"There were a lot of times when you didn't know what you were doing. Sometimes there was vagueness. Some of the stories were three times as long as they needed to be. The key was to make it relevant, to try to figure out what the piece is trying to say.

"The show was one of those moments that doesn't happen very often. It was unheard of to have a show that is funny, one that reflects your values and pays and is on regular broadcast television. It was the show of my dreams. There was no way I would have worked that hard if it hadn't been such a great opportunity." The audience response was especially gratifying. "Whenever we went to a corporation and Mike asked to see someone they'd call security and public relations. The security guards often turned out to be huge fans of his."

"Michael imagined two trains in opposite directions, our train and the other guys," explains Wald. "He wanted our train to have more fun so that people on the other train would want to cross over. Because people liked his disarming sense of humor, he got away with a lot. It was the best show on television, like Sid Caesar's *Your Show of Shows*.

"Unlike *The Daily Show* and other programs that picked up some of our ideas (not to mention talent) from *TV Nation*, this show was always in his voice. Michael knows he is coming from a personal place and even if he is a multimillionaire he's still the underdog in some way, the person who will stand up for the issue. He is smart and funny enough to go out and accomplish something important. None of these other shows are really like that.

"The thing that's so great about him is his sense of humor. It's funny in a sick way. So much of what he is about can't even be explained. Like when we did the piece about an apparent serial killer moving in to a Westbury, Long Island, neighborhood. The neighbors never complained, even when the actor playing the madman role to the hilt with chain saws and burial pits began firing his shotgun in the wee hours of the morning. When they found out it was all staged by *TV Nation*, the neighbors retained a lawyer who threatened to sue.

The show's bathroom humor failed to tickle funny bones at targeted companies. Reporter Roy Sekoff ran into trouble when he rode the "shit train" down to Texas to find out what happens to waste flushed down the toilet by the *TV Nation* staff and millions of fellow New Yorkers. The sludge wound up on the Merco Ranch in the West Texas town Sierra Blanca where it was used as fertilizer. Merco sued the production company, Tristar, Sekoff and EPA expert Hugh Kaufman for defamation. While defendants and their attorney got their poop in a group, Moore was not named in the suit." An initial verdict in Merco's favor for $7 million was reversed on appeal.

Another classic segment that remains the talk of *TV Nation* reunions was the show's decision to spend $5,000 on Washington, D.C., lobbyist Bill Chasey. While this might seem like a pittance in the influence peddling league, *TV Nation* received plenty of bang for its bucks. The Washington insider helped persuade two Congressmen, Howard Coble (R-NC) and Floyd Flake (D-NY), to introduce a resolution declaring August 16, 1994, *TV Nation* Day. Speeches drafted for them aired live on C-Span and suburban Fishkill, New York, agreed to honor the occasion by giving city employees the day off. Town businesses closed for a big parade broadcast the same night on the show.

The last-minute programming switch, which included live segments, panicked a McDonald's ad man who wasn't allowed enough time to figure out which of the company's prepared commercials best fit the show. He solved the problem by canceling his spot just before the show went on the air.

"Michael had a lot of good suggestions," says Wald. "When we were cutting he would come in and suddenly try a juxtaposition. It was great. I can tell you working for *TV Nation* made it harder to go back to regular TV. I try to incorporate humor more. I was never interested in pretty boring stuff."

Wald worries at times that the success of television may be contributing to the fact that "as a society we are getting farther and farther away from each other. I even worry that we are watching each other but from a distance. But at the same time it's a medium that does stimulate conversation and helps people get together in new ways."

Warren Littlefield shares this view. The trick is to find producers who can find ways to inform and entertain simultaneously. "I think the creative freedom we gave Michael can be a little bit overwhelming," says the studio executive who wrote Moore a creative blank check. "Michael rose to that responsibility. We didn't have network executives following him around saying, 'You can't do this, you can't do that.' We were not censoring him as he worked and what we got back was wholly creative and original. There is a lesson here.

"A broadcast standard change could be a request to say damn only twice, instead of three times. Broadcast standard issues with Michael were more global. When it was all said and done, broadcast standards accepted that the rules of engagement were going to be different, in the same way we did the episode of *Seinfeld* about masturbation called 'The Contest.' Well we've never done that before, but this is an adult show and it is an adult theme and we are not going to say they can't do this. We'll be open-minded.

"Broadcast standards saw that Michael's show was very adult and very entertaining. Conceptually they understood who Michael Moore was and they were open going into it. I said, 'Okay. Michael Moore is going to ruffle some feathers, and that is what he does.' I think we got a lot of stuff on that surprised, educated, and enlightened the audience. The pact the show had with the audience wasn't violated.

"He broke ground in many ways and that was exactly what we wanted him to do. The victory was that the system did not destroy the product. The product was able to survive the system of broadcast television.

"I had very high expectations and I went into it with a lot of respect for Michael. He didn't meet my expectations he exceeded them. I found the type of TV he was doing with *TV Nation*, resonated for me as a viewer. I accomplished a lot of the things that I went into this business to do, entertain, inform and illuminate. That was television that I wanted to do and be a part of.

"I wasn't sure what was in the mind of Michael Moore, whether he could put out enough segments, enough material. It is one thing to toil over a film, where there is one through line premise. It takes a massive amount of time to put that together and to present it. When you finish an episode in TV, guess what? You don't get to rest when you are done. You have another one to do. There are multiple segments in each episode. I didn't know if we would burn out Michael Moore, if there were ten great ideas inside Michael Moore. It turns out there were far, far more."

One of the strengths of *TV Nation* was Moore's total immersion into the project. Unlike his *Mother Jones* days, when he would simply postpone editorial decisions and duck scheduling issues, the NBC arena played to one of his strengths, last-minute decision making. He loved working in crisis situations, editing projects until minutes before air time. And while this could be hard on his staff, it often gave the show an immediacy lacking in network TV.

"I think his process was one that helped strengthen the entertainment value of his work," says Littlefield. "His approach was not a solitary one, it was not a traditional news approach. News is put on a certain pedestal. Once an idea is approved in news a segment producer goes off and executes it. Michael surrounded himself with very smart interesting people. His approach to his own ideas and those pitched by his creative staff was, 'Let's get in a room, throw things against a wall, play with it and see what we come up with.' It was a kind of guerilla approach, a real cauldron of ideas, that made for interesting TV.

"Questions raised in story meetings included setup, figuring how the piece would work, contingency planning for unexpected turns in the story line and of course, coming up with a strong ending. It was a challenging environment, where really good ideas were nurtured.

"I think the Yaphet Kotto *TV Nation* piece is really powerful entertainment, a segment that resonates to this day throughout this country. When he did a piece in a Mexican factory, Michael was just great at challenging authority. This was a lot like *Roger & Me*. He walked into a large manufacturing plant. He reached out to the people who were in that plant, identifying with the little guy. I liked his collision with the powers that be, poking, searching and exposing to some degree the power elite. I was educated. I was entertained. I haven't seen that kind of story on TV. The news division isn't taking me there.

"Inevitably *TV Nation* showed up at media events covered by NBC News and other networks. One was a Rudolph Guiliani press conference where the show's finger-licking good mascot, Crackers the Crime Fighting Chicken was asked to leave. And in some locations *TV Nation* wasn't just covering the news. It was making news.

"One day I did get a call once from the news division and they were like, 'Hey what's Michael Moore doing. We are covering legitimate news stories and we keep bumping into Michael Moore.' My approach was, 'I understand, I understand and I will talk to Michael about this.'

"I never called him. The fact of the matter was that Michael was doing his job. If Michael showed up some place where the news division was present, I knew that his take would be different. That was what he was supposed to do."

Moore's old compadre, Jim Musselman, was amazed by his success in television. "During a visit to New York, I was walking up Fifth Avenue, and across the street was Michael, being followed by an entourage of fans. I waved, but he never saw me."

Not a single segment was cancelled during *TV Nation*'s debut summer season on NBC. During an hour-long, year-end special the Peacock network's broadcast standards department did stop two segments. One was a piece on condoms. The other was a piece on anti-abortion crusader Roy MacMillan, who suggested it would be justifiable to "assassinate the Supreme Court judges" in defense of the rights of the unborn. Moore gave in after the network pointed out that not a single sponsor wanted to appear around this frightening segment that sent a disturbing message to a well armed nation. .

Although the segment never made it onto the air, the Secret Service asked for a private screening. "We'd like to review the transcript ourselves and see the context in which the remarks were made," said the agency's Eric Harnischfeger. After McMillan's 15 minutes of *TV Nation* fame was cancelled, the pro-lifer tried to clarify his remarks. This decision may have been connected to the fact that two days after

the segment was dumped a pair of shootings at Brookline, Massachusetts, family planning clinics left two dead and five injured.

MacMillan complained that correspondent Louis Theroux hammered him with hours of leading questions to come up with minutes
of footage that would win him life membership in Moore's pantheon
of wackos. Asked how he felt about slitting the throat of an abortionist, MacMillan said, "Well, it certainly would not be out of the word
of God. I think you should do it in love, and I think you should do it
to cause instant death."

MacMillan insisted that quotes like this did not give him a chance
to finish his thought. "My comment, in response to a leading question, was, 'Certainly it is more merciful to kill a person swiftly than
drawing it out like an abortionist does—one limb at a time.' I was
not advocating killing anyone. I was just saying anyone who kills,
whether it's a dove or a deer, should be merciful."

Despite his impressive fan base, the great reviews and a more than
satisfied front office, Moore would not take yes for an answer from
NBC. Stepping away from an average audience of 9 million viewers he
quickly began floundering in the choppy waters of Rupert Murdoch's
Fox TV kingdom.

Moore claimed that "despite the unprecedented amount of fan mail
they received, NBC decided against ordering any future episodes of
TV Nation beyond a holiday special." Actually, says Littlefield, it was
Moore, not NBC, who ended *TV Nation* on that network. Rather than
pursue another season at NBC, he moved the show to Fox, convinced
that he could win a bigger audience and ultimately enjoy a larger budget. Producer Wald believes Moore's decision to leave NBC for Fox,
where it was rumored he might be slotted against NBC's *Saturday
Night Live*, was not a good idea. Warren Littlefield agrees.

"I was so overwhelmed with so many things," recalls Littlefield.
"As passionate as I was about Michael and the show some of the
details fell away. Every fall the Hollywood Radio and Television Society hosted the four network presidents for a Q-and-A session. Michael
hosted it in 1994 at the end of his summer season on NBC. He was a
superstar. He was so funny and so insightful and so informative. Usually
these luncheons get so safe and it was fabulous to have him. A lot of

people were buzzing about how great Michael Moore was. This helped raise his profile at Fox. They were suitors and hot to trot. What they offered versus what we were willing to offer looked good to him.

"*TV Nation* was not a home run, it was a solid single. From a pure broadcast ratings sense we weren't sitting on a *Seinfeld* or *Frasier* or *Friends* or *ER*. In terms of the strength of an asset, a network asks how much can you monetize it. It was something we were proud of and we wanted to continue. I wasn't the only voice in the building who thought that it was great television. It wasn't an advertiser 'must have' but it wasn't a disaster. We had a history of sticking with singles that eventually became doubles and home runs. The show had an average of 9 million viewers each week which was good then and a great number today, especially when you consider that Jon Stewart and *The Daily Show* has a fraction of that number.

'We were excited, we were proud, there was creative potential. But we weren't dealing with a monster hit. Someone else came along and said here is what we want to do and they made a case that seemed more compelling than playing it out with us."

The Fox version of *TV Nation* also offered a generous helping of guerilla theater. Women cheered when the show's Johns of Justice flatbed trucks rolled into the parking lot at destinations such as Pro Line, a Texas company that had 150 women on the payroll and six men-but just one bathroom for each sex. Rather than meet a government order to install more bathrooms for women, the company attempted to fire them en masse. After this action was stalled by an Equal Employment Opportunity Commission suit, the Johns of Justice truck arrived. Correspondent Karen Duffy invited the Pro Line women to use the half-dozen Johns of Justice porta-potties at no charge. Unfortunately the bathroom break was short-lived. At the company's request, police arrived in minutes, threatening to arrest the *TV Nation* team and impound all the portable toilets.

Building bridges with sworn enemies became one of Moore's passions. For example in Georgia, he found a way to get up close and personal with Newt Gingrich. Eager for an interview with the House Leader who brought $4 billion in federal funding to his Cobb County constituents, Moore joined Gingrich in a Fourth of July Parade.

As Moore walked alongside the local hero and waved to the crowd, the congressman pointed to a nearby rooftop. "I have to warn you, there's a sharpshooter up there on the roof pointing a gun at you." Moore peeled off and caught up with Gingrich later at a barbecue. Before the Congressman could escape, Moore held up a mike and shook hands with the GOP leader. "No, you're not hallucinating, I'm Michael Moore. This is Newt Gingrich, and tonight on *TV Nation*, Newt and Mike save America."

Unfortunately, Rupert Murdoch's Fox turned out to be a step down for the show's editorial independence. Dave Wald, who believed leaving NBC was an inexplicable decision, had good reason to worry. Four segments were killed as Moore lost important battles with broadcast standards. Among them was the story of America's first family of AIDS funeral picketing, the Phelpses of Topeka, Kansas. Led by Pastor Fred Phelps of the Westboro Baptist Church (www. godhatesfags.com), the peripatetic pickets ranging from grade school children to grandparents, protested the funerals of AIDS victims being punished by the almighty for violating the Biblical injunction on sodomy. Other shows too hot for Fox were a piece on the support group for the CEO's of bankrupt savings and loans who "prospered long after their clients went bankrupt," a segment on small condoms and a reenactment of the Los Angeles riots.

In September 1995, Fox decided not to renew the show, prompting fans to picket evildoer Rupert Murdoch's New York office. The day after the final *TV Nation* episode, Moore, Glynn and producers David Wald and Jerry Kupfer received an Emmy for Outstanding Informational Series. Addressing the audience at the Shrine Auditorium in Los Angeles, the show's founder thanked "General Motors, General Electric and General Murdoch—without them, we wouldn't be there."

WE BOMBED IN TORONTO

MOORE'S PREDICTION that his staff's *TV Nation* work would effectively blacklist them from work in this industry proved he was working with a broken crystal ball. Most of his alumni would move ahead nicely in the industry. Jerry Kupfer would create the NBC pilot for a Tina Fey/Alec Baldwin show called *30 Rock*. Gideon Evans moved on to *The Daily Show*. Wendey Stanzler was a key editor for *Sex and The City*. David Wald went to work for *The Learning Company*. But for most of the *TV Nation* team there would never be another opportunity that brought with it the kind of creative chaos central to the show. Who but Michael Moore could turn being thrown out of a corporate waiting room into an art form? And who was going to fight corporate crime if Crackers was cooped up.?

Fortunately, the boss's own hiatus was brief. Two weeks after taking home their Emmy, Michael Moore and Kathleen Glynn arrived for the premiere of their long awaited feature, *Canadian Bacon*. The hard-to-hawk screenplay, finally got a break when Moore took hard-to-hawk copies of his *TV Nation* pilot to actors John Candy and Alan Alda. They liked the premise of this feature script—America declares war on Canada to give a boost to the defense industry and a president's sagging ratings in a reelection campaign.

Both stars signed on for the film and David Brown, who headed production at 20th Century-Fox and Warner Brothers with Richard Zanuck for many years, agreed to produce the film. These men who had launched the career of Steven Spielberg with *Sugarland Express* and *Jaws,* had gone on to executive produce *The Sting,* winner of seven Oscars.

A man who had taken more than one walk on the Hollywood's noir side, Brown produced Robert Altman's *The Player,* the story of a studio executive being stalked by a spurned screenwriter he can't remember. He is also famous for his description of the film business as an industry "where you can't make any money but one where you can get very, very rich."

As Moore quickly discovered, finding $10 million in financing for a movie (one of the backers was fellow University of Michigan drop-out Madonna's Maverick Picture Company) with stars like Toronto born Candy, Alda, Rhea Pearlman, Jim Belushi, Rip Torn and Kevin Pollak simply created a new set of problems. He was slipping into a quagmire film critics like to call "the terrible twos." Or as Moore explained, "It was the true sophmore jinx. Everything that could go wrong did go wrong."

Although his budget was 40 times the size of *Roger & Me,* Moore realized that the film wouldn't work if the cast and crew didn't understand that many politicians and business people had a gift for lying in public and getting away with it. To make sure that his troops understood the film's political contest, Moore wrote Stanley Kubrick in Britain who agreed to share a print of *Dr. Strangelove.* The classic was shown on the eve of principal shooting at Parkwood, an estate that had been the home of R.S. McLaughin, the founder of General Motors of Canada. Now everyone understood how the world ended, with a big bang and a bunch of wimps.

Unfortunately the screening was lost on John Candy, who was so drunk that evening that producer Brown worried he wouldn't be able to show up for work. Fortunately the star sobered up and was on the set ready to go at 6 a.m. While relations with the cast and crew were cordial (his stepdaughter Natalie had a cameo role and Kathleen, who had interned on Spike Lee's *Malcolm X,* served as co-producer, title designer and costume designer), Moore was at odds with celebrated cinematographer Haskell Wexler who he felt was "72 years-old and slightly bitter." Moore accused Wexler of deliberately pulling certain shots out of focus to keep them out of the film. When the actors stopped to rehearse in key locations like the top of Toronto's CN Tower, Wexler, according to Moore, would ask, "Are we going to make the fucking movie or not?"

Candy, siding with Moore, responded, "We're going to fucking leave."

Wexler suggested "the aw-shucks homespun character that Moore portrays is a complete falsification." There were also battles on the set between Moore and Ron Rotholtz, another *Canadian Bacon* producer who had worked with Madonna's Maverick Picture Company. "They almost came to blows," says Brown.

These were only minor skirmishes in a backstage plot line that was starting to sound like a Hitchcock film. Before post production wrapped, Candy had to head south to meet a commitment on the set of *Wagons East.* "They had him riding in 100 degree Mexican heat," says Moore. "He was exhausted."

Worried about his lead's health, Moore called and suggested the actor ditch the project and return to California. As it turned out, Candy had done precisely that a week earlier only to learn he could be held in breach of contract. According to Moore, an agent warned, "you get your ass back there or you're going to get sued."

Back on the Mexican set, Candy sounded worse. "I can barely breathe," he told Moore in a phone call. The next day the famed comic actor was found dead in his room. He was only 43.

The heart attack that took Candy's life was the kind of personal tragedy that not only devastates family, friends and fans, but calls into question Hollywood's dangerous work ethnic. There were, of course, practical issues for the production company. "We needed Candy for postproduction scenes," says producer David Brown, "and had to work around the problem in final editing." But finishing the film to honor the actor's memory was much more than a technical matter. Moore's own guilt made him realize that perhaps he should have pushed the actor just a little harder: "I wish I said 'Fuck CAA (his agency), fuck the lawyers."

While a complicated set of circumstances led to Candy's death, it was relatively easy for all concerned to pin it on the Mexico project. Assigning blame is easy when actors are pushed beyond their limits and forced to work eighteen-hour days and more. As Haskell Wexler would point out years later in his documentary, *Who Needs Sleep,* the endless overtime embedded in the movie industry is an occupational safety officer's nightmare.

Candy's death and a brain tumor that sidelined a sound man on the project made Moore wonder if anyone on the project was safe. Finally the director got a break when character actor G.D. Spradlin (playing the warmongering president of Hacker Dynamics) grabbed Moore and pulled him to the ground during a post production shoot. It was only a mild heart attack and Moore knew exactly what to do. He asked actor Kevin Pollack and the crew to call 911. Then he got down on the ground and shouted, "G.D., you cannot die, Pleaase don't do this. Come back. Please." Twenty seconds later the actor's eyes opened and he said, "There was a bright light. I was in Vegas and was winning everything."

After shooting was completed Moore headed off to Cannes. By now the film's original backer, Propaganda Films, had lost its sense of humor about Moore's bacon bits and was thinking about abandoning the project. Moore was dismayed that this division of Polygram believed the film was too political. Propaganda executives tried to boost cast and crew morale on the set with a memo pointing out that John Candy's "Uncle Buck" had made $60 million. Wrong message, said Moore, who was trying to make a "political" comedy. His anger at the Propaganda machine ultimately contributed to a breakup. After major film distributors turned down the project, Brown was forced to go with Greenwich Pictures, a small company specializing in art house films.

The preview was scheduled for a theater in a working class New Jersey town near New York. "I thought people were getting up and going to the bathroom," says Brown as members of the preview audience slipped away. When they didn't return, he began to wonder why the preview hadn't taken place in Greenwich Village or a college town that could appreciate Moore's style of filmmaking.

Convinced there was no market for the movie, the distributor limited the opening to a handful of cities. Critics were lukewarm about the film, which grossed just $132,000 in theaters-money that was never paid to the production company that had invested $10 million in the project. "I still thought it was a great movie," said Brown. "Unfortunately we never even saw the $132,000."

Despite its commercial failure, there was a lot to admire about *Canadian Bacon*, a satire later echoed by Barry Levinson's *Wag The Dog*. But it showed Moore the difficulty of creating art inside the Hollywood wagon circle.

A DIFFICULT CLIENT

CANADIAN BACON'S FAILURE TO SIZZLE and the demise of *TV Nation,* a show that peaked with NBC ratings comparable to today's *60 Minutes,* dumped Michael Moore into the Never-Neverland of turnaround. Undaunted, he quickly began working on new projects. From producers rep John Pierson to his New York business manager, attorney Ken Starr, Moore had always tapped in to first class talent when it was time to navigate around the Hollywood sharkscape, Moore decided to take time out to write a book, *Downsize This! Random Threats From An Unarmed American.* But even this Harper-Collins project quickly landed him back in the documentary world, as he brought along a film crew to record his book tour. Unable to sell the project and worried about other stalled film ideas, he turned to Starr for advice. The advisor handed him off to Douglas Urbanski, manager to the stars, film producer and former theatrical producer.

Overachieving can always be a liability for a star. At least that's the way some of Moore's advisors see it. Looking back on this period years later, his former manager Douglas Urbanski, broke the cardinal rule of his profession. "I never talk about my clients," he says. "Never. But this is different. Michael Moore holds people in his films to an intense level of scrutiny, and I believe the same standard needs to be applied to him."

Just back from a New York trip, Urbanski is having a hamburger and ice tea at Cravings, a Sunset Boulevard restaurant where it is possible to throw a dart and hit a Scientologist, a Jew, a Protestant, or a fellow Catholic like Douglas Urbanski. A lay minister who assists a priest every midday at nearby St. Victor's parish, Urbanski says, "I know Michael Moore is also a Catholic. But sometimes I have difficulty believing that."

A charter member of the Wednesday Morning Club, a lunch forum dedicated to the power of Hollywood conservative thinking, he has guest hosted for right-wing talk show diva Laura Ingraham as well as Michael Savage. One of his closest friends is David Horowitz, the *Ramparts* acolyte who has traded in his red-diaper-baby past and Berkeley digs for a home in southern California where he coauthors books like *The Anti Chomsky Reader* and *Destructive Generation: Second Thoughts About the '60s.*

But when it comes to talent, Urbanski is an agnostic. In Hollywood stars bankroll candidates and sing for their fund-raising suppers, producers decide when the balloons and confetti will fall from the ceiling at the Democratic National Convention and studio owners determine which bankable directors are entitled to a national soap box. Urbanski was ready for Moore's late night phone calls, the identity crisis, even the difficulties that he believes temporarily saw Michael Moore and his wife residing in separate Manhattan apartments, albeit in the same upper west side building.

Unlike agents, managers often oversee the personal lives of their clients, a risky business indeed. If they are not careful, they can find themselves feeding the cat or changing light bulbs in the pool house for celebrities who have a hard time navigating the uncharted waters of fame.

While Urbanski did not have to do housework for Moore, he did find that his new client was a major self-improvement project. "The Michael we have today is the Michael I had and he is not the Michael who existed before. As I have told others, Michael Moore is the L. Ron Hubbard of political movements. By which I mean Hubbard was a science-fiction writer who created a religion, Scientology. Michael is a filmmaker who decided, 'Hey I can change governments.' He got on to the enormous profit you can make from criticizing conservatives or taking money from hyping and distorting. He was doing some books that were very funny and very good. He was doing investigative work that had a humorous but serious nature. I think he attacked worthy targets like companies that have become multi-billion dollar businesses on the back of slave labor. But somewhere between *The Big One* and those television shows, Michael became money obsessed. I have known one other person as money obsessed as Michael. He had to devise another way to make sure that his projects would get financed and distributed. It was no longer a serious investigation of labor injustices in Indonesia. It was now about cash.

"When I worked for Michael no one wanted to distribute *The Big One*. He was unreliable about meetings. He would call and demand time and attention. It was free form and free association. It was very hard. At some point you have to sit down and do a story board or a plot line. At some point you have to get specific. He was good at making it look like he was in the game but when it came to sitting down and doing the work it was hard. He works in his own bubble.

"I kept asking him, 'How do you envision yourself? You have this great brain, this great humor, you have the ability to gin up people. Are you the labor organizer? Are you the guy who goes on *Today* and *Larry King* and talks about labor? It's a good topic. Are you a propagandist? If you are, then you can't be Jackie Gleason. If you don't decide who you are, I will make it my business to decide who you are.'"

"I'd love that," Moore replied. "My life would be so much easier."

Urbanski's problem was that "when it came to the rules, Michael was impossible. A director gets six to twelve months to edit and deliver a cut. Everyone else had to stick by the rules. Everything he reports on is a 'gotcha.' He is always catching people doing something wrong. But he is breaking the rules.

"Part of the reason I stopped representing him is that all of this is a recipe for a fight. If a person is not cooperative or professional you can't close deals. I could have imagined us putting together deals that he couldn't service. He was a famous face and funny and had a lot of things going for him but he couldn't service the thing and at the end of the day it would be unproductive. He is a real complainer, a bitch and moaner who thinks nothing is going his way. But he is the obstacle.

"His wife was a very nice lady. She was extremely supportive and attentive to him and extremely devoted to him and was in such frustration about getting him to function. She was vulnerable and sweet and terribly bright and almost emotionally naked and raw.

"He blamed producers for things going wrong. He didn't want to acknowledge that because of *Canadian Bacon* it would be hard to initiate interest in a new film. He didn't want to deal with the reality of it. He had a great sense of entitlement. He thought he deserved show business embracing him with open arms. No one bears grudges in the world of distribution and everyone is everyone's friend. Harvey Weinstein of Miramax and Tom Bernard and Michael Barker of Sony Classics came to the screening of *The Big One* and no one wanted to buy it. They were all terribly polite to Michael, but no one thought it was for them. His talk show pilot was never picked up despite the presence of stars like O.J. Simpson and Jon Stewart."

One of the problems with pitching the film was that it lacked both hail and brimstone. A road picture crisscrossing the land of the free and the home of the brave, this documentary alternated the tragedy of outsourcing with spot checks of bookstores to see if they were doing a good job selling the director's new work. Moore's attacks on companies like Johnson Controls leaving Milwaukee for Mexico echoed *Roger & Me*. But these scenes of Moore hugging laid-off Midwesterners were no match for a Fred Ross eviction juxtaposed with Roger Smith giving himself a fat raise.

"We tried to keep him focused." says Urbanski. "I found Michael one of the most engaging and funny people around. There were 27 Michael Moores even though there are steady themes in his work. There was the Michael who could gin up people, the nice Michael, the rich Michael, the impoverished Michael, the grandiose Michael and the slightly paranoid Michael. Some of the Michaels are pretty funny. Ultimately he had to invent a character.

"He wanted to be a screenwriter without writing a screenplay. When he told me he wanted to be a screenwriter I said show me that damn screenplay. He never wrote one.

"I don't believe that Michael Moore has politics. His work is definitely about him. He loved the spotlight. He used the words regime change and in Australia went down on a big promotion to affect their election. It is unthinkable to get mixed up abroad like that. It is inconceivable at a time of war to export the main propaganda that gives solace to the enemy. I don't view Michael as a significant figure on the landscape. He's a vaudevillian. In a sense, we're all vaudevillians."

Part of Moore's frustration, suggests Urbanski, is the difficulty he has competing with his conservative opponents. "Let's take Michael Moore and Rush Limbaugh. One of these men has to be in a chair at noon on the east coast. He has to speak with a microphone for fifteen hours a week to fifteen million people. There are three or four hours of prep time for every hour of on air time. It requires an enormous discipline, an enormous brain and an enormous type of specific talent. I have had people say to me that Michael Moore is the same as Rush Limbaugh. One talks for 15 hours a week in front of a microphone and shows you who you are. Michael fills an hour and twenty-five minutes every five years in the name of the little guy."

THINKING BIG

"People like to be in the movies. They like to be on TV. There is something about the camera, they can't turn it down. They talk. I try to be respectful. We are trying to arrive at the truth."

—Michael Moore

THE BIG ONE, edited by Meg Reticker, the talented sister of Gini Reticker who had worked her magic in the final editing of *Roger & Me*, featured two interviews with Nike Chairman Phil Knight. Unlike Moore's board meeting showdowns with Roger Smith, this footage made it to the screen in the documentary finally released in 1997 by Miramax. Moore, proud to wear made-in-America New Balance shoes, had found a CEO willing to stand up for outsourcing. A poster boy for Indonesian manufacturing, Knight explained Americans didn't want to make shoes. Unlike Nike's long-gone Maine workers, who hammered the company with millions in repetitive stress injury claims, Indonesian contract laborers were not all on a first name basis with workers compensation attorneys. When Moore made a good case for opening a Nike factory in Flint, the Oregon CEO explained that Michigan was a lousy place to build shoes. Left unanswered was why Moore himself was unwilling to move his own company Dog Eat Dog Films, from pricey Manhattan to more affordable digs in Flint.

Phil Knight's claim that his company didn't employ 12-year-olds in Indonesia fell flat when he conceded that the shoe firm did hire

14-year-olds. Nike's public relations staff tried and failed to have this statement excised. Although *The Big One,* ultimately produced by Miramax, did not come close to the success of *Roger & Me*, Moore noted that the stock of Knight's firm drifted downward after the film's release. He also promised to donate half the film's profits to Flint. Unfortunately the movie only grossed $649,000 during its first five weeks.

During the filming, Moore worried about giving himself too much space in a film that lacked the emotional impact of his first documentary. Did the filmgoing public really want to watch him signing books for adoring fans in places like Rockford, Illinois? Another difficulty was the film's political context, a drive-by targeting corporations who cut and ran for third-world labor markets, depriving Americans of their jobs. This theme worked fine for other filmmakers who enjoyed the financial support of Moore's Center for Alternative Media. They were people like Sam Riddle, who produced a movie called *Chemical Imbalance* about an African-American man born to a mother exposed to toxic waste during her pregnancy. But these protégés were not seeking the kind of mass audience so important to Moore.

Turning pathos into prime time was more than tweaking audiences with stars like John Candy or Jim Belushi. Success meant mastering the difference between the careful scripting of a feature and the serendipity of documentary filmmaking. For Moore the key was starting with a shot list that would ultimately yield an unforgettable narrative. He also depended on younger talent, including a number of gifted women editors who shared his political vision.

Among them was Meg Reticker, who also worked with Moore on *The Awful Truth* and the pilot for his Fox talk show that was never picked up despite the presence of stars like O.J. Simpson and Jon Stewart. Like her sister Gini, who had stepped in to do wonderful eleventh-hour editing work on *Roger & Me*, Meg was a fellow Midwesterner and an Irish Catholic. She was not put off by serious overtime or Moore's fusion of political and comedy writing. A Latin American studies major at the University of Wisconsin, Reticker worked on both features and documentaries. Although Moore was no longer financing his projects with bingo games, major funding did not mean he could simply spend his way out of creative problems.

"In feature films you are getting notes from the script supervisor that describe every shot along with the director's preference," explains Reticker at her Brooklyn home. "You get dailies and you begin assembling scenes and the director comes in and looks at footage. He'll ask what you think about shooting other stuff. After eight weeks it's done and there is an editor's cut.

"But with a documentary the director and the editor are trying to write the script together after the material is shot. It's a lot more work. The director's vision is of utmost importance. You could get footage that Michael has shot and cut it a number of different ways. When he is shooting he knows how he is going to use that material. Michael has more of a notion of the story he is going to tell. There were points as an editor where I looked at it, did this cut and Michael would come in and cut it a different way.

"I have had the experience of dumbing it down but this is not dumbing it down. He has an ability to entertain and be informative. You might take some material and it is too heady and too PBS. His ability to do both those things is just amazing. He is surrounded with a pool of comedy writers and political producers. They are so different.

"Much of *The Big One* is based on *Downsize This*. That was almost my script for the film. We are dealing with all the issues that appear in the book. All the stuff was Michael's stuff. It had to have his stamp of approval. There was no other TV that was like that. With *TV Nation* (her brother-in-law Jerry Kupfer was executive producer) they were creating something that never was. There was no show like that really.

"How often do you get to work on a show that meant something? It wasn't just shitty TV. Everyone had a certain political framework. Bringing together those people and pressures meant we worked tons and tons of hours. There was a lot of overtime. Michael had to sign off on everything.

"Film is such a collaborative art form. You only see what is on the surface. People see the celebrities and they think they are the heart of the process. But they are only a small part of it. There are all these people behind the scenes. Especially with the documentary. The director is really the co-director."

Comic relief was critical to Moore's strategy. "He is amazing with comic timing," says Reticker. "It not something that you can describe. He has an intuitive notion of when a joke is to be layered in, how to play things longer and shorter. Having Steve Forbes sitting there and not blinking for a minute is one example. His ability to come to Cheap Trick star Rick Nielsen's Rockford, Illinois home and shoot the shit and play the guitar with this guy is another. He has this everyman quality, relating to people."

One advantage of Moore's celebrity status is his ability to land major subjects. "Not only did Phil Knight give him an interview," says Reticker, "he let him come back for a second time. Some people, I'm one of them, thought Phil Knight was crazy to ask him back.

"When I worked on *The Big One* a lot of people were feeling sorry for the public relations people who would come down and meet Michael in the lobby at Johnson and Johnson or Procter and Gamble. They felt sorry for these women. He is just going after them. I said there is no mistake that those women are put in those positions. They are more apt at socializing. Michael is playing their game and using the language they are using. When the woman from Johnson and Johnson says we are relocating, he says, where, in Mexico?"

Another Moore trademark was using footage other directors might toss. For example, says Reticker, "when he went to the Leaf factory (that was firing workers making Payday candy bars) he told the cameramen, 'whatever you do, don't turn off the camera.'" While this approach can bring out the police and lead to security officer palms being waved in front of the lens, it also gives the editor a shift in the action that underscores Moore's message. Obviously we have nothing to hide. Why else would we be asking you to leave?

For Reticker, Moore "has the right mix of politics and comedy that takes his films to a more subversive level. He is able to take an issue and look at it in such an original and prescient way. Michael will see things before others see it. In *Downsize This*, he had the whole Enron thing figured out. Michael also makes fun of himself. He makes himself an easy target and takes it a step too far sometimes and makes an ass of himself on some level. People criticize him but it makes him more human.

"Michael really is the person that he presents, the McDonald's eating guy. He is always the outsider. He does not like to be in celebrity situations. It doesn't make him appear as likable as he might want to be. When he did his acceptance speech at the Academy Awards he was rocking the boat. He can not give in to thank yous. He has to stick to the issues.

"He is willing to rock the boat and really put himself out there. There haven't been a lot of people like that. He is willing to go out on a limb. There should be thousands like him. It's hard to know why there aren't more people out there like him. Jon Stewart is one. Morgan Spurlock of *Supersize Me* is another."

One problem for editors like Reticker is Moore's tendency to fiddle and fine-tune work until the FedEx truck pulls up in the driveway. "He works until the last minute, finessing it, playing with the writing and the music. You never get this feeling that it is locked. He is tinkering with it. Technically the sound can be sketchy because he tinkers. It's the nature of his art that he is constantly reworking his material. It's his greatest strength but it can make it hell. There's an element of him that is attracted to a rough around the edges feel to his material. It's not smooth sailing.

"I think Michael believes he is in *The Big One* too much," says Reticker in the living room of her Brooklyn home. "He doesn't like himself being in the film as much as people think he does. He wants to be part of it. He wants his imprint to be on it and I think it is always very painful for him to see himself. Especially if you look at *The Big One*. He is in it all. In *Roger & Me* and *Bowling for Columbine* and *Fahrenheit 9/11*, he is not in it that much. There were correspondents. *The Big One* is a tough one for him . . . Trying to maintain the control he wanted is impossible. Doing a film a year, his writing and his political work and his web page, it's too much."

NO REPUBLICANS WERE HARMED
IN THE MAKING OF THIS SHOW

"Clearly I am a person who suffers from a lack of ego. I mean, if I felt better about myself I wouldn't look this way."

—*Michael Moore*

WHILE *THE BIG ONE* WAS NOT a commercial success it helped Moore develop new material for his television career. Just weeks before the documentary's premiere, Michael Jackson, the BBC chieftain who had picked up *TV Nation* in Britain, put up the financing for sixteen episodes of *The Awful Truth*. Now at Channel Four, Jackson's support opened the door for a cable deal with Bravo. In addition to trying to air raucous crowd shots in Times Square (chanting lines like "The Glove Didn't Fit We Must Acquit" for one of Moore's favorite causes, O.J. Simpson), the new show also began and ended some segments in front of a studio audience. And Moore still received a great deal of attention thanks to his "Take Me To Your Leader" plot line.

From the waiting rooms at Humana Corporation where he was eager to invite executives to the soon to be announced funeral of a HMO member denied a pancreas transplant, to his attacks on air pollution from factories owned by New York's Ira Rennert, Moore had found the cheapest location in town. Why bother to slash production costs by shooting in Canada or haggling with a film board in Louisiana when America's spiffiest corporations would let you be a lounge lizard, at least for a few minutes. He proved again and again that it cost absolutely nothing to shoot in a lobby with security guards holding their hands in front of cameras or threatening to have him arrested for trying to interview a CEO. In Rennert's case, the CEO was so distraught over Moore shooting a "polluter of the year" segment in front of his New York home and office that he tried (and failed) to win a court order banning Moore from Rockefeller Center, where the company's headquarters were located. And in the case of Holiday Inn, he brought in health and fire inspectors to launch a series of complaints against a hotel trying to send pro-union workers back to Mexico. Another popular spot was the sidewalk in front of the homes of executives like Phillip Morris CEO Michael J. Szymanczk. In this memorable scene cancer victims who had lost their larynxes in surgery used their voice boxes to serenade a boss and then dropped off Christmas tree ornaments handcrafted from cigarette boxes.

Gideon Evans, an *Awful Truth* performer, even tried to stage a comeback for R.J. Reynolds superhero Joe Camel. When he showed up at the tobacco company headquarters dressed as the cigarette icon, Evans was ever so politely asked to leave. "Everyone acted as if they had never heard of Joe Camel," said Evans. "It was really sad."

Evans fared better with improv in the corridors outside the Senate impeachment hearing of President Bill Clinton. Dressed as an angry Thomas Jefferson, he told reporters who quickly gathered around for an informal press briefing, "I had an affair too. Big friggin' deal. So what are you going to do, bring me back and impeach me too." Incredibly, the merry prank that had been hatched at 6:30 that morning in New York made the evening news.

In mid-December 1998, during Bill Clinton's battle with Special Prosecutor Ken Starr (no relation to New York business manager Ken Starr, who represented the filmmaker) Moore was invited to the White House for a Special Olympics benefit via Michael Jackson of the BBC.

Just a week earlier, Moore's attempt to shoot in front of the White House gate was greeted by a flak jacketed FBI team. This time, he was warmly received.

"I read what you wrote about me," the first lady told him in the receiving line. To Moore's relief, she was not offended by his chapter "My Forbidden Love For Hillary" in *Stupid White Men*. Happily her husband did not feel threatened by Moore's description of Mrs. Clinton as "one hot, shit-kicking feminist babe."

"I've been a big fan of yours Mike, since the beginning," said the President.

Moore, who had ripped Clinton as a Republican wannabe on the wrong side of issues ranging from the bombing of Bosnia to NAFTA, was quick to offer the President unsolicited advice on how to work his way out of the Monica Lewinsky political quagmire engineered by the "right wingnuts." Later Bill Clinton emerged from the garden party's executive porta-potty to find Moore waiting to resume their discussion. After the president excused himself, Moore enjoyed the evening's entertainment. Special guests Eric Clapton, Sheryl Crow, Jon Bon Jovi, Run DMC and Vanessa Williams sang a Bruce Springsteen version of "Santa Claus Is Coming To Town" with the Clintons and the Special Olympians.

Yes, Santa was back in town checking his Monicagate list to find out who's been naughty and who's been nice. For Moore this was America the Beautiful, "black, white, men, women, an ex-heroin user, an ex-Miss America turned Penthouse scandal centerfold . . . sinners all, hoping for redemption, living life through it's scars and triumphs, no one being able to cast the first stone."

In little more than a decade since he stopped publishing *Moore's Weekly*, the writer and filmmaker had found a way to connect with a remarkable audience. The Clintons were now part of his fan base, his assault on corporate America was reaching the ultimate demographic. And back in New York, urgent matters were simmering on his editorial stovetop. As always, his strange encounters with the flak catchers were an *Awful Truth* staple, as predictable as a Fred Ross eviction at a Flint apartment. While he was busy trying to raise the pulse of corporate leaders, there was plenty of time for voice-overs that articulated how, for example, the Disney Corporation was refusing to negotiate in good faith with its trade union workers at ABC. Another segment looked at Avon salespeople traveling the Amazon to sell products to natives who were charged the equivalent of half a month's income. It was a familiar story for GM hand Moore, and it played perfectly as an *Awful Truth* segment.

Frustrated by his inability to crack the public relations front line at many big companies, Moore decided that the show needed a fresh approach. His first target was New Jersey-based Tosco Corporation that had been cited for fatal accidents at its refineries. Moore began with a busload of children who charmed the receptionists. But when sexy lingerie models showed up, Tosco's reception area suddenly became a magnet for curious officials who agreed to come back with a response on the safety matter. Ultimately families of the deceased workers received a settlement worth $26 million.

Back in Manhattan, the show's Times Square segments offered notable takeoffs on famous commercials. There was Herb Poole, paroled from Trenton State Prison after serving a 19 year sentence for first-degree murder. He was proud to hold up a Microsoft box and boast: "I only use Windows software. Where do you want to go?"

Moore also made a number of road trips. Among them was a journey to Topeka, Kansas, where he put the homophobic Reverend Fred Phelps and his crusading family of anti-Somdomites on national television. Fusing the "If this van is rockin' don't bother knocking" school of romance with a steal from *Priscilla, Queen of The Desert,* Moore took the wheel of the show's Sodomobile. Filled to the brim with gay lovers, *The Awful Truth* RV featured a "please tailgate" sign on the back and a "Buggery on Board" yellow triangle. Moore aimed to break the law by having the bad boys do it in the road in every state with antisodomy laws. Trying to save gas as they broke each state's regulations, the gay activists reached nirvana at the shared border of three southern states The lawbreakers managed to simultaneously break the civil code in three southern states with their romantic activities.

But the best in show was saved for Topeka, where the Sodomites pulled up to a Reverend Fred Phelps picket line. They found him with many of his minions who had picketed the Wyoming funeral of Matthew Shephard, tragically beaten to death by homophobes. Why did they want to torture the friends and family of the young man with signs that read "No fags in heaven," "Aids Cures Fags," and "Save the Gerbils." Because, said Pastor Phelps, "He (Shepherd) was not a good man. This was not a good thing to do. He's in hell now."

Phelps did not accept Moore's personal invitation to hop aboard the Sodomobile and make whoopee with the guys. But he saw no reason to call the police since these New Yorkers were literally on the highway to hell.

Sodomobile driver Moore scored an interview with another family member who proudly boasted that her longest journey for the funeral of a gay Aids victim was for author Randy Shilts' rites in San Francisco.

"I missed that one," Moore deadpanned. "How was the food?"

CRACKING UP

PLAYING CHICKEN IS ONE OF THOSE GAMES that is always more dangerous than it looks, particularly for Crackers, one of the stars of *TV Nation* and *The Awful Truth*. The Corporate Crime Chicken, who sped around the nation in his personal Crime-mobile RV, was determined to "give those corporate crooks a lickin'." Enthusiastic viewers of the poultry fuzz phoned in more than 30,000 tips that helped create a new list of America's most wanted corporate criminals. The seven-foot-tall chicken cop could intimidate CEOs by simply showing up and ruffling his feathers.

Crackers appeared at a Rudolph Guliani press conference to find out why First Boston had been given tax breaks in exchange for a promise to keep jobs in New York. Unfortunately, like General Motors, the bank was busy dumping the same jobs it promised to protect. Over in Brooklyn, Crackers scored a major victory for the little ones when he persuaded a baby walker manufacturer to start making safer models.

In Detroit, Crackers met his match when he led strikers on a march against the owners of the Detroit Free Press and the Detroit News. A riot began as the security staff swung their billy clubs at strikers charging the newspaper's door. When an NBC cameraman and sound recorder were attacked by the police, Crackers tried to rescue their equipment. But he was intercepted by security staff who picked him up and tossed him ten feet off the loading dock.

"It was the first time any of us had seen a chicken fly," said Moore, who was protected by two pairs of security guards. "Please Mr. Chicken, don't cause trouble," a little child told the crime fighting bird. "People might get hurt." Poor Crackers was treated and released at a hospital. But that didn't hurt as much as a meeting later that night at Tigers Stadium where the *TV Nation* icon learned that other mascots wore outfits complete with cooling systems.

When the Crackers actor, John Derevlany, complained about being overheated and stressed out, Moore told him to chill. One of the problems was that Crackers did not find any crimes to fight in cooler places like Alaska. "One of Michael's problems was his view that America was the Midwest in the summer at 90 to 100 degrees," says Derevlany. "It was a really bad summer. I'd get up in the morning and read about all the heat-related deaths in places like Chicago. But I believe he had a plan to go to mid-range Midwestern cities because he could make the newspapers more easily. His unusual idea was that this kind of publicity could reach the Nielsen families in these communities and help boost his ratings. The idea was that a town like Cleveland had two or three viewers polled by Nielsen. If he could get on the front of the local *Plain Dealer,* there was a chance he could make it into the Nielsen households."

For Derevlany the heat was oppressive. "It could get over a hundred degrees in there. I couldn't take it. The head was a solid block of plastic. At the Henson Company characters are in their suits for only twenty minutes at a time. I was inside my suit for two to three hours." To cool things off and avoid a labor grievance, the show ordered a battery powered fan and then strapped on a vest with twenty pounds of ice. Although viewers loved Crackers's forays into the heartland where he persuaded Ohio regulators to put a cork in an offal-smelling chicken processing plant that was grossing out the neighbors with its nauseating operation, he longed for ocean breezes and lower humidity. Another victory took place at Doe Run Inc., a battery maker forced to shut down because of toxic lead emissions that threatened the community of Herculaneum, Missouri.

Unlike other enthusiastic colleagues eager to pitch in for the cause on a moment's notice, Derevlany resented "working on Labor Day for a Labor Day special. Michael presents himself as a friend of the working man. But the problem with the liberal media is they treat people like shit. Also he had a weird kind of contempt for New York and California. He had this weird intense passion against anyone who had a college degree, because he didn't. He felt that was a symbol of a privilege that shouldn't be afforded to people who didn't deserve it. I sort of agree with him in a way, but all of us who went to college are not silver-spoon babies. I worked two or three jobs to pay for college. When he does his stump speeches he jokes about taking all your fees from you. At USC he said it was $50,000. The speaking was a big thing for him. He would go on rants about college kids to a room full of college kids.

"One of Moore's biggest problems with *TV Nation* was realizing its limitations. To head off network censors he relied heavily on photo finishing, turning in shows for review just hours before air time. Another approach was to simply 'quit' the show, not show up for a few days to keep the network from screwing with him too early. And in some cases he would simply plead his case, often with good results. His colleagues were amazed by his ability to talk his way on with segments that appeared to be unlikely candidates for prime time television. When the network killed a segment on right-to-life advocates who wanted to shoot abortion doctors, Moore still managed to get the program on the BBC."

When *The Awful Truth* was launched on the Bravo network, Derevlany did not renew his contract. In some ways the decision to leave was difficult. "In Hollywood everyone is trying to present themselves as being as friendly as possible. They try to avoid conflict. They don't want hassle. At the end of the day all they care about is numbers. It is amazing that he got as many episodes on as he did.

"He had a good staff of writers. I was shocked when I saw *The Big One.* You can see on *TV Nation* how much a great staff of writers and editors helped him out. Pieces were scripted and you had all these jokes. With *The Big One* he was just recording his book tour and trying to make a film about it. There was no master plan to it." Derevlany believes Moore's great strength is self-promotion. "He is perfect for it. He actually has an opinion that he can effectively argue and he is funny. People love him and they hate him and they love to hate him. It is a perfect storm of media. Everything you want in a host. He uses it for a common good and for his own profit. We need more people that are effective.

"One of the problems with Michael was that he would go off on tangents. He wanted to talk about how O.J. was innocent as part of a two-minute intro to one show. It got edited out. This was all part of our endless writers meetings which was him endlessly ranting late into the night. We would listen but I just wanted to go home.

"Michael did do some great stylistic things. He would have the camera pan from the interviewer to a subject in a single shot instead of having one camera on each person. This rotation pan is much more immediate and real. It connects you instantly. When he asks a question you simultaneously see the subject's response.

"One of the problems, of course, is that in television we are pushing the limits of what is real and what is not real anymore. You need such dramatic images. It almost doesn't matter anymore whether it has any connection to what you are talking about. It's kind of like a tabloid show using Irwin Allen disaster movie footage to illustrate a point."

Moore's success brought considerable talent to his door. "Famous documentary directors wanted to get in on the show," says Derevlany. "People were calling me to find out how they could get involved. I tried to warn them." He also worried about the ability of television to carry a progressive message. "Liberal arguments don't work as well on TV because it is a lazy medium. They make more sense in print than on TV. The grand conservative images, waving the flag, our troops blowing shit up are much more compelling than seeing a bunch of people protest.

"One of Moore's great contributions is how to make that liberal argument compelling visually. Dropping TVs in the desert may be what you have to do at a time when everyone is okay with conservatives lying to us. People are more accepting, we are inherently this conservative country with a thing for religion. Clinton never got a majority. Everyone is predisposed to believing what they want to believe. If you want to tell people things are not okay you have to deliver a lot of humor and striking visual appeal.

This may be part of the reason Crackers was receiving up to 30,000 calls a week on his toll free number. "That's a ridiculous amount of people contacting a chicken," says Derevlany. "It was encouraging but also sad to see how many people were in such desperate straits that they were turning to Crackers. There might have been a kind of love-hate thing. Michael liked to keep everything focused on him. If any of the correspondents did too much better than him, he was worried." Derevlany was also concerned about the fact that Moore appeared to have a "self-destructive side. Most famous people do. You don't take big risks unless you have a self-destructive side."

After Derevlany left the show, talented writer and performer Gideon Evans decided to fill his webbed feet. His specialty was taking on companies that benefited from vast goodwill in the marketplace. Evans knew how to prove otherwise. Following up on leads that his brethren, underpaid Disney World characters such as Mickey Mouse and Goofy were victims of unfair labor practices, Crackers booked a flight to Orlando. Workers complained wages were so low they qualified for welfare, slept in their cars and showered in the company locker room. A big complaint was Disney's failure to meet its legal obligation to wash costumes. One performer, unable to pay the dry cleaning bill on his own costume, broke out in a groin rash. And, Crackers pointed out, the Disney hotheads were unhappy about sweltering summer days when the temperature inside costumes routinely cracked 100 degrees.

Evans, producer Tia Lessin and a film crew armed with inconspicuous handheld cameras, entered the park as backpack-carrying tourists. Crackers suited up in a men's room stall and made his way past Cinderella's castle. Walking briskly to stay ahead of security guards in hot pursuit, the poultry man was soon surrounded. "We have a situation in Fantasyland at Dumbo four," radioed one of the officers. In less than a minute the seven-foot-tall chicken was bobbing above a sea of Orlando's finest. While tourists tried to move in to grab Crackers' autograph, the Disney posse hustled the chicken backstage. When producer Lessen tried to intervene she was promptly handcuffed as her camera crew quickly fled the park to protect their film for the show.

"We have all this barbecue sauce and we're getting ready to fire up the grill for you," wisecracked one of the guards, as a Disney photographer began shooting Crackers. Forced to remove his chicken head, the detained performer was also photographed under his alias, Gideon Evans. After nearly two hours in custody the performer and the character were both permanently banned from the Disney Empire. "If we ever see you here again," a guard told Crackers and liberated producer Lessen at the exit, "we'll be hauling you to jail."

After the segment aired, a suited Evans showed up in front of an *Awful Truth* live studio audience in Chicago to answer questions about the Disney character liberation movement.

"What is the average temperature inside the chicken suit," asked a young man.

"It's as cool as a mountain breeze," replied Crackers.

THE FIRING LINE

NOT EVERYONE WHO JOINED Michael Moore's television revolution was a perfect fit. In fact the number of fired employees, particularly in the upper echelon, suggested that Moore's human resources department was not always finding the kind of people he really wanted to work with. His approach was probably best summed up in a comment made to office manager Barbara Moss.

"Barbara," he asked, "do you have any heroes?"

"Sure," she replied.

"Don't have any heroes. They'll just let you down."

In fact disgruntled employees discovered that the boss's sense of humor could indeed wear thin when it came to homeland security around the Dog Eat Dog world headquarters. Perhaps the most outspoken critic of Moore's leadership was Alan Edelstein who worked briefly for *The Awful Truth*.

Nominated for an Academy Award for his half hour PBS documentary on vaudeville performers of the '20s, Edelstein was the last segment producer hired by Moore for his *Awful Truth* team. A veteran of the *Great Projects* PBS and cable series, which focused on the building of American highways, dams, and bridges, he was delighted to bring home a bigger pay check. But Edelstein also worried about producing at weekly television's fast pace.

Moore believed that too much of what passed for TV news was the product of an elite, college educated crowd that came from the book-end states on the East and West coasts. Hailing from Midwestern fly-over territory he was intrigued by the idea of hiring young talent who had not necessarily been brought up on the Who, What, When, Where, Why and How of journalism school. Simply winning good reviews and fan letters wasn't enough. He wanted his viewers to take to the streets, to the polls, to the halls of Congress. Like a union organizer, he wanted his viewers to take personal risks for a brighter tomorrow. The man from *Roger & Me, Mother Jones* and *Moore's Weekly* was willing to take on any union, political party, media icon or religious group regardless of its political bent. Simply being a liberal Democrat wasn't good enough.

Moore was not dazzled by applicants with a social register pedigree, boarding school background or Ivy League degree. Unlike Ralph Nader, his personnel search engine wasn't aimed at elite colleges and law schools. "It was almost as if you got points for having a blue collar back-ground, not finishing college and, of course, being from Michigan or at least the Midwest," recalls Moore's first Crackers, John Derevlany.

For *The Awful Truth,* descending from NBC and the BBC to Fox and ultimately Bravo and Britain's Channel 4 created a significant cre-ative challenge. But with a better time slot on Bravo, he was able to worry less about direct network competition and focus more on build-ing loyalty to characters like Crackers, the Crime Fighting Chicken.

A return to some of the elements that had made the *Michigan Voice* a Molotov cocktail on the newsstands, the show was fun to watch and frequently ground breaking. It relied heavily on the talents of a young group of actors, journalists and producers who knew how to realize Moore's vision week after week. Start with a Mike Wallace style Q-and-A, throw in a dash of Mel Brooks, paste on Alfred E. Neumann's *Mad Magazine* goofy grin and you had the makings of an *Awful Truth* segment.

Moore, busy with a pilot for a late night show with Fox while also planning feature and documentary projects for theatrical release, saw himself as a pioneer who could help usher in a new golden age of tele-vision. Like his fellow Catholic, Bishop Fulton Sheen, who mesmer-ized audiences from Bangor to Barstow, the director was uniquely talented and uniquely difficult. He was happy to compare his work to shows like *Seinfeld* that started with low ratings.

Moore's wife and coproducer Kathleen Glynn told Edelstein it wasn't worth working on the show if he wasn't on the same page politically as *The Awful Truth* team. But the new hire never felt that he had to be radical to succeed. Moore's programs were driven by fact, not fiction. His Believe It or Not show benefited from his tradmark sense of humor. The key was to tell an important political story with an eye toward entertaining as well as informing viewers. And for new hires like Edelstein the show was certainly not a Stalinist dictatorship. The challenge was to find interesting stories missed by the networks that would draw right-wingers, leftists, centrists even libertarians who could learn something from reporting available nowhere else. For half an hour each week they could put aside their differences and laugh at the witty insights of correspondents who were not machine groomed.

At 44, Moore was one of the oldest members of the staff. His work as a filmmaker and creator of *TV Nation* attracted young idealists. But when he joined the staff in the summer of 1998, Edelstein never felt that he was working for a god. " I did enjoy *Roger & Me*. As an entertainment it holds up in more than one viewing," he explained. "But the problem with Michael was that he was kind of grandstanding and patronizing. There is just this feeling that he is being manipulative in a way that crosses a certain line. For example he lasted about four months at *Mother Jones*, so there is a certain amount of game playing here. It's about a person who is pissed off about being fired but it is also about how to turn this into something filmic."

Moore, of course, was not the first filmmaker or writer to turn a bad job into a fruitful story. The problem for Edelstein was that his new boss felt a " supreme need to entertain and be comedic. He is also a journalist and the two are kind of at odds if you want to be taken seriously."

For Edelstein, who was used to working on long-form documentaries, the deadline pressure at *The Awful Truth* was intimidating. Another problem was that promising assignments didn't always work out. And in some cases breaking news disrupted the schedule.

"He always likes to position himself as someone who is tangling

with the authorities," says Edelstein. "Nothing got killed production
or budget wise but some things didn't work out. I remember he did
a satirical piece about teaching high school kids how to shoot better.
But then the Columbine High School Massacre took place in Little-
ton, Colorado and the segment was cancelled."

Edelstein was surprised to discover that the brazen television personality tended to be dispassionate in the office. "I had read and
heard that he was difficult. But I really didn't tangle with him. The
only problem I noticed was that he was not always available for his
producers. There is a lot of this in show business but Michael gets
more criticism for it because he is supposed to be of the people."

Edelstein's first piece for the show focused on the thought that Bill
Clinton's Secretary of Defense, William Cohen, was not a tough guy.
The cabinet official wrote poetry such as "The Wound" lamenting a
car striking a deer:

"Forgive me for I know what I have done.
I have taken a child of the woods in the gun sight of my hood."

Determined to have Cohen go *mano a mano* with our enemies, the
producer arranged for North Korean, Iraqi and Afghanistan diplo-
mats to confront the Secretary on the Pentagon lawn. Eager to draw
the American military leader downstairs for an arm wrestling match,
the North Korean official shouted through a bullhorn:

"Your poetry is for wusses. Our poetry is strong."

"It was a very thin premise that didn't make a lot of sense to me,"
says Edelstein. "We had news footage of him disco dancing and stuff like
that. He always looked very ill at ease. It was pretty much a visual sam-
pler of Cohen looking like a jerk. But it didn't get into politics much. The
segment was sort of a spoof showing other secretaries of defense looking
real macho. It was not something I would have assigned."

When the producers gathered to screen their work, Moore pref-
aced the meeting by telling everyone not to take it personally if he
tore their work to shreds. Edelstein was relieved when Moore did not
lambaste his Cohen piece.

In the late summer of 1998, a second segment proved much more
difficult to pull together. In the tradition of *Saturday Night Live*'s
"Weekend Edition," Moore was intrigued by the idea of faking news

stories. His idea was to attack the Taliban's decision to ban television by dropping tv sets to the deprived viewers of Afghanistan. Although Edelstein enjoyed helpful Taliban contacts, the producer discovered "it was a pretty dicey time to produce such a piece and they eventually shot it in Arizona with Mexicans." Although the segment was labeled as a "pre-enactment" viewers were not told that the TV sets were being dropped in the American Southwest, thousands of miles from their intended recipients.

"In a sense," says Edelstein, "Michael thinks he pioneered doing explicitly phony interviews. While he is certainly part of the trend that led to the creation of *The Daily Show,* I think it actually goes back to *Weekend Edition.*"

Although *The Awful Truth* never did get its television airlift off the ground in Afghanistan, Edelstein believed the complexity of this project explained why he was receiving fewer assignments than his fellow producers. This excellent theory held up until he was fired, presumably because of a budget crunch. Edelstein quickly returned to a longer film project of his own. Conveniently this personal narrative wove in global issues including a look at the political impact of fundamentalist groups like the Taliban.

In much the same way Moore worked his *Mother Jones* firing into *Roger & Me,* Edelstein decided to integrate his brief stint at *The Awful Truth* into the story line. Eager to include his old boss in this work in progress, Edelstein headed for the University of Massachusetts to film one of Moore's campus talks. And that is when he learned The Awful Truth about trying to film a former employer.

"I was sincerely angry about being fired and the way it was handled. But confronting Moore on camera was something I wouldn't have done if I hadn't been working on this film."

Moore's Amherst, Massachusetts, appearance combined his stand-up shtick with scenes from *The Awful Truth* and *TV Nation.* A few minutes into the speaker's routine, Edelstein began asking questions through a megaphone. When the filmmaker asked why he had been fired, Moore quickly convinced the audience that Edelstein was a plant on hand to liven up the appearance.

"If I'd been more experienced I would have really dug in," said the former *Awful Truth* producer, "But I am not confrontational by nature. And I hadn't really thought through what I was doing. The crowd was intrigued. They thought this was funny. They let him do his thing. The scene is interesting to watch but very poorly shot."

Learning the difficulty of shooting and interviewing simultaneously, Edelstein hired a friend to accompany him to Moore's 57th Street Manhattan office on December 4, 1998. Borrowing a page from Moore's playbook, Edelstein invited New York reporters to cover the showdown over his firing. But playing lobby lizard wasn't any easier for Edelstein than it was for Moore. After waiting around the office for a drop in appointment, Edelstein was finally greeted by one of the boss's minions. She explained, in a scene familiar to fans of Moore's own work, that the CEO was out.

Edelstein returned several days later and filmed a brief hallway encounter with the filmmaker's publicist. Later that day Moore called Edelstein to explain that he had been fired for gross incompetence: the William Cohen piece was so terrible that the entire segment had to be reshot. Edelstein asked why none of this was mentioned at the time. Moore apologized for the way the firing was handled.

Several weeks later Edelstein showed up in Harlem to record an *Awful Truth* shoot comparing American racism with South African Apartheid. As Moore spoke to Harlem residents on the street, the Brooklyn freelancer was right behind him. In a conciliatory manner Moore asked the disgruntled former employee if he wanted to talk further. "Call my office after the New Year and we'll set something up."

Unable to reach Moore by phone in January, Edelstein decided to film another live *Awful Truth* audience event at the University of Illinois in Chicago. This time the show's producer noticed Edelstein standing in line and hit the eject button. "I guess it was illegal and he told the police I might be a dangerous person," said the ex-employee. "The officers followed me out the door to my rented car where I was frisked and told to leave the campus. They were told I might be armed and dangerous."

Returning home with memorable footage of himself being thrown out of the Chicago show, Edelstein was surprised to run into Moore and Glynn in the lobby of a New York theater. "I was waiting for friends to come out as they were going in," says Edelstein. "Glynn looked at me and said, 'So I guess you are stalking us now.' I said, 'I am waiting for some friends.'"

"A couple of weeks later a card was stuck in my door by a New York police detective asking me to call." Edelstein was instructed to come down to the precinct station. "That was the beginning of a long weird pissing match. Moore decided that he was going to play hardball with this guy who was annoying him. He claimed that I called the office thirty times. Actually I called the office one or two times at his request and I never raised my voice."

When Edelstein showed up at the precinct station he was detained on trespassing and harassment charges, placed in a holding cell for nearly ten hours and, at one point, handcuffed to the cell bars. After being released on his own recognizance, he pled not guilty. "The complaints made to the police were total fabrications. He didn't have anything to back it up.

"When I was offered a plea bargain I turned it down and a couple of weeks later he dropped the charges."

Edelstein believes his run-in underscores one of the weaknesses of Moore's films. "He lied quite egregiously to the police to have me arrested. There were things that he said in the complaint that were true. Going to the University of Massachusetts with a megaphone was a fact but it was also a college prank. The other things he said about me threatening his family were not true. He lied about that."

Edelstein sued Moore for malicious prosecution. "That is something I would not do under ordinary circumstances. But part of it was a game. It was misusing the court system but I generated a much higher level of interest from the media. Like his case, the suit was thrown out.

"His films are a much more subtle version of the problem I had with him. There is some truth and half truths and outright lies. Whenever he is called on this he says I'm an entertainer and I can take license. To me the chronology problems in *Roger & Me* are pretty outrageous. Other people don't feel that way. I think the way he has edited it and narrated it is certainly not journalism. It doesn't wash and it does undercut what he is trying to do.

"I think he is skilled at getting under people's skin and generating controversy. He is masterful at that. He knows how to work the boundaries between facts and half truths. It's a very unsettling experience regardless of your politics, an interesting mix of propaganda and journalism.

"Is he more truthful because there is a lot of propaganda and misinformation on the network news? If you accept Michael Moore as a pamphleteer or propagandist I have no gripe with what he is doing. There is a legitimate place for that kind of thing in society.

"Many would argue that TV news is an instrument of the establishment. But lying doesn't correct lying. I think in *Fahrenheit 9/11* his portrayal of Iraq prior to the invasion is essentially a lie. Happy kids flying kites is not Iraq under Saddam Hussein. He doesn't want to acknowledge that because it doesn't serve his purpose. It's the same thing with Bush's speech at a fund raising dinner with wealthy donors where he says 'You are my base.' Bush was making fun of himself. If you see the clip that is masterful propaganda but it is not rigorously honest. He is looking for ways of making a point and that is legitimate. But it is not legitimate journalism.

"Moore has found a working class niche which has not existed since the 1960s. It is fine to strongly identify with workers who are oppressed. There is a certain freshness and excitement that people get out of his stuff. He portrays himself as the authentic voice of the working class and he has a sense of humor and a maverick quality that is missing from a lot of the left-wing journalism."

Edelstein's film includes scenes of his legal battle with Moore and journalists who interviewed him, including the *New York Times* and *Good Morning America,* as well as footage of the University of Massachusetts showdown. "My film is not really about Moore. It is a very large and unwieldy project. It's a much wider frame. It existed before I ever worked for Moore. It is basically shot and it needs to be edited. It's not a Michael and Me story. It is very complicated because I have great material to use in my film and that was the driving force to do this. I don't hate him. It is being done more for artistic reasons than out of anger."

"YOU ARE THE ONLY PERSON I'VE EVER SEEN DIVE INTO A MOSH PIT AND COME OUT WITH HIS TIE STRAIGHT"

"If you're listening to a rock star in order to get your information on who to vote for, you're a bigger moron than they are. Why are we rock stars? Because we're morons."

—Alice Cooper

FOR RALPH NADER, the decline of civic activism, was the end of the Democratic process. Americans, he explained, had no choice. "Without protest movements aimed at protecting the rights of citizens, the nation would inevitably move down the path to dictatorship. When I started out in Washington exposés on subjects like auto safety would lead to Congressional hearings led by Abe Ribicoff, Gaylord Nelson or Warren Magnuson. Legislation would be passed that would protect our environment, improve auto safety or give airline passengers protection from being bumped from flights. Today when there is a big exposé on *60 Minutes* on a consumer issue I call them up to get the reaction and find out they got maybe four calls. These exposés don't have legs. The new generation of civic leadership, replacing people like Martin Luther King, César Chávez and Joan Claybrook, are not being covered in the same way. Their causes don't get attention. No one is finding out about their causes.

"The masterminds of abusing our society will be protected because no one comes out to protest. I've tried to do something about loan sharking and usurious payday loans in the black community, a terrible rip-off. No one, not even the Democratic Black Caucus which includes people like John Conyers, will get behind this cause. There couldn't have been an easier issue. Even Dennis Kucinich wouldn't join. The problem is you have safe seats on both sides of the aisle so nothing happens."

What's behind this attention deficit disorder on progressive causes? "The problem," says Nader sitting in the board room of Washington's Carnegie Building, "is that there is an absolute vacuum in leadership on these kinds of issues. Overall, Michael Moore is definitely a plus. But the problem is that if you become the issue rather than the subject your message is defused. J. Edgar Hoover tried to make King, rather than civil rights the message, and slander him."

The politics of character assassination, an old American tradition, steals time from critical items on the national agenda. A shortage of progressive leaders to fight for these causes in the manner of the Flint sitdown strikers or the antiwar and antidraft protests of the '60s makes it harder to reform American politics. Issues like national health care, flood protection, global warming and rebuilding the public schools are swept aside by the drumbeat of militarism in Iraq. Simply getting attention for an issue like electoral reform and meaningful campaign spending limits becomes harder because there is less room for these stories in a wartime era.

For Ralph Nader, the man who proposed the hardening of airline cockpit doors in the '80s, the spectacular costs of government inaction represents the collapse of the two-party system. A pariah to many progressives who feel that his attacks on the "lesser evil" theory of democracy are washed-up rhetoric, Nader argues that the issues hew to a peculiar aspect of the American character. Airlines, willing to risk bankruptcy, not to mention the lives of their own customers and innocent victims on the ground rather than spend a modest amount of money to harden their cockpits against coordinated attacks by Middle-Eastern hijackers, symbolizes the problem.

"There are so few places that you can go today to seriously discuss our political future," says Nader. Once you get past public television hosts Charlie Rose and Dennis Wholey you find a vacuum. In a presidential campaign the only way I could reach young people was to go through Jay Leno, David Letterman and *Saturday Night Live.* I can't get in the presidential debates so I have to settle for Jon Stewart. That is where it's at.

"Getting people to pay attention to serious issues is always a problem. When Bill Maher asked me what the big issues are I said the avian flu epidemic and he said, 'Come on.'

"One of the problems is that Hollywood is a negative for the Democratic Party. What the Hollywood/Michael Moore matrix does is provide relief for the Republicans to perfect their politics of distraction. I have been told that the only way to reach young people was through MTV's Rock the Vote. I will never agree that you have to steer kids into serious politics through rock music, by going through their menagerie."

Moore disagreed. Early in the 2000 campaign, *The Awful Truth* host made the rounds of Iowa caucus venues, offering to endorse the first candidate willing to leap into a portable mosh pit. The fact that some of the candidates had never heard of a mosh pit or crowd surfing was no problem. Moore assembled a jiving group of young people on a flatbed truck and drove them to campaign rallies. George Bush was his smirking self, suggesting that Moore "get a real job." Senator Orrin Hatch flatly refused although he did stand still long enough for Moore to body slam him in front of a camera. John Mc-Cain was also a dud and Gary Bauer thought the whole thing was a joke.

That left one major candidate—a black, homophobic, pro-life, anti-gun control Zionist named Alan Keyes. After persuading two of Keyes's aides to leap into the mosh pit, Moore went to work on the selling of the candidate. More than one person had died crowd surfing, and the Republican's Secret Service agents had no confidence in the TV star's guarantee of safe passage. But after his daughter Maya carefully explained the process and offered her encouragement, the conservative, wearing a long leather jacket, fell backwards into the screaming crowd of Keysters. After crowd surfing the pit and doing a couple of body slams with a high-school student, he walked out with the endorsement of Moore's show.

He was also high-fived by a TV crew member who said, "You

know, you are the only person I've ever seen dive into a mosh pit and come out with his tie straight."

Clearly politics made strange futon fellows. How had Michael Moore ended up in the curious position of throwing his show's weight behind a Republican of ill repute? "We knew Alan Keyes was insane," Moore told the media after an endorsement for the Republican flashed on *The Awful Truth* TV screen with the look and feel of a Powerball lottery winner. It was official—Michael Moore's show was backing a Republican neocon. "We just didn't know how insane he was until that moment."

During the Republican debates several days later candidate Texas Governor George Bush politely asked Keyes what it felt like to leap into that Mosh Pit. A more judgmental Gary Bauer suggested that Keyes was homicidal: "I was a little surprised this week to see you fall into a mosh pit, while a band called The Machines Rages On or Rage Against The Machine played. That band is anti-family, it's pro-cop-killer and it's pro-terrorist. It's the kind of music that the killers at Columbine High School were immersed in. Don't you think you owe an apology to parents and policemen on that one?"

"Actually, I don't," said Keyes. ". . . Until you told me this fact, I had no idea what that music was . . . I disclaim any knowledge of it . . . I was willing to fall into the mosh pit. But I'll tell you something. Do you know why I did that? Because I think that exemplifies the kind of trust in people that is the heart and soul of the Keyes campaign. It's about time we got back to the understanding that we trust the people of this country to do what is decent. And when you trust them, they will in fact hold you up—whether it is in terms of giving help to you when you are falling down, or caring for their own children. So I thought that as an emblem of that trust, it was the right thing to do. And anyway, my daughter thought it was a good idea."

She may have been right. Underdog Keyes came in a surprising third in the Iowa caucuses, ahead of non-moshers John McCain, Orrin Hatch and his nemesis Gary Bauer.

While Rage Against the Machine proved to be an asset for the Keyes campaign, it was never part of the Nader Super Rally lineup. After the primary, Moore attempted to broaden Rage Against the

Machine's audience by directing their next music video in front of the New York Stock Exchange. As the band played on, four officers put Moore in a choke hold. Angry protesters responded by hurdling police barricades and storming the steps of the exchange. Their invasion was halted when security officers lowered steel gates at the building's entrance. The officers let Moore go as they futilely chased the protesters, now cast as extras in the video.

Returning to his TV show, Moore went to work on a segment featuring his sister Anne, an attorney who lost her job in the Nevada County, California public defenders office after protesting the fact that defendants were pushed into abandoning worthy cases, even when they were not guilty. She discovered that only one out of 900 cases represented by the public defender had gone to a jury trial in 1998. Other defendants had been forced to accept plea bargained prison sentences or probation.

While the show continued to highlight problems with the American legal system, Moore turned his attention to the presidential election. He argued that Bill Clinton's eight years in office did not make a good case for the election of another Democrat. "Bush and Gore Make Me Wanna Ralph," he argued while throwing his baseball cap in the ring for his old boss Nader.

"Ralph is definitely one of a kind," he explained to his fans. "Before you all send me a lot of mail about how weird Ralph is 'cause he doesn't own a car or is a 'sell-out' because he's got a few million dollars, let me say this: I used to work out of his office, and Ralph is definitely one of a kind . . . Ralph is at least half as crazy as Jesse Ventura—and about a hundred times as smart. I'd say he's also saved about a million or so lives, thanks to the consumer and environmental legislation he has devoted his life to . . . Between Gore and Bush, and himself, he's the only person running who would guarantee universal health care for all, the only candidate who would raise the minimum wage to a decent level."

Moore rejected the notion that a vote for Nader would help elect Bush, a Republican determined to appoint Supreme Court Justices who would end a woman's right to choose an abortion. "I will go so far as to say that George W. Bush, if for some reason he is magically elected, will never do anything to make abortion illegal," said Moore. "If 70 percent of the country favors legal abortion, trust me, that party boy is never going to cook his goose on this issue."

The Democrats, argued Moore, had a poor record on abortion rights. It was Jimmy Carter who stopped "abortions for women or wives in the armed services. He also stopped any further funding to birth control groups overseas that offered abortion as an alternative. And he ended all Medicaid payments for poor women in need of an abortion.

"Clinton," argued Moore, "misunderstood his mission: he was supposed to support a woman's right to choose, not his right to choose women. It is now twice as hard for a woman in America to obtain an abortion as it was when Clinton took office. The anti-abortion terrorists have been so successful in their campaign of violence against abortion clinics and doctors and hospitals who perform abortions that a woman can now get an abortion in only fourteen percent of the counties in the United States. Terrorism has scored its first victory on U.S. soil by assassinating enough doctors and firebombing enough clinics so that no one wants to perform an abortion."

In the fall, Moore joined the Green candidate's Super Rally campaign lineup along with headliners like Patti Smith, Jello Biafra and Iris Dement. The filmmaker was given the choice assignment of introducing the candidate at superrallies in key cities such as Portland and Chicago.

On *The Awful Truth*, Moore reminded his audience that mainstream candidates were an easy target for all kinds of unsavory pressure groups. Unlike Nader, the competition would quickly bank money from questionable supporters. To prove his points he opened four bank accounts during the 1996 presidential campaign including "Satan Worshipers For Dole, Hemp Growers of America, Abortionists for Buchanan, and Pedophiles For Free Trade. Each group wrote $100 checks to the four leading candidates. First to cash his check was Pat Buchanan. Right behind him was Dole. President Clinton's team had no problem taking money from the hemp growers and of course Ross Perot found himself in the embarrassing position of accepting financial support from the free trade pedophiles. While each of the candidates returned the money after Moore broke the news of his stunt, their inability to catch these donations strengthened his case for Ralph Nader.

In Wisconsin for the 2000 Nader/LaDuke campaign, the film-maker explained that his candidate would never cash these kinds of checks. And he quickly discovered there was another hidden benefit to joining the Green campaign, Nader's three-hour speeches. After providing a rousing introduction, he was able to enjoy a leisurely dinner with friends in Madison and still have plenty of time to return to the auditorium before the final standing ovation.

Nader welcomed support but had difficulty persuaded the film-maker to say a few unkind words about the politics of democrats like Hillary Clinton. Although Moore had trashed Bill Clinton on *The Awful Truth*, the first lady was sacrosanct. "He told me he couldn't say anything critical about Hillary," says Nader. "I asked why and he said, 'because I've got this thing for Hillary.'"

In cities like Boston, the filmmaker was a key reason why a sellout audience was happy to pay $10 to support the Nader cause. "He is the son my mother wanted to have," said Phil Donahue, as the new Green Party advocate walked on to the stage wearing jeans, a T-shirt, sneakers and a baseball cap to a standing ovation. "His name is Michael Moore."

Moore began by attacking two of the four major networks for not carrying the upcoming presidential debate. One of Nader's biggest problems, the subject was ideal fodder for the speaker who quickly brought smiles to the faces of his audience: "For those of you who will be watching *Dharma and Greg* instead (of watching the debates) I would like to give you a short preview of what you will miss:

Mr. Bush: 'I support the death penalty.'
Mr. Gore: 'I support the death penalty.'

Mr. Bush: 'I support, NAFTA.'
Mr. Gore: 'I support NAFTA.'

Mr. Bush: 'I support the World Trade Organization.'
Mr. Gore: 'I support the World Trade Organization.'

Mr. Bush: 'I support an increase in the Pentagon Budget.'
Mr. Gore: 'I support an increase in the Pentagon Budget.'

Mr. Bush: 'I am not for universal health care.'
Mr. Gore: 'I am not for universal health care.'

"Back and forth, this is what it is going to be Tuesday night. All I am hoping for and I think the appropriate thing is that after the debate Al Gore goes over and gives George Bush one of those big Tipper tongue kisses.

Mr. Bush: 'I love you.'
Mr. Gore: 'I love you, man.'

"You know it would save us all this time and money between now and November 7, let's just elect both of them. Bush can run the country Monday, Wednesday and Friday and Gore can run in on Tuesday, Thursday and Saturday, and on Sunday Cheney and Lieberman can take over."

Moore estimated that according to the Zogby Poll, five percent of America, 14 million people, "no chump change" supported Nader. He did particularly well in Alaska (17 percent), Connecticut (11 percent) and Oregon (8 percent).

"I have to tell you something. I am not going to vote for Ralph Nader because I want the Green Party to get the 5 percent so they have federal funding which I hope they get because it would be a cool thing. I am not voting for Ralph because it makes me feel good or righteous or because he hangs out with Pearl Jam. I am voting for Ralph Nader because it's the right thing to do, because he believes in what I believe and that is the only reason you should vote for someone for President of the United States.

"I am voting for Ralph Nader because he has never lied to the American people. Can Bush and Gore and Lieberman and Cheney make the same claim. I am voting for Ralph Nader because he has promised to end the drug war. Bush and Gore have only promised to end their own personal former drug use. I am voting for Ralph Nader because he is the most qualified candidate, and that again is the only reason why you should vote for someone for elective audience.

"Why is Ralph Nader the most qualified candidate? Ralph Nader is responsible for more laws than Bush and Gore combined. Is there anyone here in the audience who can tell me about one piece of legislation that Gore was responsible for in the U.S. Senate other than voting for Scalia to be on the Supreme Court?"

Moore drew cheers from the audience as he summarized Nader's legislative crusades that led to passage of everything from the Freedom of Information Act to the Environmental Protection Agency.

"Ralph Nader is personally responsible for saving the lives of hundreds of thousands of people because of this legislation. How many lives has Al Gore saved? How many lives has George W. Bush saved? He is in the business of executing people, not saving lives, sitting like a coward behind the Governor's desk in Texas, the multimillionaire son of a multimillionaire signing pieces of paper to execute the poor in Texas.

"You know, 225 years ago a bunch of revolutionaries were right here in this city and I am sure a lot of people said, 'Hey you can't win. They got a king and an army and they are bigger and stronger than us.' I think about 25 percent of the people believed they could win. The other 75 percent said, 'You can't win.' And when Rosa Parks took her seat at the front of the bus what if she had thought, 'I can't win. There is only one of me'?

"Any great change that has occurred in our history of all of our great leaders has occurred because they believed they could win and they would listen to no one else who thought they couldn't win. Change only occurs because you have the courage of your convictions. I am tired of talking about this presidential election like it is Las Vegas. I don't want to hear any more talk about the odds of winning or not winning. This is not Las Vegas. This is a presidential election in the democracy of the people of the United States. No more talk about this winning business.

"'But Mike, a vote for Nader is a vote for Bush.' Hey I didn't go to college, help me out with this:

"A vote for Nader is a political Molotov cocktail that we need to throw into a corrupt and bankrupt system filled with its dirty money.

We need to do this right now folks. We are turning into the United States of America, Inc. brought to you by McDonalds, GE and Nike. We have turned our country over to a group of corporate criminals none of which have spent a single day behind bars.

"We all know and can collectively agree about the nightmare George W. Bush would bring if he is elected as president of the United States. But let me say this to the people of Massachusetts. Let's look at the nightmare we have gone through after the last eight years of Clinton/Gore. Let's not forget the facts. The record speaks for itself under George Bush we had thirty-eight million Americans who had no health care.

"Under Clinton/Gore we had forty-five million who had no health care. Under Bush we had one million Americans in jail. Under Clinton/Gore we now have over two million of our citizens in jail. One of seventy adult men is in jail. Twenty percent of African Americans have had their voting rights stripped from them under Clinton/Gore and nearly half of those in prison are there because they participated in an activity that both Gore and Bush have admitted to doing themselves.

"You know a man came up to Ralph and said, 'Mr. Nader I want to vote for you but we've got to stop Bush.' Nader asked, 'When you send your congressman to Washington D.C., do you expect them to vote their conscience?'

"'Yes, I do.'

"'Then why do you expect less of yourself?'

"Many of you will be voting for the first time in your lives. You are being told that you have to settle for less. You are being asked to compromise your conscience you are being asked to do what you don't think is right because of some strategic chess move to block someone else from getting into office.

"You have to understand that your parents who voted for George McGovern in 1972 ended up learning a very bad lesson, which is I think we have to settle for less, and settling for less got us Carter which led to Reagan and Bush because they saw how weak we were because we were willing to settle for less and that led to Clinton and Gore and the political gene pool just keeps getting depleted more and more so that we no longer have a Thomas Jefferson, but we have a Joseph Lieberman who is at the behest of the pharmaceutical companies and the insurance companies. That is what we'll have after Gore. Young people do not allow this to happen. Don't vote your fears, vote your dreams and your aspirations. And please now lets give a big Boston welcome to a man who will tell you the truth, Ralph Nader."

For Matt Zawisky, an advance man on the Nader campaign, Moore was the perfect warm-up act for the presidential candidate. Zawisky had been a big fan of Moore's work before he met Nader during a campus visit at the State University of New York in Genesco. After graduation he helped found Democracy Rising, a grassroots organization that staged superrallies to support causes like public campaign financing. From there he went on to join Citizens Works, another public interest group fighting corporate crime.

Zawisky was one of a group of campaign aides who urged Nader to bring back the former editor of *Moore's Weekly*. "He brought us youthful credibility from *The Awful Truth*, *TV Nation* and *Canadian Bacon*." Like Nader and Moore, Zawisky fought hard against General Motors. In his case the battle was over the fate of Poletown, a Hamtramck, Michigan community bulldozed to make way for a Cadillac plant designed to bring jobs to the Detroit region. After the residents, including Zawisky's uncle, were evicted, the GM plant failed to flourish and was ultimately closed, yet another example of the auto giant's inability to rebuild the community's economy.

"Moore brought this sort of working class giant that has not been awakened since the '30s to the campaign," Zawisky says. "Michael's uncle was a huge influence in the Flint sitdown strike. This lineage combined with his humor and media savvy really scares the right and made an important contribution to Moore's appearances.

"Ralph is perceived as negative and a spoiler. Michael brought in new support through his plain language that builds bridges. Michael's style, his stories, his celebrity factor, his ability to charm audiences all helped the campaign. Ralph is focused on the 800 pound gorilla that is corporate power. He needs more people like Moore to connect to that message, to fight for health care and against political corruption."

By the end of the 2000 political campaign, Moore was beginning to worry that Nader could indeed throw the election to Bush. While personally committing himself to the Green Party candidate, he gave students at a Florida State University rally in Tallahassee special permission to cross over and vote for Gore. Then on a plane headed for Los Angeles, he called the Nader campaign office and suggested that the man he had been boosting at super rallies across the nation throw his support in swing states to the Democrat. As part of the deal Gore would have to sign off on key portions of Nader's platform including universal health care and an end to tax cuts for the rich.

"Mike," said one of Nader's advisers. "Are you okay? . . . Ralph will be crucified if he backs Gore and Gore will be crucified if he changes his positions at such a late date. It's not going to happen."

HOW MUCH IS THAT UZI IN THE WINDOW?

Getting Charlton Heston Ready for his Closeup

"Why do many people around the world hate us?"
—Suggested discussion topic from the
Bowling for Columbine *Teacher's Guide.*

EAGER TO REACH A BROADER AUDIENCE, Moore wrote a new book called *Stupid White Men,* which began with a lengthy account of the "coup" that put "El Presidente" Bush in office. The fact that Moore had campaigned for Ralph Nader in the 2000 election did not detract from his central premise. To those who suggested that Nader was the reason Al Gore lost the election, Moore replied that the credit really went to Florida Governor Jeb Bush who shoplifted the White House for his brother. Al Gore, he added, might have also strengthened his own case if he hadn't made the mistake of voting for the Senate confirmation of Antonin Scalia to the Supreme Court. "Don't write me and tell me about the kind of Court we 'might' get under Bush thanks to Nader," said Moore. "We already have it thanks to Al and his Democrats."

The September 11, 2001, Al Qaeda attacks on the World Trade Center and the Pentagon forced Moore and Glynn to abandon their plan to fly home from Los Angeles. On their way back across America in a rental car, they learned that one of his line producers, Bill Weems, had died on the American Airlines flight that hit the twin towers. Another victim, Barbara Olsen, wife of Theodore Olsen, the attorney who argued George Bush's winning case at the Supreme

Court (and went on to become Solicitor General) had appeared with
Moore on Bill Maher's *Politically Incorrect*. The conservative author
was enroute to another appearance on that show when her United
Airlines jet was flown by an Al Qaeda hijacker into the Pentagon.
To honor Olsen's memory, Maher left an empty chair on the set. "I
agreed with her on nothing," said Moore, "and cried when I saw that
empty chair."

Moore and Glynn drove across Arizona and New Mexico, and as
they descended the Continental Divide, Rush Limbaugh was on the
air suggesting convenient bombing candidates for the United States
Air Force. "I am sure he is on his way down to the nearest recruiting
station to sign up," suggested Moore, "for surely he would not expect your son or daughter to risk their lives for freedom while he just
sits back and enjoys his new half-billion dollar contract."

Their route continued on to Oklahoma, where they headed down
the Will Rogers Turnpike. "I think I know what he would say about
all this," wrote Moore, "let alone what he would say about this state
naming a toll road after him."

By the time they reached Columbus Ohio, where they had dinner
with old Flint/Michigan *Voice* Al Hirvela, there was a message waiting
from HarperCollins. His new book, *Stupid White Men,* dedicated to
Hirvela, was off the press. Unfortunately, publication was being delayed in the wake of the Al Qaeda attacks. For Moore, who had been
attacking the President in a series of letters on his website ("Keep crying, Mr. Bush. Keep running to Omaha or wherever it is you go while
others die, just as you ran during Vietnam while claiming to be 'on
duty' in the Air National Guard"), the postponement made sense.

"I have absolutely zero interest in going out on a book tour this
week . . . I just can't go out there and have my name attached to
something that is 'on sale.'" Accordingly he instructed his webmaster
to remove everything from his site that led browsers to purchase any
of his own films, TV shows or books.

Back home in New York, Moore balked at his publisher's request
to rewrite the book and pay $100,000 to reprint 50,000 copies. His
publicity campaign was backed by outraged librarians who fought

for releasing *Stupid White Men* without changes. The book, which Moore did not alter, finally came out in January 2002. It sold over 4 million copies—a phenomenal bestseller. His 47-city publicity tour peaked in Portland with a crowd of 5,000. Another 5,000 were turned away, and traffic was so bad that police had to shut down an interstate freeway. To the surprise of its publisher, *Stupid White Men* even hit the top of the bestseller list in Germany. Offering advice on everything from guidance counseling for men on how to urinate without annoying the women in their life (tip number one, lift up the toilet seat) to solving the Mideast crisis, the book was peppered with letters from Mike. One renewed his call for the American government to cut out $3 billion in aid to Israel and ante up $6 billion to fund a Palestinian Marshall Plan. He suggested that the leader of the Palestinian Liberation Organization give nonviolent civil disobedience a try in the tradition of Gandhi and Nelson Mandela.

In his letter to Yasir Arafat, Moore pointed out that the old eye-for-an-eye, tooth-for-a-tooth approach to international diplomacy would never extinguish that burning Middle Eastern ring of fire. "If as I suspect you would prefer peace and quiet to constant war and displacement then you must lay down all arms, lay down your bodies in the middle of the road and then just wait. Yes the Israelis will beat many of your people. They will drag your women by the hair, they will sic dogs on you, they may even get out the firehoses (and other tricks they've learned from us Americans). You MUST NOT FIGHT BACK. Trust me, when the pictures of your suffering at the hands of these brutes go out across the world, there will be such an outcry that the Israel government will be unable to continue its oppression. If you want, I will come and join you in your nonviolent protest. It's the least I can do after helping finance the bullets and bombs that have killed your people."

Unfortunately Arafat, his datebook full with the suicide bombers of the intifada, didn't have time to respond to Moore's generous offer. Unable to put his body on line to bring peace to Israel and Palestine, he returned to making a documentary about an explosive subject, America's laisséz faire approach to gun control. Letting the bullets fall where they may, America was losing 50 young people and children each week to gunfire. Assault weapons, drive-bys and the mass merchandising of ammo in super stores had created a new participant sport. "If it bleeds, it leads," was the mantra of the TV newsroom.

The 1999 Columbine High School murder of 15 students by two crazed teenage assassins was too dark for a TV movie of the week. But the subject was perfect for Moore's Dog Eat Dog Films, which began shooting a documentary on the nation's soft spot for firearms. Moore was a National Rifle Association lifetime member, and his state was home of the Michigan Militia that had nurtured Oklahoma City bombers Timothy McVeigh and Terry Nichols. His Bravo cable followup to *TV Nation*, *The Awful Truth*, had ridiculed the National Rifle Association with a touring gun safety character called Pistol Pete. Designed in the color purple, this six-foot-tall, six-shooter character was able to march right in to the office of NRA friendly Congressman John Dingell (D-Michigan) alongside reporter Jay Martel without being asked to show ID by Capitol security.

Moore also created a parody about a sharpshooting school aimed at teaching would-be campus killers how to use bullets intelligently. The key was lots of after-school target practice. Instructors would also teach kids how to prioritize. When confronted with a quarterback, a cheerleader and a straight-A nerd, it was vital to know who to shoot first. Obviously it was the quarterback, because he was the person most likely to take out the shooter before he could do real damage.

Moore's work on his new film came at a remarkable time in his own life. The success of *Stupid White Men* ended a financial drought that had followed the end of *The Awful Truth*. His talk of selling his New York apartment and returning to Michigan ceased. No longer did he have to worry about vacating his New York office in the middle of the night. And as work progressed on *Bowling For Columbine*, Moore continued to reap a warm reception from women who were intrigued by his notion that they outlived men, a gender in decline due to disgusting personal habits. In the summer of 2002, after his mother died, he returned to his boyhood home in Davison to discover a copy of his book "sitting out there with the page marked where she had left off, and she was on the chapter about the end of men and their attitudes towards women, and I'm sure she loved that."

In August 2002 the director flew to the Telluride Film Festival to screen *Bowling For Columbine*. He also tried, at his family's urging, to end his period of mourning and resume his self-appointed role as America's corporate gadfly. In front of a television audience Moore parried columnist Robert Novak's suggestion that he was out to bring down capitalism and turn America into a socialist haven. "Bob," he replied, "that is exactly what I intend to do and, considering more people have bought my book than any other nonfiction book in America this year, I guess that means that the majority of Americans agree with me on this point, so look out Bob 'cause we're going to seize your money first!"

Moore's *Bowling for Columbine* brought him back to many of the themes that made *Roger & Me* a classic. This time, instead of searching futilely for his subject, Moore succeeded in interviewing National Rifle Association President Charlton Heston, who graciously welcomed a fellow lifetime member. Like his famous Christmas Eve showdown with Roger Smith at the General Motors headquarters, this interview proved that when all else fails, try the front door. Or as Woody Allen puts it, "Ninety percent of life is showing up." After more than two years of failing to arrange an interview with Heston, Moore was convinced the Michigan born actor would never agree to talk. Following a shoot in South Central Los Angeles, the team had left their hotel enroute to the airport for a flight home when they passed a vendor hawking Hollywood star maps.

"Hey," said one of the crew members, "let's get a star map and see if we can find Heston."

"No," said Moore, "let's just get to the airport; I just want to get to my seat."

A chant went up in the crew van: "I want a star map, I want a star map."

After picking up a map, Moore realized "it's like they're challenging me, like I don't have it anymore. So I took their dare and drove up the hill. I get out and ring the bell and out of that little box came the voice of Moses . . . You can hear my voice shake because I'm like, 'Holy shit.'. . . He told me to come back the next day, and I thought,

for sure somebody'll put an end to this. And we show up at 8:30 and
the gates open." It was a perfect matchup, possibly Heston's greatest
supporting role, as he articulated the NRA's mantra for mass audiences
in the wake of the Columbine massacre and repeated them for Moore
personally. Heston's sincerity and willingness to open up was an investigative reporter's dream. From his point of view America's astonishing
pace of gun homicides was partially attributable to ethnicity. Gun control
would never work in this country because the American melting pot was,
unfortunately, in meltdown. As long as differing races did not know how
to get along Americans would be inclined to shoot first and ask questions
when they got around to it. Right or wrong, Heston's view won standing ovations from members who understood, as California's Jerry Brown
once put it, in this country you don't mess with a man's cars or his guns.
Even Moore himself shared Heston's view that gun control alone would
not end America's culture of violence. As the director explained:

"I believe that if we were able to get rid of all guns in America
and have strong gun control laws that we would still have the central
problem of being afraid of each other. In America it's every man for
himself and to hell with you and me."

Audiences lined up to see the film as it played some houses for
more than six months. Moore's $21 million box office gross was a
record for a serious documentary. Since he wasn't an elected official,
the National Rifle Association couldn't throw millions of dollars into
a political campaign against him. Instead, an attorney working with
the National Rifle Association, David T. Hardy co-authored *Michael
Moore Is a Big Fat Stupid White Man,* which briefly made the *New
York Times* bestseller list. The book's publisher was a Harper Collins
imprint, Regan Books, which also hit the bestseller lists with Moore's
Stupid White Men. The Rupert Murdoch company had found profit
centers on both sides of the Michael Moore controversy.

A *Bowling for Columbine* "press conference" highlighted the fact
that the Columbine shooters had purchased their bullets at a Denver
area K-Mart. The superstore pulled ammunition from its shelves after
two badly injured Columbine survivors visited the company's Troy,
Michigan, headquarters with Moore to "return the merchandise."

Predictably, the film prompted a backlash from fans of Charlton

Heston. They accused Moore of ambushing the NRA president shortly before the announcement of his retirement due to Alzheimer's. NRA members also organized a national boycott of K-Mart after the chain stopped selling ammunition. Moore continued his crusade against big box firearms dealers by publishing the names of Wal-Mart shoppers felled by gunfire while trying to take advantage of low prices and plenty of free parking. His online petition gave fellow Americans an opportunity to lobby the nation's largest retailer to stop selling guns and ammo. This grassroots effort offered a new twist to the concept of caveat emptor. Moore wanted buyers to beware of an ex spouse or fired employee that could be waiting at the exit, aiming to use their freshly bought Wal-Mart piece to blow them away.

During the fall Congressional campaign, Moore continued to campaign against George Bush's party. One of the most critical Senate races was in Minnesota. On the morning of October 25, 2002, Minnesota Senator Paul Wellstone, his wife Sheila and their daughter Marcia boarded a KingAir turboprop in Minneapolis and flew north to Eveleth for a funeral. In the midst of a reelection campaign, Wellstone, a former Carleton College political science professor, had voted against the war in Iraq, against George Bush's tax cuts, against the Patriot Act, against everything that made life worth living for the American Enterprise Institute and Fox's Bill O'Reilly.

Wellstone appeared as a white knight eager to introduce labor legislation on Moore's aptly named TV show, *The Awful Truth*. The new law aimed at curbing the wretched excesses of outfits like Walt Disney World, where broiling summertime workers accused the company of giving new meaning to the word sweatshops. Moore even promised his viewing audience that Wellstone's running mate in his next Senatorial election would be none other than Crackers, the show's seven foot tall corporate crime fighting chicken. Returning the compliment, Wellstone's television ad campaign borrowed liberally from the documentaries of a filmmaker he greatly admired, a working class hero who had won hearts and minds from Sundance to Cannes—Michael Moore. The Senator was proud that his TV ads, crafted in the underdog spirit of Moore's hit documentary, *Roger & Me*, were winning over independent voters.

When Wellstone's plane crashed short of the runway, killing all aboard, Minnesota lost a senator, and America lost a gifted politician. Joining the bereaved was President George Bush, who praised Senator Wellstone as "a man of deep convictions, a plain-spoken fellow who did his best for his state and for his country." A few weeks later, Wellstone's last-minute replacement Democratic candidate, Walter Mondale, was defeated by Republican Norm Coleman, giving Bush the GOP majority he needed to take control of the Senate.

As Tom Delay and Bill Frist became the House and Senate majority leaders, Moore continued work on his film about President Bush and 9/11. He also continued to promote *Bowling For Columbine* to the Academy Awards electorate while traveling abroad to push his film.

In November and December 2002, the director delighted crowds at London's Roundhouse theater with a "one and a half man show" called *Michael Moore: Live*. His suggestion that black passengers could have easily foiled the Al Qaeda 9/11 hijackers offered a new slant on his wimpy white man thesis. The thought that Samuel L. Jackson or Morgan Freeman would have easily saved the day sidestepped the fact that whites fought back bravely on United flight 93 before it crashed in Pennsylvania. But this was only one part of an act that proved a graduate of an average British university could easily one up an American Ivy League alum during a trivia quiz focusing on politics and geography. This "Stump The Yank" segment was followed by a call to a Kuwait MacDonald's searching for clues on Osama bin Laden's whereabouts and a cry for the audience to cut up their supermarket loyalty cards.

His audiences applauded Moore's negative comments on Israel but failed to honor his call for a pledge that the Holocaust would not be repeated. "He stopped in mid-sentence," wrote one critic, "noting the way the crowd reacted to the deaths of Palestinians compared to the deaths of Jews."

Moore's suggestion that there might be anti-Semitism in the room was a much discussed moment in the show that also featured a section called "Lies They Tell You."

"One of the things they tell you is that there is a special someone out there for you. Let me tell you there isn't a special someone out there. Think about it. I love you, your friends love you and anyone in the room would be happy to sleep with you. That special someone, they're just going to fuck with your head."

Offstage, Moore was quick to use his bully pulpit to point out that most of his critics come from the left. "Whose quote is it that the liberals are the cops for the right?" he asked a reporter. "The purpose of the liberals is to police the political discourse, so that the left end of the discussion, goes no further than just a tiny bit left of center, and then to marginalize everybody else out here as if they are not part of the debate."

Was there any truth to the rumor that the BBC was picking up extraordinary expenses for Moore and his family? Yes, he replied, this whispering campaign was remarkably accurate. The filmmaker and his entourage were making the most of their opportunity to exploit the ruling class. "It's trying to take as much money from them as possible, and to make them bleed . . . The Ritz (Hotel) likes the idea that they've got this presenter from (BBC) Channel 4, this prime-time show . . . oh it's this guy, then look who's trailing behind him . . . and this is what really bothered them because I had black and white people that I brought over, all looking like me and dressed like me, walking in and out of the Ritz, I love it.

"I heard that I'm the highest-paid presenter in the history of Channel 4 . . . When I go back home and say I got more money than any presenter on Channel 4, they'll say, 'God, that's fucking great! . . . Back home we call it fuck-you money. OK? What that means is, the distributor of the film can't ever say to me, 'Don't you dare say this in the interview or you better change that in the movie because if you don't you're not going to get another movie deal.' Because I already have my home and my family taken care of, and enough money from this film and book to make the next film, I'm able to say, 'Fuck you.' No one in authority can hold money over me to get me to conform."

Back home, Moore flew to Aspen, Colorado, to receive an award from the U.S. Comedy Arts Festival and the First Amendment Center on February 23, 2003. Moore was asked by former Bill Clinton press secretary Joe Lockhart about his remarkable ability to go head on with shoe titans, the gun lobby and auto companies. "It's pretty easy to say there has never been a filmmaker like Michael Moore. He's a journalist, he's a comedian, he's a provocateur, he's an activist . . . most people love him, some people hate him but no one can deny the power of Michael Moore's work."

Moore replied, "Guys like me are not on TV . . . people who come from the working class, men or women. We don't own networks or studios. We don't have uncles in the business. How do we get our foot through any kind of a friggin door. I am constantly thinking . . . we've got to take this further, we can't stop here. This thing has got to move forward. What else can I tackle? What are the doors that the media is afraid to open? I've got to go ahead and open those doors. I will do it at my own personal risk.

"I realize . . . the publisher of the book or the studio who will give me the money for the film will hate me at some point along the way and realize at some point that they have fucked up in giving me the money to do this and it is at that point that I know I have opened the right doors. But I am not doing things purposely to just make them mad but this is a weird relationship . . . *TV Nation* was on the GE network then it went to Rupert Murdoch network (Fox), *The Big One* was distributed by Miramax which is owned by Disney. *Roger & Me* was distributed by Warner Bros. and now this film [*Bowling for Columbine*] is United Artists and MGM, which is owned by Kirk Kerkorian.

"There is some weird sleeping with the enemy going on here. The irony of it is never lost on me. I know why they are doing it and they know why I am doing it. They are doing it, because they are in the business of making money and I make them money." Ignoring the failure of *Canadian Bacon*, he claimed to be "one of the few filmmakers who can say every single film I have made has made lots of money . . . I have never had any red ink on any ledger for my work. For that very reason, even though they have political agendas that are the opposite of mine, they don't operate like you and I. We have feelings and politics, that we care about. They care about the bottom line, how much money did Mike make for us today.

"'Give him another roll of film.'

"'But he is going after our stockholders.'

"'It doesn't matter, give him another roll of film.'

"I am doing it because through these large media entities, I am hoping to reach as many people as possible. I do not create my work for the church of the left. I create my work so that we end up with a country that is being run by a set of values and a political agenda . . . that in the words of the man who is currently occupying federal land at 1600 Pennsylvania avenue that truly leaves no one left behind.

"What truly bothers me about this equation, this set up with the corporate masters who put my work out there often reluctantly . . . is that they know that ultimately it's not a dangerous act to put Michael Moore out there. They are so convinced that they have done such a good job of dumbing down and numbing the minds of the American public, that . . . when they watch *TV Nation* or *The Awful Truth* or this movie or DVD or whatever, they will laugh, they'll cry and turn it off and switch it to *Help Me I'm A Celebrity, Get Me Off This Island* or whatever this new show is, and that's what bothers me. That they are so sure that the American public is so apathetic that they won't revolt. I'm betting on the fact that the people will revolt . . ."

WHEN YOU WHIZ UPON A STAR

Michael Moore, Disney and George W.

THE FILMMAKER'S 45-SECOND ATTACK on George W. Bush at the 2003 Academy Awards was only a trailer for Moore's next project, *Fahrenheit 9/11*. Returning to the format of *Roger & Me*, it offered Moore's fans a predictable mix of social history, class warfare, militarism, management mistakes and, most of all, victims who told their personal histories with irrefutable honesty. In March 2004, while he was completing his new documentary, the filmmaker agreed to parody himself at the Academy Awards. A fiery Moore talk was rudely interrupted by a *Lord of the Rings* monster who bashed in the big guy who had gone on stage without his trusty sidekick Crackers. This scene was quickly upstaged in real life by *Fahrenheit 9/11*'s backer, The Walt Disney Company. In May, just days before the Cannes Film Festival, the studio announced it had no intention of letting the film be distributed by its Miramax division. This generated priceless publicity, which was leveraged when the film won the Palme D'Or at Cannes. The film's New York premier was a homecoming of sorts for Moore. On hand were the man who taught him how to use a Nagra sound recorder during the filming of *Roger & Me*, the Reverend Jesse Jackson, role model Spike Lee, a wide awake Tony Bennett, Yoko Ono, Salman Rushdie, Mike Myers, Lauren Bacall, Tom Brokaw, Al Franken, Leonardo DeCaprio, Chloe Sevigny and dozens of other celebrities waiting in line to pose with the prize winner and give him a big hug.

Veteran author and *Slate Magazine*'s "Hollywood Economist," Edward Jay Epstein, points out that Eisner was eager to "generate the illusion of outside distribution while orchestrating a deal that allowed Disney to reap most of the profits." The Weinstein Brothers purchased the film rights through a startup called Fellowship Adventure Group. A new team of distribution companies agreed to take a smaller cut on the project thanks to all the Disney generated publicity. *Fahrenheit 9/11* brought in a $228 million worldwide box office and $30 million in DVD royalties with net receipts totaling $78 million. Epstein says after paying Moore $21 million, the Weinsteins an estimated $16 million and deducting $11 million in costs, the studio walked away with roughly $30 million, all donated to the Disney Foundation, which has not disclosed where the money wound up. Perhaps this is why Eisner gives the film he refused to distribute an A: "The reason it is a hit is it's entertaining... I loved it."

With the kind of coverage usually accorded a Tom Cruise or Julia Roberts movie, Moore's film quickly became part of the calculus of the 2004 presidential election. The idea that Michael Moore, whose last campaign was a losing bid for reelection to the Davison School Board, could influence a presidential election seemed preposterous until you stopped to consider that over 20 million had seen the picture. Enthusiastic supporters put on benefits so others could see the film whether they could pay the price of admission or not. And Moore urged buyers of the *Fahrenheit 9/11* DVD to pirate as many illegal copies as possible.

Moore's former *Mother Jones* colleague Bruce Dancis, now arts and entertainment editor at the *Sacramento Bee* and a widely syndicated reviewer of DVDs was impressed: "Michael's movie played an important role in letting the country know about the false premise of the Iraqi war, there was no connection between Al Qaeda and the Iraqi leadership. Unfortunately the film went off on tangents on the Saudis and Bin Laden family. But it did show what an inattentive President Bush was and how his desire to get into a war was not based on anything real. That is an important lesson."

Was it just possible that Michael Moore's greatest dream, the political secret weapon he always spoke about, was actually going to send George Bush into early retirement? Would John Kerry take Moore's avuncular advice? The filmmaker's theory was that sparring over undecided voters was a waste of time. The real way to win an election was to motivate the 50 percent of the electorate that didn't bother voting. Eager to do his part, he spoke of abandoning his chance to win another Academy Award for Best Documentary by releasing the film to television before the election. Under Academy rules, that would prevent *Fahrenheit 9/11* from being nominated. Instead he would seek a nomination for Best Picture, a category that was less restrictive.

At the July Democratic national convention John Kerry did not follow Michael Moore's game plan. When the Republicans met in New York to renominate George Bush, experienced speakers knew exactly how to rally the convention and bury the trash talk of people like Alan Keyes who called Vice President Dick Cheney's daughter Mary a lesbian sinner guilty of "selfish hedonism." On hand to cover the convention for *USA Today,* Moore was seated next to Rabbi Shmuley Boteach, a conservative radio talk show host on the Liberty Broadcasting Network and author of *The Private Adam: Becoming A Hero in A Selfish Age.* After Secret Service agents waved off reporters trying to interview the director, Moore borrowed a pen from Boteach to take notes. Taking advantage of his time alone with the star, the rabbi asked why he had told the *New York Times* that Israel was on his private axis of evil. The filmmaker claimed he had been misquoted. "That quote was taken completely out of context. I believe strongly in Israel's security and Israel's right to defend itself."

When the Rabbi suggested that "the impression, sadly, is that you're an anti-Semite," Moore was aghast: "Of course, I'm not a hater, and you would be surprised at just how little you and I disagree on all the issues and on the Israel issue in particular. I really want to correct that, because I am not an enemy of Israel . . . I like Israel and I've visited twice, the first time during the first intifada . . . I regard the Jewish people as the most oppressed people on earth . . . After I made *Bowling for Columbine,* I discovered that Israel had one of the lowest levels of violence . . . even though there are so many guns around."

Their conversation was interrupted by Senator John McCain, who didn't realize Moore was in the audience. The featured speaker blasted the director as a "disingenuous filmmaker" portraying Iraq as an "oasis of peace" under Saddam Hussein.

Vice President Dick Cheney pointed at Moore as the convention crowd turned toward the ambush journalist with the anger of hometown fans taking on an umpire who had called a third strike against their team's clutch hitter. Boos and catcalls gave way to a chant, "Four More Years, Four More Years."

"Not four more years," replied Moore raising two fingers toward the crowd, "two more months."

Was the director offended? "Nah, I take it all in good humor," he told the rabbi. "These people are Americans, just like me. They love this country, just like I do. I bet that if we all sat down together we'd discover just how much we agree on all the issues." Moore was quick to point out in *USA Today* that Bush supporters buying ads attacking John Kerry's Vietnam record and wearing Band-Aids embedded with purple hearts had done the same thing to John McCain four years earlier. In that primary campaign they suggested McCain's five-and-a-half years in a Vietnam POW camp made him mentally unstable. They also challenged McCain's patriotism and spread rumors that McCain's adopted child from Bangladesh was a "black baby."

Why was McCain targeting Moore instead of Bush? The answer had a lot to do with the way some Americans construct their nightmares. What made Moore a threat to George Bush and other politicians was his potential to influence people who normally didn't pay much attention to politics, potential voters beyond the reach of 30-second political spots. He could also connect with young people who had every reason to buy the wisdom of people like Bush and Charlton Heston. For example Chris Moore (no relation), an NRA loyalist running Moore's Military Surplus in Davison, Michigan, had to nod his head in agreement with the filmmaker's suggestion in *Bowling for Columbine* that offering guns as a premium for opening a new bank certificate of deposit "seemed a little strange." Even people who sued Moore, like Terry Nichols' brother James Nichols, believed "the pen is mightier than the sword, but it's always as well to have a sword handy." Was there a limit to the American arms race? Of course, said Nichols, who believed the Second Amendment did not protect a homeowner's right to keep a nuclear device in the basement. "There are a lot of wackos out there."

Michael Moore claimed that on a good day his website was getting more hits than the White House. The filmmaker's speaking fee now eclipsed the price for Rev. Robert Schuller, the cleric who tried to inspire Flint's downtrodden with a come-to-Jesus rally in *Roger & Me*. With *Fahrenheit 9/11*, America appeared to have renewed Moore's option. He had become the country's best known iconoclast, offering helpful hints on foreign policy in bestselling books like *Dude, Where's My Country?*

"Hey, here's a way to stop the suicide bombings—give the Palestinians a bunch of missile-firing Apache helicopters and let them and the Israelis go at each other head to head. Four billion dollars a year to Israel, four billion a year to the Palestinians—they can just blow each other up and leave the rest of us the hell alone."

Of course before they blow each other up, Moore wouldn't mind if the Israelis would accept one special assignment. He was eager to hire the Israelis to "find Osama bin Laden and kill him . . . We give the Israelis billions of dollars a year. They're better at this assassination stuff than we are."

A MESSAGE FROM MICHAEL

Sex, Lies and Videotape

DURING THE LAST WEEK OF SEPTEMBER 2004, with just six weeks left during the Presidential campaign, Michael Moore left his Torch Lake, Michigan home and headed south along the Lake Michigan shoreline to Elk Rapids. Here on a balmy Sunday afternoon he kicked off a 60-city campaign tour that would spread across 20 battleground states. In Antrim County he headlined a fundraiser for two local Democrats running for sheriff and the state legislature. The latter candidate, Jim McKinney, the former Charlevoix school superintendent, was running against Kevin Eisenheimer, who had defeated John Ramsey, the father of the late Jon Benet Ramsey in the June primary.

The event was a tune-up for his "Slacker Campaign" created to lure apolitical younger voters to the polls and rally the Kerry Troops. Traveling by private jet, Moore would take his campaign to an audience of more than 300,000. Part of the estimated $700,000 tour cost was covered by roughly $200,000 in speaker fees. The balance was financed by Moore personally and his generous friend Harvey Weinstein. With his entourage of advance men and women, security people, publicists, book and DVD sales managers, drivers and gofers, the campaign had the look and feel of a Bruce Springsteen tour blended with the rhetoric of Tom Hayden.

Driving south to Big Rapids beneath a canopy of oak, ash and maple beginning to go Technicolor, Moore was defeating F. Scott

Fitzgerald's argument that there were no second acts in American lives. Two decades earlier he had failed in his effort to sell the *Michigan Voice* in the Midwestern hinterlands. Now as he drove onto the campus of Ferris State University, the children of Michiganians who had passed over Moore's running critique of the Wolverine State's power elite were lined up to hear his world view.

After selling out in Big Rapids, the Moore machine headed east to Mount Pleasant, the home of Central Michigan University. As the crowd surged through security, his stepdaughter Natalie Rose, approached clerks at the Moore bookselling stand to take down numbers on sell-through of his collected works. Reporters were handed press passes with a picture displaying the filmmaker with a motion picture camera slung over one shoulder and a shotgun on the other. Team members wore "all access" dog tags featuring a picture of *My Pet Goat,* the children's book George Bush was reading at a 9/11 No Child Left Behind photo opportunity in Orlando when he learned that Al Qaeda had struck the World Trade Center. At the lectern was a large print version of the same title.

Thanks to tight security it took the audience nearly two hours to reach their seats. During the wait the spectators watched signs flash on the projection screen behind the podium. "Before you leave, register to vote and find a volunteer and commit your time to get W out of office." Students near the front tried to figure out why someone was stacking underwear and ramen on a table behind the lectern. By the time Moore arrived on stage, doing a jerky disco dance to the strains of "Vacation" by the Go-Gos, latecomers were still being seated.

"I never danced once in high school," Moore confessed to the audience. That may have had something to do with the fact that he only went on two dates at Davison High, and in each case he was asked out. Then with a look at the crowds still filing in he added, "We honor the slackers. We honor them for their tardiness but some people have to go to work or school in the morning.

"I love coming to Central Michigan. This is the place where all of my friends went because they were turned away from [the University of Michigan in] Ann Arbor. I know we have some of our Republican brothers and sisters here, and let's do unto them what they do not do unto us and welcome them with open arms. They are really pissed because they only have a few months left, four more months."

Moore thanked the crowd for their warm reception. This was a vast improvement over the Republican National Convention, where Moore felt like all 10,000 delegates had a rope in their hands. "On the boo meter I got louder boos than Saddam Hussein. Clearly Republicans love Saddam more than they love me. And they never mentioned the name of Osama Bin Laden."

Moore conceded that he was secretly flattered by John McCain's two pinkies down review of *Fahrenheit 9/11*.

Of course all this trash talk about his film sidestepped the political heat that was in the room. Father Moore was on the stump to answer a question that cut to the heart of the American experience. Was God a Democrat or a Republican?

"Republicans," he explained, "are up at the crack of dawn trying to figure out which minority group gets screwed today. On our side we never see the crack of dawn. They are up at five a.m. and have instructions from the almighty. We live in a country where the majority wants a clean environment, where the majority believes women should be paid the same as men and where the majority believes women should have control over their own bodies. The majority of Americans take the liberal position on just about everything. The majority of Americans think it is a dumb idea to pollute the water. The majority of women do not support assault weapons. The majority of Americans already agree that the war was a mistake. We don't have to get up at five a.m., because the majority of Americans are against this war. We have to let them know that the cool thing to do this year is to get out and kick some W ass.

"Republicans are angry. They control the White House, the Senate, the House, the Supreme Court, the majority of congress and two cable news channels. God you are incredible. We want to be you except without the mean spiritedness."

Moore believed that the Republican party had lost its franchise with the almighty. He argued that the Republicans had forfeited their right to political leadership in America because they were no longer the party of Abraham Lincoln and Dwight D. Eisenhower. "Republicans are not Republicans. They are the radical right. The FBI wanted to see if any of the 9/11 terrorists had bought any guns. The only time John Ashcroft stood up for the rights of people in this country was when he stood up for the gun rights of the terrorists. John Ashcroft put a stop to violation of the rights of the 9/11 hijackers" by immediately terminating the FBI's inquiry into their firearms shopping history.

Even worse, argued Moore, the President had failed America when he promised to "smoke" Osama Bin Laden "out of his hole."

"Mr. Bush," asked Moore, "where's Osama? If a dog got loose and killed 3,000 people and the dog catcher didn't catch him, wouldn't you want a new dog catcher? There is no way Bush can continue this war. He's going to bring back the draft and you're going to be drafted. In the Kerry administration there will be no draft."

Moore rejected the notion that Kerry was a flip-flopper. He countered that the real flip-flopper was George W. Bush, who had become a nation-building fanatic after opposing the concept during the 2000 Presidential debates with Al Gore. In fact, this state-sponsored enterprise was operating as a kind of Homeless Depot, knocking down private residences across Iraq with wayward bombing raids. "On the first 50 air strikes we were zero for 50 on our targets. We killed a lot of civilians."

Was Kerry's patriotism at risk in the Iraq debate? Certainly, not, suggested Moore. A simple bit of rhetoric would clear the air, suggested the would-be Kerry speechwriter. He was more than willing to put words in the Democrat's mouth.

"I have had only one position. I listened to you and I supported you and you didn't make the right decision and you should leave office."

Standing a few feet away from an Army Reserve recruiting sign on the auditorium wall, Moore turned his attention to America's men and women in uniform. "I was walking down the street in New York and I ran into a soldier. He told me, 'I was on a ship off Iraq when the war started and I saw you on the Oscars and I booed with all my buddies. Now I want to apologize.'"

Quoting himself, Moore told the audience his instant response: "We the American people apologize to you for sending you into harm's way when we shouldn't have.

"You are supposed to believe the commander in chief. Bill Clinton lied about a blowjob. Bush lied and we've got 1,050 dead soldiers for this. If maybe he had told them the truth we wouldn't be at war."

Playing media critic, Moore also attacked the television establishment for failing to create the kind of reality show that made *Fahrenheit 9/11* such a hit. Why did audiences have to pay $9 or $10 at a cinema to see Saudi beheadings, Iraqi prisoners being tortured and gruesome shots of Iraqi civilian neighborhoods being blown up?

"I had two freelancers and a couple of video tapes and I did it in a couple of days. There are five networks over there and they didn't show this. I don't agree with the copyright laws in this country, so when *Fahrenheit 9/11* comes out on video you know what you have to do."

Moore went on to give the Republicans equal time by presenting a series of commercials he was offering pro bono to the GOP. The first commercial zeroed in on Arlington Cemetery. "58,000 Americans died in Vietnam but John Kerry wasn't one of them. If he had truly loved his country he would have died. Vote Bush."

Another ad showed footage of former Democratic Senator Max Cleland who "claimed to have lost two legs and one arm. He still has one arm. If he was a real hero he would have lost the other arm.

"You should not be getting your news from a guy in a baseball cap with a high school education. Let me address the slackers, fellow slackers, would-be slackers, and the fifty percent who don't vote. Tomorrow we will read that news that says three more Americans died in Iraq. I'm not a Democrat, I rarely vote for Democrats. I'm on a 60-city slacker uprising tour. My goal is to get as many nonvoters to vote as possible. I'm voting for John Kerry."

Moore was delighted that the same poll showed 40 percent of the Republicans who saw *Fahrenheit 9/11* enjoyed it. There were also hopeful signs at the grassroots level. As he prepared for an appearance on the *Tonight Show* with Jay Leno, Moore was greeted by a stagehand he first met at the Kodak Theater after the Academy Awards ceremony.

"I never thought I would see you again," the crew member told the director. "I want to apologize. You were right."

"You don't have to apologize. All you did was believe the president that there were weapons of mass destruction. I just took a wild guess, and it turned out I was right."

This view was echoed by long-term political allies. "His view," said Dan Kildee, now treasurer of the city of Flint, "has been if we are going to be Democrats let's be Democrats from the inside out and change our party. Unity means united to fail. We need to have huge fights within the Democratic party over health care, over fundamental issues we care about. If we don't move the party we can all sit home and pine away about creating some progressive third party. I don't think I'm going to live that long."

To those who promised to register and vote, Moore promised instant gratification. After handing out clean underwear and ramen on stage to one young man, Moore realized the would-be voter was French. "Thanks for the revolution," Moore joked as he demanded the return of his ramen and and Fruit of the Loom.

NOVEMBER 2, 2004

"I don't know if I can believe half the things he says."
— *Osama Bin Laden impersonator*
on Saturday Night Live

ALTHOUGH *FAHRENHEIT 9/11* HAD A GENUINE IMPACT on George Bush's election campaign, it was not enough to help defeat the president in crucial battleground states like Ohio and Florida. However, a Harris poll showed that 70 percent of the independent voters who watched the film gave it favorable marks. What would have happened if Moore's movie had reached a wider audience? While this remained a speculative matter, there was one clear victory for the filmmaker. His record-breaking documentary opened up a new market for politically oriented DVDs from all points of view. Some of these movies couldn't have even been financed let alone distributed had it not been for the surprise success of *Fahrenheit 9/11*. While Bush's victory was attributed to the "moral values" of Christian conservatives on election day, exit polls showed that opposition to the war in Iraq had helped Kerry win in battleground states such as Pennsylvania, Wisconsin, Minnesota, New Hampshire and Michigan. Michael Moore's film helped mobilize that anti-war movement.

Many Christian leaders believed that "family values" included support for America's combat operations in Iraq. But other Christians like Michael Moore argued that this war was morally unjustifiable. When leaders of the Christian right warned their congregations not to see *Fahrenheit 9/11*, they were promoting the same kind of religious mind control that was at the heart and soul of Muslim fundamentalism. These prophets believed that state controlled media was an adjunct to their religion, which explained, for example, why Egyptian television aired a series promoting the vicious blood libel and anti-Semitism of the Protocols of the Elders of Zion in 2004.

Censoring one's opponents to make room for a self-serving world view meant that freedom of the press belonged to those who owned media conglomerates. From the executive suite at the Walt Disney Company to the Church of the Nazarene there was a belief that the gospel according to Michael Moore was heresy. For his part, Moore encouraged his viewers to seek out information from all points of view. In the months and years ahead he would continue to champion a new generation of documentary filmmakers who believed, as he did, that America and the world needed to hear from journalists who didn't pledge allegiance to Rupert Murdoch or the National Broadcasting Company. Moore believed that the Bush administration had made it impossible for the American public to hear and see the truth. He believed that Bush "lies" on subjects like Iraq's "weapons of mass destruction" were not exposed by the mainstream media until it was too late to undo the political and military damage. The administration also censored media with its unprecedented secrecy. For example, despite the best efforts of the General Accounting Office, Americans still don't know which energy company executives had been in closed-door meetings with Dick Cheney to rewrite energy policy.

Critics, bestselling books, websites, documentaries and MICHAEL MOORE LIES bumper stickers promoted the notion that the filmmaker was America's village idiot, a college dropout who dared to attack a president with degrees from Yale and Harvard Business School. Why, Moore never spent a day in uniform-yet he called George W. Bush a National Guard "deserter." In Michigan angry Republicans led a legal campaign to have him indicted for bribing voters by handing out free underwear. Although this complaint was thrown out by the courts, it confirmed Moore's ability to satirize American politics. Even people who believed that Moore told the truth argued that his documentaries were little more than serial entrapment. A comedian portraying Osama Bin Laden on *Saturday Night Live* added a humorous twist when he explained three days before the election that the only American journalist to see him regularly was Michael Moore. "Frankly," Osama's double told his audience, "I don't know if I can believe half the things he says."

The truth about Iraq, assault guns or buying drugs from Canada, all topics central to Moore's world view, were subjects that demonstrated how difficult it was for Americans to abandon their biases. For example, on Election Day 2004 nearly half of all American voters would go to the polls believing that Saddam Hussein was one of the terrorists responsible for destroying the World Trade Center. Despite overwhelming evidence to the contrary, this faulty view was crucial to Bush's reelection. Now Michael Moore's job was similar to the work of nuns who had schooled him back in Davison. America needed to do its homework and begin to realize that reliable information was only available to those who demanded it. The success of his films as well as the work of a new generation of documentary filmmakers was critical.

During the election campaign Michael Moore drew crowds that equaled those of Ralph Nader. And he had no problem making a public appeal against Nader. On *Real Time with Bill Maher*, the muckracker and the host personally got down on their knees and begged Moore's old boss, the man who had also employed his stepdaughter Natalie as an intern, to bow out of the campaign. As Nader snatched Moore's "Made in Canada" baseball cap off his head, his 2000 campaign ally pleaded, "Ralph, Ralph, don't do this. Don't do this, Ralph. Come home Ralph." After the Maher appearance, Nader asked Moore what he thought he might make on *Fahrenheit 9/11*. "He told me that after it's all over, with DVDs and everything else, worldwide, it will be $35 million. With the producers', exhibitors' and distributors' share, plus what Disney held onto, agents commissions, etc., there is no way he could make that much. He's one of the few rich people I know who exaggerates his wealth. Why would he try to do that?"

Nader also continued to press Moore to stop rewriting the history of the 2000 campaign. "He claims that I misled him by promising that I would campaign in the safe states that were already in the Gore camp. But the fact is we campaigned together in places that were up for grabs such as Michigan and Wisconsin. He never retracts a lie. We stepped in to save him when he was at his lowest point psychologically after being fired by *Mother Jones*. Now he has closed the door on the those who incubated him. He won't even return our phone calls when we ask him to join us on an important cause by signing a petition. We can't rely on him to fight the good fight. It's all about the hubris of money and fame. Just like Citizen Kane, it went to his head."

YOU CAN'T GET INTO HEAVEN
WITHOUT A PERMISSION SLIP FROM THE POOR

*"To much of corporate America he's the scariest man alive. If Michael
Moore shows up with a camera go running for the hills."*
—Joe Lockhart, Bill Clinton's press secretary

GEORGE BUSH'S NOVEMBER VICTORY gave Michael Moore an opportunity to return to his day job, sending misbehaving corporations to the
woodshed. Before turning back to filmmaking, he tried to look on
the bright side of John Kerry's defeat. Quoting a friend's Romanian
grandfather, he told his loyal troops, "Remember . . . this is such a
great country—it doesn't even need a president!"

In post mortems, some film executives suggested that Moore's film
may have actually helped the Bush campaign. "I'm just not sure it
didn't also mobilize the Republican side," said Jon Feltheimer, head
of Lions Gate Entertainment which distributed the film after Disney
backed out. Journalists such as *Vanity Fair*'s Judy Bachrach advanced
the remarkable theory that Moore's film had triggered a Republican
backlash that ultimately cost Kerry the election. Angered by Moore's
negative portrayal of Bush, they responded with grass roots organizing and fund raising that strengthened the President's reelection
campaign.

This view ignored many other important factors in Kerry's defeat,
such as his handling of the Swift Boat attack ads that questioned
his military service during the Vietnam war. It also ignored the fact

that Kerry had sidestepped key domestic issues like raising the minimum wage, the Republican assault on civil liberties and Bush's coddling of his friends in the oil industry at the expense of consumers. In much the same way that Al Gore had stumbled when he refused to let Bill Clinton campaign for the Democratic presidential ticket in 2000, Kerry had failed to take advantage of some of his party's best opportunities. With Bush embedded in the White House for another four years, Moore returned to filmmaking. He also received a confidential call from an editor at *Time* magazine. Moore and Mel Gibson had been tentatively named men of the year in recognition of their maverick cinematic achievements from opposite sides of America's body politic. While Gibson had backed out of financing *Fahrenheit 9/11,* they remained friendly. These Catholic directors independently produced two of 2004's most controversial and commercially successful films. Both movies were also denounced by critics who either refused to see them or did not share Gibson's and Moore's values. Their cinema controversies encouraged Americans to look into their hearts as they reexamined spiritual and personal beliefs, not a bad idea in a democracy.

Gibson's approach in his film *The Passion of the Christ* suggests that the hand of the Jews was all over the arrest, trial and crucifixion of Jesus. It also raises cries of anti-Semitism. Although it is true that Gibson's father, who worships at a private church on the actor's estate in Australia, has been a holocaust denier, the man of the year co-candidate is personally convinced that six million Jews did perish in places such as Auschwitz and Buchenwald.

Time's eagerness to enshrine these two directors in their pantheon alongside the likes of Ghandi, Martin Luther King and Albert Einstein, depended on the willingness of both Moore and Gibson to fly to Los Angeles for a photo shoot and interview. Both agreed, but after finishing with the editors, Gibson flew home to Australia where, Moore believed, divine intervention changed the course of history.

"Something happened overnight. He goes to his little church and he must have talked to God and he said, 'No f***ing way you're doing this. Mel calls up and says, 'I'm not going to do it. I thought it over and it is not the right thing to do,' and so they put Bush on the cover."

Dipping into his baseball hat collection, Moore returned to the talk show circuit as the blue collar guy from a blue state. On the speaking circuit he continued to command tens of thousands of dollars for personal appearances where he demanded that America raise the minimum wage.

Moore's documentaries had opened the doors for a new generation of acolytes attacking the power elite like McDonald's in *Super Size Me*. Echoing *Roger & Me*, producer, director, star Morgan Spurlock landed in voice mail hell when he tried to interview the fast food chain's CEO about the dangers of a month long hamburger diet. Then, in a surprising twist, the 60 year-old McDonald's chieftain died of a heart attack at a convention in Orlando just weeks before the film's release. His 44 year-old successor died of cancer less than a year later.

While Moore shared top honors at the People's Choice Award with Mel Gibson, the man who had backed out of backing *Fahrenheit 9/11* ("I feel a kind of strange kinship with Michael," declared the actor-producer after the ceremony) this consolation prize was certainly no match for *Time*'s Man of the Year honor. After disqualifying himself for the best documentary Academy Award by releasing *Fahrenheit 9/11* on pay-per-view television before the presidential election, Moore failed to win a Best Picture nomination. Two documentaries attacking the filmmaker, including *Michael Moore Hates America*, also failed to win Best Documentary nominations.

Back home in Davison, Michigan, the high school hall of fame committee chair put out a feeler to the filmmaker's sister. "Do you think that if we elected Michael to the hall of fame, maybe he wouldn't come and you could accept the award for him?"

That was the problem with inviting a firebrand name like Michael Moore to the dais. You never knew whether you were going to get a mannered performance or if you'd have to call security.

Like Phil Knight at Nike, Moore showed little interest in moving any part of his growing film company, Dog Eat Dog Films, from its Manhattan base to Flint. The idea of relocating in the Midwest did not seem practical. And the idea of getting behind a John Kerry or an Alan Keyes no longer seemed to make any sense. The Republican who won the endorsement of *The Awful Truth* during the 2000 Iowa Caucus took a body blow from his daughter Maya Marcel-Keyes. This Brown student who talked her dad into trying out Michael Moore's Mosh Pit came out as a lesbian on Valentine's Day 2005 at a Maryland political rally. She added that her less-than-cool parents had kicked her out of the house and refused to pay her college expenses at Brown. (The Tides Foundation in San Francisco quickly stepped in with an offer to help her out financially.)

In the summer of 2005 Moore returned to northern Michigan, where he organized the first Traverse City Film Festival a short drive from his Torch Lake home. He also spent time in Davison, where he and Kathleen Glynn had just added another property to their real estate portfolio—a Main Street Victorian where his mother was born. Although the couple continued to work in New York, Davison proclaimed itself one of Governor Granholm's "cool cities"—the aerie of one of America's most loved and hated filmmakers.

At Davison High School's hall of fame, which features other local celebrities like Ken Morrow, a hockey star on the 1980 American Olympics dream team, Citizen Moore is missing. A former administrator, Kay Shepherd insists this oversight is unintentional. Another Davison High student, Sheryl Leach, who invented Barney the purple dinosaur, isn't in the hall of fame either. "Some people think they both should be inducted," explains Shepherd. "But the nominating process is a little complicated. Still, it could happen."

Flint Journal film critic Ed Bradley isn't surprised by this slight. "The same thing happened during our first Flint Film Festival, which took place at the time *Fahrenheit 9/11* was coming out." Rising from his chair in the Journal cafeteria to return to the newsroom, he says, "If they had premiered *Fahrenheit 9/11* here it would have been a bonanza for Flint. Media would have flown in from all over the world to see it. Flint would have been on the front page, on international television. The festival would have received incredible press. It would have helped attract attention to all the young filmmakers. Michael would have been a big help. It would have been great for Flint's image. I just don't get it"

But Flint Film Festival director Greg Fiedler has another view. "I thought *Fahrenheit 9/11* was a great film. Our arts council supported

Roger & Me with a grant. Michael's work is very important. But he would have drowned out the voices of other young filmmakers. Yes, we would have made more money, but this is not a commercial venture. We're trying to encourage new talent. Christopher Robin Hood, director of *Coping*, the audience choice winner, is terrific. He's a Flint native who could easily turn out to be our next Michael Moore."

Moore returned to Flint in November to receive the Genesee County Progressive Caucus first annual Paul Wellstone Award. The award ceremony at Mott Community College was just 500 feet away from the site of Moore's now demolished birthplace, St. Joseph Hospital.

In his hour-and-twenty-minute acceptance speech, Moore hinted that the Sisters of St. Joseph were the guiding light that convinced him to dedicate his own life to the least fortunate among us. "The bible is very clear. You cannot get into heaven without a permission slip from the poor."

Paul Wellstone had turned his own life into an object lesson, voting his beliefs regardless of the political consequences. Moore believed that redemption meant finding another political leader who could resume Wellstone's mission. And now, it appeared, help was on the way. Moore confessed that the "only good thing to come out of that tragic plane crash is the fact that my good friend Al Franken is now considering running for Wellstone's old seat in 2008."

No longer relegated to Jay Leno's couch, America's politically minded comics weren't mired in the political pessimism of Mark Twain or the cowboy shtick of Will Rogers. Although none of them had actually been elected, performers like Jon Stewart, Steven Colbert and Bill Maher were giving voice to the progressive agenda. The Republicans might have a lock on Fox News, but the Comedy Channel appeared to be in the hands of the Democratic National Committee. And in Franken's case, comics appeared to be viable candidates for the party of John F. Kennedy, Bill Clinton and Paul Wellstone.

As a film essayist, Michael Moore had stunned Washington D.C. and Hollywood by demonstrating that documentaries could quickly impact the American agenda at a surprisingly affordable cost. While Moore's sense of humor endeared him to the crowd that night in Flint, it was also clear that his career trajectory was no laughing matter.

Roger Rapoport

When George Bush wanted to strike back at Democratic Congressman Jack Murtha for demanding withdrawal of American troops from Iraq, White House Press Secretary Scott McClellan ridiculed the renegade for "joining the likes of Michael Moore."

Moore's Wellstone night performance went live for an hour and twenty minutes on C-Span. Once again he had become a matinee idol for Middle America, campaigning hard for politicians who could revive the spirit of Jack "Ask What You Can Do For America" Kennnedy. But not everyone in his hometown considered him an oracle. "I get along with the guy fine," said postman Wallace Rose, the father of Natalie Rose and first husband of Moore's wife Kathleen Glynn. "I don't have a problem with him. But he grew up in Davison, I grew up in Flint." From his booth vantage point in Lone Star Steak House off Miller Road, the decorated Vietnam War Vet and former Democrat looks up from his Cobb salad and asks: "Do you understand the difference?"

The whiteness of middle-class, low crime, Davison contrasts with low-income, African American Flint. And his view of the racial and economic divide between Flint, the hole in Genesee County's economic donut, and Krsipy Kreme Davison, is not the product of a couple of hours of cultural anthropology in a multiplex.

Like Moore, he is the nephew of a GM sitdown striker who helped create Flint's United Auto Workers in 1937. He is also an alumnus of AC Delco, the same company that employed Moore's father. But in recent years his politics have downshifted into George Bush territory. "I was the kind of guy who used to just turn off Rush Limbaugh after ten minutes and say he's full of shit. But a few years ago. after the 2000 election, I was driving back from Montana and I started listening to what he was saying about NBC, ABC and the mainstream media. That was when I started to pick up on the bias. I listened to him preach an ideology that made a lot of sense.

"You will vote for the left to fix a situation but they are never going to solve a problem for you. If you are going to be a successful black person you are not going to be a Democrat or a liberal."

A graduate of Flint's Kearsley High School, Rose grew up in Carriage Town, a middle class neighborhood where Hubbard's Hardware store handed out free bats to kids who broke theirs playing baseball. On a drive through his old neighborhood, he shows off Atwood Stadium, home of high school football and baseball and for one memorable day each year, the scene of a Detroit Tigers exhibition game. It was also the venue for a memorable John F. Kennedy speech. "It was strong on national defense," says Rose. "If someone gave that speech today you would say he'd be a Republican."

Baby boomers jumped on bikes to head downtown for coney islands or pick up baseball cards at his dad's shop, Glen Rose Variety. After his brother was hit by a car, Wallace Rose's father took a job at General Motors, where the health benefits took care of major medical bills. "In those days you could hire on at the metal fabrication plant and if you didn't like it you could go to another job. That was just the way it was. There was always an opening."

Following an honorable discharge in 1971, the decorated vet rejected a chance to take a job with General Motors in favor of warehouse work and later moved to Genesee Welding. Rose was driving a truck through Lake Orion on July 30, 1975, when, by coincidence, his Teamster union leader Jimmy Hoffa was in town for his last lunch. "I kept having nightmares that somehow after he was abducted I was called in to take away his body."

Making GM level wages without the hassle of assembly line work, Rose "was a Democrat because of special interests. That was prime time for liberal thinking. Democrats are a party of special interests, unions, tree huggers, teachers and unions."

After leaving the welding company he joined McDonald Dairy and also worked as a dog trainer before hiring on at the Post Office. Now living in the unincorporated Mount Morris area, he delivers mail in Mott Park, one of the city's better neighborhoods. His previous route in North Flint was a much tougher assignment. "Flint is a hell of a tough town. It's a dangerous town. It's like living in Bagdahd or Watts. I am street smart and I know how to survive here. But I wouldn't want to raise a family here. When I am on my mail route people come up and ask, 'What the hell are you doing here in this neighborhood after dark.' They are worried that I might get shot. As a white person I have to be accommodating, you know, 'Hey, how's it going.' You have to show respect and also demand respect.

One of the postman's biggest problems is big dogs, the ones let loose by kids who like to watch a mailman sprint. "I've never been scared in my life. But when one pit bull came after me I had to put him in a headlock. Yes I could survive in the neighborhood where I work, but I wouldn't want to live there."

Rose is talking just a couple of weeks after a five year-old girl was shot and killed while riding with her family on an ill-fated auto test drive. Afterward, two of her relatives were shot in a related homicide. "Yes you have unemployment here," says Rose. "But you didn't have people killing each other during the Great Depression when unemployment was much worse.

"The people in *Roger & Me* who were getting evicted, weren't all GM workers. Some of them were on welfare. They were victims of LBJ's Great Society that decimated black communities in this country. It created a new class of victims. Simply giving people more government money does not solve a problem caused by taking the man out of the family. The single parent household doesn't work. It means women have to have more babies to increase their welfare benefits. Women can't teach family values by themselves. They can't do the man part. Since Martin Luther King there has not been effective black leadership. Jesse Jackson was going to run for president until the Democratic Party realized we can't have a black man as president.

"Race has become an industry in this country. Al Sharpton is an extortionist pointing at me, a 58 year-old stupid white man saying I'm the problem, that I'm biased. I work with black families every single day and get along with them well. And I listen carefully. I am entertained by black people but I am not in favor of anyone who is trying to take advantage of the system. The only person effectively speaking out about this is Bill Cosby.

"There are many different affirmative action programs. But it doesn't always work. Great Lakes Cemetery in Holly awarded contracts to a minority construction firm, but they couldn't build sewers."

Rose does not believe that social engineering will ever have the economic impact Democrats sell to the electorate. "I have a family friend, a woman who was on welfare. She did everything she could to get off it. She went to see *Bowling for Columbine*. That's the movie where Michael alludes to the fact that Michigan's former Republican Governor John Engler cut social services to people on the welfare rolls.

"Moore suggested that those cuts created a domino effect that ultimately led to the tragic death of a six year-old, the focal point of his showdown in Beverly Hills with the NRA's Charlton Heston. Because an impoverished Flint mother was stripped of her welfare benefits, she was forced to move her family to a relative's home. There her little boy found an uncle's gun, brought it to Beecher Elementary School and fatally shot six-year old Kayla Rowland. In the documentary, Moore chides Heston for staging an NRA rally in Flint after Rowland's death. Well my friend was also a single parent and she didn't put her family in that situation. Compare that with the family involved in the shooting. Some people decide this is not going to happen to them and will try to get out of the system."

Is there an answer to random violence in a city victimized by shuttered auto plants, high welfare rolls, kids not graduating from high school and single parent households?

"There are only so many good ideas out there, Republican or Democrat." says Rose. "One of the downfalls in our political system is that it's too partisan. Let's get on the right side and see what's good for the country. Let's see if we can make it work. Down the road, if it's not working, let's see if we can change. Right now the only debate in this country is on the right over immigration. Democrats are waiting until the debate is over to see what the Republicans agree on and then say it is not working.

"Another trick of the left is to keep you in a state of fear, whether it's Iraq or global warming. We get bombarded about global warming by *Time* and *Newsweek*. The mainstream media is one of the worst enemies we have in this country. If it hadn't been for the new media, the Fox Channel and talk shows, we'd be in the dark. I don't listen to anyone who doesn't validate what they are saying. Laura Ingraham will make a statement and validate it. Rush Limbaugh also does a great job of that.

"You're much further ahead to go with a good idea that benefits the people whether you are a Democrat or a Republican. The left will always tell you to vote for them to fix a situation. But they are never going to solve the problem for you. Look at a problem created by liberal America, the great society. It's a mindset. Anyone with common sense would see that because of automation and globalization this was going to come to a head. Take a look at the communications industry in this country. At one time they had as big a workforce as General Motors. Because of technology they got rid of 80 percent of the phone operators. GM and the union saw automation coming and they settled on contracts they shouldn't have accepted. They set up a job bank where workers are paid for showing up and not doing anything productive. When GM asked for relief, the union refused to give them any. GM was wrong on that contract. My father and my uncle used to argue about this. Dad believed that one day the union would wreck the company.

"Why would someone want to come to a city like Flint with a UAW mentality? Why would Nike want to move here for that? If you haven't found your niche in Michigan, it is time to move on. They need people to work out in Wyoming.

"It's true that people are jealous of Michael Moore's success. If you take someone like him who was struggling, he'll admit as much as anyone else he got lucky with *Roger & Me*. But he did it on his own. No one gave him anything."

The sun is setting over the Flint River as Wallace Rose finishes his tour of the city that has become a derogatory nameplate for inner city America. It's still possible to see the USA in one of Louis Chevrolet's convertibles. But the combination of higher gas prices and global warming have persuaded a lot of loyal GM customers to start thinking about a Toyota Prius. Does Rose have any answer to this and other chronic economic problems well documented by Moore and Glynn?

"Yes, I do. You are responsible for your own actions. Don't depend on the government to support you."

Despite his busy schedule, Moore tries to make time for mentors and old friends who helped him from the beginning. While he didn't make it to the Sisters of St. Joseph memorial service for Sister John Catherine in January 2006, he did send a wonderful email. He had hoped to get back to Nazareth to see his favorite teacher, the one who had taken such pride in his accomplishments. His email was filled with the kind of love that touched other nuns like Sister Janet Kurtz and Sister Mary Ellen Gondeck, head of the Peace and Justice Committee. Sharing the email at a table in the dining hall, Sister Mary Ellen said, "From the very beginning of his success, he had donated to our women's shelter in Flint, the hospitality house." Moore's generosity to the Sisters of St. Joseph was important. But the nuns were equally grateful that he kept calling for advice on how to best support the goals of the Peace and Justice Committee.

"Peace prevails, where peace has been learned, met, experienced, modeled," declared the nuns in their policy statement. "We invoke God's call as presented to us in the Book of Deuteronomy: 'Choose life, then, that you and your descendants may live.'"

After Hurricane Katrina burst the levee in New Orleans the film-maker asked the sisters for the names of Louisiana charities that might be better at relief work than the Red Cross. "And," said Sister Kurtz, "he sent his own office staff down to New Orleans to help in the recovery."

Sister Kurtz, back from a 21-year mission in Peru, continued to live modestly at the Mother House. "I couldn't live with myself if I was real comfortable and living the good life. I don't identify with wealthy people. We weren't there for that. That's not our mission."

But the idea that Moore's net worth could easily exceed the annual budget of the Sisters of St. Joseph did not diminish his accomplishments. As the nuns began moving their trays down the cafeteria's dinner line, Sister Kurtz said, "We need people in both arenas, people who can help others. I know he has given money to the rabbit woman in *Roger & Me*. Rather than use his intelligence to fill his pockets, he uses his influence to be a modern day prophet."

Sister Mary Ellen, who ran into Moore at GM shareholder meetings in the '80s believes that Moore's sense of humor has made it possible for him to deliver his serious message to an appreciative audience. "A prophet like Michael steps out and speaks the truth."

WHERE MONEY ISN'T EVERYTHING

"When we started this film (Roger & Me) we didn't think we were going to get a Warner Brothers deal. We didn't think we'd get this or that. We just thought we'd save our town. We got all this other stuff but we didn't get to save the town. That's what makes it painful to watch . . . that sense of . . . personal failure. We probably set our goals a little too high thinking we could save our town with this movie. It's kind of a crazy idea but you know things aren't going to get better unless we have a lot of people with crazy ideas."

—Michael Moore

PHIL KNIGHT STILL HASN'T SHOWN UP with a shoe factory. The murder of six year-old Kayla Roland at Beecher Elementary School continues to play out for late night cable audiences watching reruns of *Bowling for Columbine*. And Flint remains the buckle on the rust belt.

But wait a minute, who's this driving up in his Buick SUV? It's Moore's old compadre, the man he helped elect to the Flint school board at age 18, the nephew of Flint's Congressman Dale Kildee. Yes, it's Dan Kildee—handsome, funny and optimistic. Why is this man smiling? Could it be because he knows that Flint is the first city in America to effectively guarantee that homeowners cannot be evicted for simply failing to make their mortgage and tax payments?

Meet Dan Kildee, the Treasurer of Flint, Michigan and head of the county's Land Bank. "I hope you don't mind taking the elevator," he says. "It cost us $150,000 and I figure if enough of us ride it we can get the price down to $10 a trip. Walking out of the spotless Land Bank lobby onto downtown Saginaw Street, scene of the memorable parade where the governor, Miss Michigan, UAW leaders, exotic dancers and bands marched their way through an unforgiving downtown landscape of abandoned storefronts and boarded up hotels, Dan Kildee sounds hopeful. Flint unemployment, 23 percent at the time Michael Moore shot that *Roger & Me* cavalcade of celebrities, bureaucrats and wannabes, is now down to 8 percent. And while it may not be time to break out the Dom Perignon, feel free to pop open a Pabst Blue Ribbon.

Handsome apartments in a renovated building next door to the Land Bank are bringing new tenants downtown. "We were worried that seven hundred and fifty dollars a month might be too high," says Kildee. "But that doesn't seem to be a problem." Kildee, leads the way uptown on his city of hope tour. First stop, the Durant Hotel, named for a co-founder of General Motors. Opened in 1920 and closed in 1973, this property slowly made its way up the speculator stairway to heaven. Writing off the building for tax breaks and then reselling, these do-it-yourself captains of the inhospitality industry made profits off an eyesore that contributed nothing to the city economy.

"The Land Bank acquired it," says Kildee "and this fall we will start reconstruction from the inside out. The building will be housing for three hundred graduate and international students. They will be able to live downtown, attend the University of Michigan's Flint campus and get affordable housing. And, for the first time in decades, the building will be producing tax revenue for the city."

New coffee shops are opening downtown, over 1,300 homes have been rehabilitated, and thanks to the Land Bank there's a sensible reason to buy a Flint home in an uncertain economy. This city may be the first in the country to unequivocally boast that it is foreclosure-free for homeowners. Move in to a Flint home and no matter what happens to your job, the Land Bank will find a way to keep the lenders and tax assessor at bay. This city agency will do everything necessary to insure there is no sheriff's sale of your property simply because you can't make your mortgage or property tax payments. In Flint, it appears money really isn't everything.

After showing off some of the Land Bank's rehabilitated housing, Kildee swings down along the manmade channel that guides the Flint River through the former heartbeat of middle America. "Another place where Michael's message and ours intertwine is right here. We call it Chevy in the Hole. At one time there were twenty-five thousand people working in factories along this corridor. We had the biggest concentration of GM jobs anywhere in the world.

"We didn't try to attract new industries, or plan for a different kind of economy or teach our kids not to assume jobs at the auto plant were a given after high school. The things we are doing now through different means would have never started under the old GM model. In the past the leadership of the community came out of GM. The government, the school board, the banks were dominated by General Motors. Our community was able to get on without thinking. We were completely asleep as a community. That was why the old days were so much worse.

"Now we have this huge tract of open land. They turned a river into an open sewer. One of our plans at the Land Bank is to take all of this, renaturalize the river and create a walkable riverfront. It will go from being a real detriment to the community to a beautiful area."

Rebuilding Flint has forced city officials to concede that what used to be good for General Motors is no longer good for the auto company, much less its hometown. "One of the problems with such a heavy reliance on General Motors was structural unemployment," says Kildee. "Periodic recessions meant layoffs that could last for years. General Motors was always going through up and down cycles. There was a time when our town had twenty-five-point-one percent unemployment and the second highest per capita income in the United States. The fact is that good times in Flint were really not all that good for a lot of people.

"In the 1980s, General Motors went after tax assessments in every community where they had a plant. They had the most expensive lawyers and all sorts of experts to fight these towns that were struggling to make ends meet. In the end they received about half the tax abatement they were seeking. For example in Flint their assessment dropped 38 percent."

Not satisfied with lower taxes, the world's largest industrial corporation found a better way to save money in its hometown. It slashed employment from a peak of 79,000 to just 15,000 GM jobs (another 3,300 work at bankrupt supplier Delphi).

"No longer," says Kildee, "is this a center for high paying, low-skilled jobs. The days when someone could graduate high school and sign on at GM for a good job with good benefits are gone. Periodic layoffs were a big problem but people knew that they would be re-hired on the strength of rising car sales and end up with a home, three cars in the garage and a boat and a cottage up north."

Flint, once the auto company's largest employment center, was also a magnet for workers from outside Genesee County. "The city became a victim of that former system," says Kildee. "The idea that we can go back to a county with 197,000 people and seventy-nine thousand GM jobs is an impossibility. We have this legacy of reliance on a single industry which supplied high wage, low skilled jobs. The reality is that Flint may have to end up being a smaller city."

In 1970 just 7,000 residents of Genesee County worked elsewhere. Today over 45,000 Genesee County workers take advantage of economic development in southeast Michigan by commuting up to two to three hours to work in other counties.

"While unemployment today is lower, the total size of the economy and per capita income is lower. It's hard to characterize any of that as positive. Finding ways to attract new business means competing with cities across the Midwest and around the country."

Across town Kildee swings past the fifteen-year-old world head-quarters of the Delphi Corporation. Purchased by the Land Bank for just one dollar, this class A office space is already beginning to bring in established businesses and startups. With rents running only one dollar a square foot, Flint can now vie for new business with lower-cost competitors around the country.

"Our focus is not on chasing development," says Kildee. "There is always going to be another city that can give bigger tax credits. The idea that a Toyota or a Honda is going to come here and be our savior isn't realistic. I don't believe in the growth model. Higher population is not an indicator of quality of life. Just look at Mexico

City. Our focus is on improving people's lives, making sure they live in friendly neighborhoods where they can walk to schools, parks, libraries and stores.

"Communities have become obsessive about competing for jobs, a singular definition of quality of life. We have become so obsessed that we have contributed to the culture that Michael has railed against. We use all kinds of tax breaks and public resources to get these jobs with no promise that their presence will contribute to the quality of life in the community. There is marginal evidence that heavy industry contributes to the quality of life in a community.

"It is better to use public resources to clean up neighborhoods, tear down abandoned houses, and improve schools. We want to reinvest in our community, rebuild neighborhoods and create a safe feeling. These things have an immediate impact on the people who have decided to be here. We want to make Flint a better place for people who already live in our community."

For Flint and many other cities, the problem starts with speculators lured by the prospect of get-rich-quick schemes based on no-money-down foreclosure acquisitions. A perfect lose/lose scenario for homeowners and their hometowns, it leads to evictions, loss of tax revenues, abandoned properties, declining neighborhoods and suburban flight. Everyone loses, including local businesses and community schools and churches. According to Kildee, here's why:

"Foreclosure destroys a city's tax base through goofy tax auctions. You've probably seen those ads that explain how to make money in real estate with no money down. If you didn't pay and were two years late on your tax bill, the city would sell a tax certificate for as little as $100 to some infomercial-watching, eBay-using speculator. If the owner came up with back taxes, the interest penalty went to the speculator. If he didn't, the speculator got the house and rented it for a few hundred dollars a month to a tenant who would be evicted if they missed a payment. Often the speculator would resell the property at a small profit, and the new owner would typically default. Once again Flint would take title to the property, sell to another speculator in a foreclosure auction and the entire cycle would repeat itself.

"For fifteen years," says Kildee, "properties circled through the old system. When we changed the legal system, the county took title and won the right to rehabilitate these abandoned houses that could be resold for up to one hundred thousand dollars. The income from these sales underwrites the Land Bank and allows us to rehabilitate more houses. Alternatively we demolish eyesores and sell the vacant lots to neighbors who annex the property and maintain it."

"We can take the worst house on the block and turn it into the best one. Unlike the foreclosure properties, where houses go into decline, this benefits the entire neighborhood. We have developed a system that preserves neighborhoods, redevelops vacant and abandoned urban land and protects homeowners from predatory speculators who won the right to evict people for just a small amount of back taxes." Flint put a stop to this process by unbundling the system, looking at all the laws governing this process and replacing predatory speculators with the Land Bank. "First," says Kildee, "instead of allowing foreclosure, we step in and put the owner into a program where they are held harmless. The Land Bank pays the back taxes and then works out a long-term, very low-interest repayment plan that insures owners can remain in their houses. Since the banks don't want to take back these properties, residents are virtually guaranteed they don't have to move.

"In five years the county has taken ownership of fifty-four hundred tax-foreclosed properties that would have gone in to the hands of speculators. Had we not rewritten the system, seventeen hundred families would have been subject to losing their homes. At the same time we aggressively go after those abandoned properties that are ruining the landscape of the city, the kinds of places that showed up in *Roger & Me*. And we've completed a mechanism to make the whole process completely self-financing for the county.

"Roughly ten to fifteen percent of the abandoned properties acquired by the Land Bank can be rehabilitated and sold. This income pays for the acquisition of additional commercial and residential sites that would have been lost to speculators. We use Brownfield financing from the government to pay for demolition and cleanup of abandoned sites," says Kildee.

"This work can easily be collateralized because the Land Bank owns a great deal of property with economic value. We have twenty-nine-hundred properties and a few hundred with economic resale value. The income and tax revenue from the houses we can sell allows us to pay for the demolition of houses that are eyesores. Those lots are then annexed by neighbors or community associations who maintain the area.

"Last year we had five-hundred-fifty vacant properties managed by neighbors. Rather than pay some contractor to mow the lawn and keep it free of debris, we pay people in the neighborhood through a block club. They are taking care of everything else, the property that is hurting them the most. Our Clean and Green program is a cool way for us to pay neighbors to take care of their own community.

"Today there are thirteen hundred families who previously lived next door to a burned out abandoned house that are now adjacent to a green garden or a pocket park. The job of the Land Bank is to take the land and transfer it to a new owner. The effect of that transaction is to improve the value of the neighborhood rather than take the value out.

"As I travel around the country, I find *Roger & Me* has helped make this a more dramatic innovation. Their impression is that if you can make urban land reform work in Flint, Michigan, they can do it in Little Rock, El Paso or Dayton. Knowing what they know about our city from Michael's movie, we are famous for vacant and abandoned property. It helps that people have an understanding of how bad things were in Flint."

Heading back to his office for a dinner appointment, Kildee is proud that Flint is slowly becoming a poster child for urban land reform. Already the Charles Stewart Mott Foundation is funding pilot projects in five other Michigan cities. And the story he tells around the state suggests why other cities and Washington's Brookings Institution are studying Flint's innovative answer to regressive property tax laws.

"Unless someone wants to lose the home they own in Flint, it's almost impossible to be evicted. We prevent homeowners from losing their property. I won't foreclose on them. I put them on a payment plan that strings out as long as you can imagine. Foreclosing on an owner-occupied property might get me some cash right now. But in the long run I am eating my seed capital.

"The impact of maintaining home ownership is measurable and positive. We also don't evict tenants who can't pay their rent. However we are aggressive about foreclosing on vacant and abandoned property. When we sell them the taxes go into a pot of money to pay for more demolition and more cleanup.

"Although Flint had a big loss in GM jobs, the city has not had a correlating income loss. Because the city's workforce was older, most of the workers left with a pension, health care or a retraining program at a job bank. There were also many substantial employee buyouts. What looked like a big cliff has been more like a downhill grade.

"The whole trend in our economy puts places like Flint in the crosshairs. We are just trying to figure out what we can do to make life more livable for people in this town. Part of our work is job generation. We try to make life a little bit better for people who have stuck it out in a neighborhood, sent their kids to school and done the right thing. We want to be sure they are not penalized by having to live next to some big abandoned house."

This comeback story that offers hope at the local level for creative communities willing to reform outdated tax codes, rewrite city ordinances and most important, keep speculators from preying on the poor. In a bipartisan spirit, both Republicans and Democrats have signed off on a progressive redevelopment program that does not rely on banks, traditionally reluctant to lend in economically depressed communities. Happily this program is also self financing.

"The old foreclosure system was designed for the agricultural economy," explains Kildee as he heads down into one of Flint's pretty neighborhoods where oaks provide a convenient canopy on this sunny afternoon. There are no crack houses here or derelict homes. Kids are playing ball on front lawns while their parents read the paper and chat on their cell phones. "It didn't work in a place like Flint. We have had to come to grips with a different kind of economy. Fifteen or twenty years ago people were just waiting for General Motors to announce they were going up to fifty thousand again. The message of *Roger & Me* in 1989 was not received very well by a lot of people who now understand its truth. Some people thought Michael's film hurt Flint. But it had the effect of getting people to focus on the fundamental economic problem. Life was only better for people making those GM wages. Everyone should have known those jobs weren't going to last. For the people who were not part of the GM largesse, life was very tough in Flint."

Fifteen minutes east of Flint, one of the most famous artists to come out of Davison, Michigan, the hardest working man in performance poetry offers another perspective on the heartbeat of America. John Sinclair, just in from Berkeley, California, is on hand at the Davison Eagles to emcee the first annual I Chews the Blues Festival. Like Dan Kildee, he takes a grassroots approach to political reform. But in his case the grass is smoked.

As a pig roasts on a barbecue spit, the blender crew whips up mango smoothies and the concession stands does a brisk business in Gatorade and Bud Light, John Sinclair is surrounded by old friends who haven't seen him since a 1989 high school reunion. It's a grand homecoming for Sinclair, a tall man with a stylish white goatee who will never forget the genius who introduced him to black music, Flint's WBBC disk jockey, Ernie "The Frantic One" Durham. "We're so glad you're here," says an admirer. "We're so proud of what you've done."

Greeted by his eldest daughter Sunny and granddaughter Beyonce, Sinclair is quickly surrounded by old friends and classmates eager for him to autograph his Blues Scholars CDs, books of poetry, memoir and a remarkable booklet-CD set published by the repository of the Sinclair Collection, the Bentley Historical Library at the University of Michigan. It was a good thing that Alvin Bentley, the conservative Republican Congressman (he was nearly killed in 1954 when four Puerto Rican nationalists opened fire on the House Floor, wounding him and four colleagues) never knew about this counterculture collection donated after his death.

The John Sinclair story, an archetypal journey of drugs and rock and roll along with plenty of doing it in the road, was the antithesis of University of Michigan Regent Bentley's world view. Biographer Cary Loren writes, "In 1963, 22-year-old John Sinclair ate a portion of peyote buttons (peyote was still legal then) and had his first psychedelic experience.

In the moment of the peyote experience he chronicled his trip in a small student notebook as *The Realization of Peyotemind and After*: 'Under peyote I realized the most profound truths of my life and I know that the realizations will stay with me and influence the course of my life.'

"Already primed with an appreciation of beat-era poetry, literature and jazz, Sinclair was now poised to help define the landscape of the unfolding '60s and stake his commitment within a support group of unified artists, musicians and writers. *Peyotemind* become an interior outline of thought and manifestation."

The old adage that "if you can remember the '60s you weren't really there" certainly did not apply to John Sinclair, a folk hero in Davison and beyond. The Johnny Appleseed of the marijuana movement and founder of Trans Love Energies, Sinclair nearly turned the '60s into a religious experience. His martyrdom in Jackson Prison and his path to freedom in the hands of John Lennon, Yoko Ono, Bob Seger, Stevie Wonder, Phil Ochs, Archie Shepp and other musicians, as well as poets like Allen Ginsberg, made him a Davison legend. But at the same time, the White Panther cofounder also recognized that recreational drugs were not a quick fix: "When Tim Leary told Jack Kerouac that LSD would change the world, Kerouac replied, 'Coach, walking on water wasn't built in a day.'"

Admiring well-wishers told him his passion had made them realize the error of their ways. "I was a campus young Republican when I first heard you speak," one autograph seeker told him while the Rusty Write Blues Band performed in the background. "Your poetry and talk got me thinking, and now I'm on the other side."

"Thank you," said Sinclair. "I am so glad you're here."

The poet's crusade to liberalize marijuana laws was also praised by other fans pleased to see he was selling a new book by former White Panther leader Pun Plamondon. "Glad to know he's not selling for Amway," said one man as he headed over to the smoothie line.

For Sinclair, who opened the show reading poetry backed up by the blues music of fellow Davison native Mark Adams and the Fabulous Windbreakers, the festival was an emotional homecoming. Now on the road performing more than six months of the year at clubs, concert halls, bars and college venues, Sinclair lived and worked in New Orleans for 12 years after leaving Michigan in 1991. After George Bush and Dick Cheney won the 2000 election, Sinclair decided to become an expatriate blues scholar. He moved to Amsterdam, where his online radio show broadcasts from local cannabis clubs. He's found a welcoming audience for his work across Europe in clubs and art galleries. And in Sinclair's eyes, permissive Dutch drug laws are the bomb.

Although he has been ahead of his times in many ways, Sinclair has never been a slave to popular culture. The former president of the University of Michigan Flint's film society seldom sees movies. "They aren't making the old kind of Fellini, Goddard films, interesting movies about life." The last feature film he took in was Clint Eastwood's *Bird*, the 1988 Oscar-winning biopic on the life of jazz legend Charles Parker. A year later he also caught *Roger & Me*: "I admire Michael Moore. He works in this hostile field where the only reason they let him do it is he makes money."

Sinclair is also down on the networks and cable. "I really don't like television, being absorbed by someone else's thing. I can do a lot in two hours, read newspapers, write, listen to music. Turn off the TV is what I say. It surrounds people with an artificial environment. You have no idea of its effect. It's carefully selected to sell you things. It replaces other emotional events in your life with how you'll feel about owning a new car. It's the bad driving out the good."

Turning to the crowd, a lively mix of kids, teens, college students, families and senior citizens, Sinclair feels at home in his hometown. "This is my idea of a great festival. People who you never heard of playing and having fun. This isn't about business, it's about playing music for your friends. No one is making a million. I don't give a fuck about someone who has a million because they are different. They worry about their taxes. I am still focused on how I get dinner just like the average person in America."

Unlike other band leaders, Sinclair doesn't travel with an entourage. The makeup of his Blues Scholars group depends on his venue du jour. At each show he relies on old friends to join him for live performances where he reads his poetry.

"I've spent ten years trying to figure out how to do it." The result is a considerable distance from rap music which he dismisses as "third grade Mother Goose rhymes done with a machine gun. Walt Whitman got rid of rhymes a hundred and fifty years ago. Rap is Negroes acting bad before an audience that is seventy percent suburban whites who don't like poetry."

Sinclair's decision to move to Amsterdam is his personal protest against the Bush administration. "Look at the way the Republican brain trust bullied the Democrats into dropping the recount and the Supreme Court locked Bush into place. Then he goes around the world fomenting war and calls it democracy. That's one of the reasons Bush people and the big corporations hate Michael Moore. They hate him because he is powerful in the realm of ideas where no one else has any. They want you to be stupid. If you can demonize a whole population you can get away with anything. That way when they say go invade Iraq, people will say, 'Good, I'll send my son.'

"Moore goes against the grain in a country where you can buy a Congressman for two hundred thousand dollars. The President doesn't cost a whole lot more. What it's all about is less people getting more money. Now they don't want to pay taxes.

"Moore chose movies because people want to watch movies. He makes a difference because his films are different. I'm not a threat because when I got out of prison I chose poetry."

In several important ways Sinclair shares Moore's political and artistic interests. "Vote Democratic," he says, "that's a good first step. We've got to get these thugs out of office. They wanted to impeach Clinton for a blow job. But when Bush blows up Afghanistan and Iraq, that's no crime."

While he doesn't go to the movies, Sinclair has been coproducing a film with Steve Gebhardt since 1991. It's called *The Life and Times Of John Sinclair.* For Gebhardt, who has produced documentaries on the Rolling Stones and John Lennon, the project is a cultural overview of the '60s and the decade's most famous marijuana bust. An earlier Gebhardt project, *Ten For Two,* focused on the 1971 John Sinclair Freedom Rally in Ann Arbor. Although the film was briefly released in Britain, it was never shown in America because of the John Lennon deportation proceedings.

Assisting Gebhardt by doing research, transcribing dialogue and scoring the documentary, Sinclair has also helped raise money for the project. After raising $50,000 in finishing money, the producers are busy marketing the project for a 2007 release.

"We couldn't get it accepted at film festivals," says Sinclair. "There is a scene near the end where people in Amsterdam are laughing and smoking one ounce joints. This isn't what they are looking for. They like films about people who are fucked up. They don't want people who are unrepentant. I don't think the movie will be a success. The grandfather of recreational drugs is not what they are looking for today."

As the blues bands play into the warm Davison night and Harley riders roll more joints, Sinclair digs into another pork barbecue sandwich. Is there a chance that he might be able to find hometown backing for his film project? "Actually," he says, "we did approach Michael Moore's foundation. When I applied I thought he would give us some money. I was shocked when he didn't reply."

Was it possible that the Davison filmmaker ignored the poet because he doesn't like to get high with a little help from his friends?

Sinclair shakes his head: "That explains it. I can't believe I never thought of that. Moore doesn't do drugs."

AFTERWORD

A to Z—Where Are They Now?

Osama bin Laden remains at large.

Anne Bohlen teaches film at Antioch University in Yellow Springs, Ohio. She is also working on a documentary about the atomic energy industry in Ohio.

George W. Bush won a second term, appointed two conservative justices to the Supreme Court, claimed that a $283 billion projected deficit for 2006 proved his tax cuts were working, vetoed federal funding of stem cell research and attended but did not speak at the funeral of one of his most generous campaign contributors, white collar criminal of the decade Ken Lay.

Alexander Cockburn, columnist for *The Nation,* writes on a computer. He is the co-editor of *Counterpunch* which *Out of Bounds Magazine* has called "America's Best Political Newsletter." This website offers a kaleidoscopic view of national and international issues from a leftist perspective. *Counterpunch* Books include *The Case Against Israel.* Leader of the pack, Cockburn suggested Moore lives in a "stew of self-aggrandizing hypocrisy in which you've been marinating for years." After reminding Moore of his willingness to plead his case after the *Mother Jones* firing, Cockburn mentioned the autographed books sent to his old friend. "To Alex," read the inscription on *Downsize This,* "You were there when it mattered and when few others were. I will never forget that." "Yes indeed," said Cockburn, "I was there when it mattered and this lends a certain strength to my response and to what I would write in my next book if I felt like sending you one, namely 'To Michael—who has never been there when it mattered.'"

Bruce Dancis is the entertainment editor of the *Sacramento Bee.* Reporters for his section have favorably covered Moore's films and interviewed the director on several occasions. "Moore tells them he has a lot of respect for the fact that I was a draft resister," says Dancis. "And he's also mentioned that getting fired from *Mother Jones* was one of the best things that ever happened to him."

John Derevlany lives in Culver City, California, not far from the Sony lot. He is busy writing animated shows, primarily Canadian and European coproductions, for children include *Wayside School* on Nickelodeon and *Gerald McBoing Boing* for the Cartoon Network. He also has a ukulele website. Derevlany believes that writing for kids makes sense because, in a sense, it's too late to reach adults. "They really are our best hope."

Gideon Evans left his job at *The Daily Show* in 2005 to make TV pilots including one for the Comedy Channel with *Supersize Me* star Morgan Spurlock.

Mel Gibson killed his chances for another shot at *Time*'s Man of the Year honor in July 2006, when he launched into an anti-Semitic tirade against a police officer who pulled him over on Malibu's Pacific Coast Highway. Gibson apologized for his Jew-hating remarks and also said he felt bad about hitting 87 mph in a 45 mph zone.

Kathleen Glynn, who remains Michael Moore's producing partner, told the *Flint Journal*'s Ed Bradley she is not jealous of her husband. "At a certain point, you buy a car from a salesman, and you don't think about the 200 people who made the car. You see a movie or a TV show, and there's the star of the show and the other things are kind of seamless. You don't recognize them, and you're not supposed to."

Busy with her own production company, Blue Lake Films, she is developing two films. *Local DJ*, the autobiography of Flint radio star and Michigan band promoter Peter C. Cavanaugh, is characterized as "*Almost Famous* meets *Woodstock* . . ." In addition she is busy with a script about Marlon Brando's formative years. Glynn's charitable work for breast cancer is another passion. Her impressive art bra was auctioned off at an Alden, Michigan benefit. She also exhibited her quilts at a Flint exhibition benefiting the Way to Women's Wellness Foundation.

Ben Hamper lives in Suttons Bay Michigan, a short drive from Michael Moore and Kathleen Glynn's Torch Lake home. His turn-ons include "isolation, Latina's Pizza (Flint), Catholic girls, happy hour, Lou's Bar (Sutton's Bay) . . . .and beer frames."

Adam Hochschild's *King Leopold's Ghost* sold over 300,000 copies and became a documentary. It is also in development as a feature film. His *Bury The Chains* was a finalist for the National Book Award.

Dan Kildee, treasurer of Flint, Michigan and head of the city's Land Bank, is spreading the word on the city's innovative program at cities around the country.

Phil Knight has been named the 70th richest man in America by *Forbes Magazine*. With a net worth of $7.3 billion, he is also the wealthiest shoe salesman on the planet. Nike and its sister lines control 40 percent of the nation's athletic shoe market. The company continues to make its shoes outside the United States and has no plans to open a factory in Flint, Michigan.

Jerry Kupfer's new sitcom, *30 Rock*, starring Tina Fey and Alec Baldwin, debuted in the fall of 2006 as NBC continued its drive to pull itself out of the network ratings basement. The program focuses on behind the scenes life at *Friday Night Bits*, a late night TV comedy show.

Warren Littlefield was stunned in 1999 when his superiors at General Electric ". . . overlooked all" his "good work . . . when circumstances beyond my control caused NBC to stumble. That's all right, I tried to tell myself, GE's strength is making toasters and jet turbines, not 'must-see TV.' Still, their ingratitude stung me like one of Jay Leno's trenchant monologue jokes on *The Tonight Show* program I helped to revitalize." He left the network to join Barry Diller and Bill Gates to create Sony TV. Eager to head off on his own, he then formed the Littlefield Company based at the Paramount TV, before relocating to Touchstone Television, a division of the Walt Disney Company. In the spring of 2006, his company completed *Our Thirties,* a pilot about a group of San Francisco friends making their way through life in their 30s.

Would it make sense for Moore to return to network or cable TV today? "Television never precludes you from also doing movies, and with a successful television base you wonder how many more millions of people would have seen the movies which are really important, powerful films. When I looked at *Columbine* and *9/11,* I said, 'Wow, how brave Michael Moore is.' He was so far out in front of the rest of the country today. Looking at Bush's disapproval ratings, the horrific track record of this administration, the number of lies, the deceit of people who have been a part of Bush's administration and the number of people who have fled, it's clear Michael was years ahead of the rest of the country. I myself as a registered independent found myself not wanting to be critical of Bush at the time. I was hoping that he was a leader who could take us through this national tragedy and that here was a leader with wisdom and truth and guidance. Michael said, 'No I am going to show you another side of the story.' Today we realize just how out in front of the American public he was and how many resented him for being so bold and outspoken.

"The seeds of *Columbine* and *Fahrenheit 9/11* can all be found in *TV Nation.* It all comes down to his appetite. Clearly he has established a strong basis in the theatrical market. If he wants to do television that door will be open to him for quite some time. It's a grind and you better be unbelievably passionate about not sleeping if you want to feed a monster called television. The creative demands are enormous and from the outside looking in it may appear to be a fun exciting and glamorous life. The fact of the matter is it is like running a marathon every day. The ultimate thank-you is 'I want you to keep making shows.'"

Conrad Martin, director of the Stewart R. Mott Charitable Trust, continues to receive a large number of grant proposals from aspiring filmmakers for "Michael Moore style documentaries." He has turned the phrase "Michael Moore interview" into an adjective like a "Ken Burns interview." It's the bumbling amateurish ambush interview. Still based at the Mott House across the street from the capitol, Martin continued to be an eyewitness to history. In early 2006, right-to-life marchers were being picketed by pro choice advocates including one wearing a coat hanger on top of her hat, inexplicably hung up in a chain link fence guarding the capitol area. At his desk he recalled a Michael Moore talk at a Nation Institute dinner where the celebrity was greeted with catcalls when he suggested the audience was "delusional if you think Bush would change reproductive rights. There is no difference between Bush and the Democratic Party." Martin believes that despite Moore's inexplicable lapses in judgment like this one "the good he has done far outweighs the bad."

The Mott Foundation director believes that the failure of Moore's campaign to oust Bush suggests that *The Big One*'s rhetoric plays better abroad than it does at home. Martin finds that Moore is "worshipped in Europe because he feeds into the European view of trailer trash Americans. Like Woody Allen, the American iconoclast does much better in Europe. The response to his documentaries helped form the European sensibility of America."

Unfortunately, in the United States, one of the ironies is that Moore, "pisses off blue collar people even though he defends them. Blue collar organizers have problems with the way Michael is portraying blue collar people, i.e., killing rabbits for food." Another problem is the fact that some swing voters see Bush as a "dumb f*** like me. I don't want someone smarter than me to be president. I will vote for people who understand me . . . People do not like being talked down to."

An additional problem is that many younger Americans don't understand what they are being asked to give up. "Pro-choice has floundered with a new generation of women who don't understand what it is like to be without that right."

Stewart Mott divides his time between homes in suburban New York and Bermuda, Mott continues to fund charitable activities through his Washington based foundation. Areas of special interest include investigative journalism, the environment, nuclear energy and abortion rights.

Jim Musselman, president of Appleseed Records in West Chester, Pennsylvania produces recording artists such as Pete Seeger, Holly Near, Donovan, Tom Paxton, Jack Elliott, Christine Lavin, John Wesley Harding and many promising young artists. Appleseed's five-CD "Songs of Pete Seeger Set" includes Bruce Springsteen, Ani DiFranco, Bonnie Raitt, Joan Baez, Judy Collins, Arlo Guthrie and Tim Robbins in his singing debut. Musselman helped Bruce Springsteen produce his 2006 *Seeger Sessions* CD, which some critics called the Boss's best work in recent years. Independently financed with no outside corporate backing, Appleseed donates a percentage of its profits to charitable causes, including $150,000 from the Seeger set. He is currently working on another project with Springsteen.

Ralph Nader is still typing on his trusty manual Underwood he used to pound out the manuscript for *Unsafe At Any Speed* and refusing to write on a computer. "It's my little reminder of the false promise of modern technology. One hundred and twenty years ago, citizens of the United States didn't have cars, phones or even email or faxes. Blackberries grew wild on bushes. And yet, a group of living breathing human beings, starting with poor farmers in west Texas in the late 1880s banded together to challenge the forces of darkness, the giant banks and railroad companies. It was what historian Lawrence Goodwyn called the Populist Moment. Thousands of farmers alliances built into a nationwide movement of more than 2 million people that shook the political and economic system to its core. Instead of the Internet, the word was spread through a series of lecturers, people speaking directly with people. And according to Professor Goodwyn, it was the last time we've seen such a grassroots challenge to the economic and political system in the United States. Despite all of our lovely web sites and hand-held devices and ringtones on our cell phones and 400 channels on our DirecTV and instant access messages and . . . Despite all of this where are we. . . ? As long as the ribbons hold out, I'll continue to write my books and letters and ideas on my Underwood." For supporters willing to donate $100 toward retirement of his 2004 "civil liberties debt incurred fighting off the corporate Democrats who drove to push us off the ballot in many states" Nader is delighted to "sit down at my manual Underwood typewriter and type to you a personal thank you note" and send it to you along with a copy of Professor Lawrence Goodwyn's *The Populist Moment*.

Bernard Ohanion is a magazine editor working in Washington D.C.

Reverend Fred Phelps of Topeka, Kansas leads his extended family on picket lines at the funerals of Iraq war veterans from coast to coast. He believes that America's decision to turn the country "over to fags" is the reason God is sending our soldiers "home in body bags." After the Michigan legislature banned picketing of military funerals, Phelps retreated from that state which lost more than 60 men and women in Operation Iraqi Freedom.

John Pierson teaches film at the University of Texas. In 2005 he starred with his family in the documentary *Reel Paradise*. It tells the story of their move to Fiji where they opened the island's only movie theater and showed films gratis. The film was directed by *Hoop Dream*'s Steve James and executive produced by Kevin Smith, the director of *Clerks*. Many of the clients who benefited from Pierson's representation over the years generously supported the project. Michael Moore was not among them. When Pierson called to ask for help, his old friend from *Roger & Me* days said, "I can't believe this is happening." In the fall of 2006, on his way to deliver a keynote address at an independent filmmaker's conference in Los Angeles, Pierson reflected on Moore's conspicuous absence from the midterm elections. "It's a wonderful irony that the Democrats are taking over and he's nowhere in sight."

Staff Sgt. Raymond J. Plouhar, the Flint Marine recruiter from Lake Orion, Michigan featured in *Fahrenheit 9/11*, died from wounds suffered in a June 2006 roadside bombing in Iraq's Al Anbar province. Plouhar, who had left active duty to become a recruiter after he donated a kidney to his uncle, loved the Marines. "I remember when he fell in the bathtub and cut his chin when he was seven years old," said his father. "The only way I could get him to go to the hospital was to tell him it was a MASH unit."

Kevin Rafferty is currently working on a documentary about the rise of the American conservative movement told in cinema verité style. He has a special interest in America from 1946 to 1954 before "the conservatives seized control of the megaphone from the Democrats. This was a seminal moment. I remember when the *Howdy Doody Show* was crowded off television because of the Army-McCarthy hearings. I was pissed off because I couldn't watch Howdy Doody" along with Buffalo Bob Smith, Clarabell and Princess Summerfall Winterspring.

Among Rafferty's favorite historical vignettes on the project is the story of Harry Truman's whistle-stop campaign in 1948 when "one hundred out of one hundred papers said Tom Dewey was going to win. They weren't sure he could pay the train fare when he rode out to California and was met by Lauren Bacall and Ronald Reagan." Rafferty says that if "I played my cards right, I could have been the head of FEMA." But he has no regrets about failing to line up politically with his uncle George Herbert Walker Bush or cousin George W. "In my own family there are five siblings, two are social workers and all five are left wing activists. None of us are Republicans."

Rafferty believes that Michael Moore's success reflects a major shift in the American economy. "America used to make autos. Now we make intellectual property. We are still good at making movies. Everyone and their cousin is a documentary maker. Film schools are springing up everywhere. Because of Michael there is now a great interest in theatrical distribution. My hat is off to the guy. I have had a pleasant working relationship with him." Rafferty has no regrets about bartering Moore's work on *Blood In The Face* for his work with Anne Bohlen on *Roger & Me* (particularly after Moore helped arrange a $25,000 grant for a Rafferty film with a single phone call). But he adds, in retrospect, "we should have exchanged points."

Gini Reticker was nominated in 2004 for an Oscar for *Asylum* and an Emmy for *A Decade Under the Influence*. She continues to focus on women's issues. Her film about Muslim women training to become Morocco's first female religious leaders, *The Class of 2006*, aired on PBS's *Wide Angle*.

Meg Reticker's busy editing schedule included *Come Early Morning* about a southern woman's restless search for romance against the backdrop of her many burdens.

James Ridgeway, Washington correspondent for *Mother Jones*, is the author of *Five Unanswered Questions About 9/11*.

Natalie Rose's July 2006 wedding at a Traverse City, Michigan bed and breakfast brought tears to the eyes of her mother, Kathleen Glynn, who designed the bridal gown. Stepfather Michael Moore offered her politically conservative father Wallace Rose an opportunity to switch positions on the walk down the aisle. But Rose rejected Moore's suggestion that he take Natalie's left arm, while Michael escorted her from the right. "I've got my reputation to protect," said Rose.

Fred Ross continues to work as a deputy sheriff in Flint, Michigan.

Roger Smith is retired and lives near Detroit.

Douglas Urbanski, described by others as a "raconteur and impresario," and self described as a "Catholic, Conservative, Capitalist," has produced films such as *The Contender*, which starred Gary Oldman, Jeff Bridges, Joan Allen, Christian Slater and Sam Elliot (two Academy Award Nominations, winner Special Excellence Award from the Broadcast Critics Association) and *Nil by Mouth*, written and directed by Gary Oldman (Cannes Film Festival Winner, also of two British Academy Awards: Outstanding British Film and Best Screenplay). In addition to his other films, Urbanski was one of the top stage producers in the world during the 1980s, with his plays receiving over 30 Tony Award nominations and winning many other prizes and acclaim. Currently he is preparing for production on *Chang & Eng,* a feature film written and directed by Gary Oldman. Besides advising celebrities and those in political life, he has also become the nation's busiest and most sought-after guest host for conservative talk radio programs. During 2006 he spoke on national radio, delivering his own brand of political analysis, theology and cultural explanation, routinely filling in for the likes of Laura Ingraham, Michael Savage, Tammy Bruce, Rusty Humphries and Jerry Doyle

David Wald is managing producer at Learning Matters, where he creates documentaries used in education.

Matt Zawisky, the Nader advance man and organizer, studied the possibility of the progressive left coming up with a viable third-party candidate who would actually qualify for the debates. He was intrigued by Moore's talk of a double assault where the left took over the Democratic party and, on a parallel track, launched a viable third-party ticket. Could this third party actually help push America back toward core values like national health care and a decent minimum wage? Might it be the secret weapon for Americans who no longer want neocons, paleocons and white collar cons cutting the deck?

Is it possible that Moore, the filmmaker and Nader, the troublemaker, could emerge as a viable ticket in 2008? For Moore, who has dismissed talk that he might be presidential or vice-presidential kindling, the idea is ridiculous. But Zawisky thinks "a Nader/Moore ticket would be terrific. Michael has proven that he can bring people to the polls through his movies. It's like Schwarzenegger, The Terminator. The toughest part is getting people to vote. It's much different than building a viable progressive/ populist movement. The hardest part is getting past five percent, which gets you the campaign money, the media and of course the debates. Once you get past five percent, it's like a snowball. People want to be with a winner, and its easier to be perceived as a winner when you are at 15 or 20 percent. Those kinds of numbers would do a hell of a lot more than a couple of Democratic presidencies. It would help push the trajectory to the left, and the Democrats would have to respond more to Ralph's platform. It would be the best ticket in the sort of political culture we are in. It would be very beneficial for Ralph's message. It fills that celebrity void and can balance the money situation and open the doors to the media and the debates. It is going to take another generation to build a sustainable third party, and we have to keep a long-term focus before this will come to fruition. There would be a lot more traction because of the scandals."

Would Moore, who doubted that Americans would vote for a candidate running on the "eat out more often" platform, be game? "It remains to be seen. I think he kind of changes with the political winds. If Michael would come on board for the people, it would be huge."

Anne Zill is the Director of the Center for Ethics in Action at the University of New England, which promotes women's leadership and a different set of ethics than those currently in vogue at the top levels of government and industry. She is also the President of the Fund for Constitutional Government and an advisor to the Stewart R. Mott Charitable Trust.

Zill is also the director of the Art Gallery at the University of New England and has curated two exhibitions at the United Nations, *The Progress of the World's Women* and *The Ingredients of Peace*.

She is "interested in the connection between our right and left brains, the rational and the instinctive, the linear and the creative. I think people learn best when both lobes are engaged, the right allowing the promise of transformation. And human beings need it badly if we are to avoid the destruction of our planet before we've moved beyond. We do have in us our own gods as it were, since our brains are big, but not if we allow the destructive elements of our nature to dominate. I am one of those connectors in life who is aware of the need for good human beings to connect with others of like mind."

THINK ABOUT WHAT YOU'VE DONE

"I want people to worry and be happy."

—*Michael Moore*

IN AN ERA OF INSTANT MESSAGING and Bluetooth equipped commuters resembling secret service agents, Michael Moore wants to have a word with you. He'd like you to join him on his latest house call to the powers that be. And in the process he will share many of the unpleasant secrets that corporate executives, politicians and bureaucrats would prefer to keep locked in a safe.

In what has become the media's longest coming of age story, Michael Moore has blended his reportorial gifts with a wacky sense of humor that has astonished and delighted audiences from Davison, Michigan, to the White House. Like Lance Armstrong and Woody Allen, he is a celebrity in Europe. And from Cannes to Telluride, his moviemaking remains an inspiration to a generation of young directors. Even his victims have to crack a smile when they have a look at his satire which has inspired, outraged and confounded his many friends and enemies. He is hard to ignore and even harder to explain.

Moore's own problems—his inability to save Flint, Michigan, get assault rifles off the street, stop widespread corporate crime or defeat George Bush—are the classic investigative reporter's lament. Even his success stories, like persuading K-Mart to remove guns and ammo from its shelves, aren't clear-cut when you realize that this decision triggered a boycott that helped push the chain into Chapter 11 bankruptcy.

As I researched and wrote this book, it was clear to me that the story Michael Moore has offered movie audiences around the world has little to do with his own story, the one he has chosen not to tell. The narrative addressed in these pages is not your average celebrity biography. Like an archaeological dig, it required a look at court records in Sierra Blanca, Texas, interviews with members of the audience at his memorable one-and-a-half-man show in London (get it, a guy who takes up 1.5 seats!), a visit to the Sisters of St. Joseph Mother House in Nazareth Michigan, a trip to the Disney studios in Burbank, California, talks with Ralph Nader and editors at *Mother Jones* magazine, visits to Moore's extended media family in places like Culver City, California, Brooklyn and Washington, D.C., as well as a trip down memory lane in Flint, Michigan.

This journey included more than 200 interviews with agents, managers, producers, publicists, bosses, personal friends, colleagues, editors, actors, journalists, teachers, office managers and employees who were in the room when many of the incidents described in these pages took place. Most of them had never spoken publicly about Moore in the past. Some decided to go public after years of refusing interviews. And in this, the era of background, deep background and off the record interviews, it's a pleasure to report that nearly all of these sources insisted on being quoted. Some even shared their personal archives, determined to make sure that their stories based on written records, notes, video, audio and reminiscences became part of *Citizen Moore*. Collectively their accounts create a drama as intriguing and complicated as any Michael Moore movie.

Journalists tend to look to the future and are often wary of sitting down and reviewing their past, thinking about what it is they've done. History is a convenient way to underscore a point, but personal history is another matter. Moore's mistakes, some of them chronicled in this book, remind us of a fact he doesn't like to acknowledge: Like many of the people he attacks in his work, our nation's most prominent gadfly is a victim of his own success story. The director's errors demonstrate how easy it is to undermine his own best efforts.

For his millions of fans around the world, there is nothing quite like a cinematic moment with the filmmaker. For some his work verges on the hypnotic. The extraordinary group of people who lent their talents to this project have helped me go beyond Moore's official biography, his films, books and public letters, to shed light on many of the unanswered questions about Michael Moore. And in the process, I hope, this book shreds some of the myths about the so-called liberal/conservative debate in this country. As Moore's own shifting politics demonstrate, Americans on the left and right have engineered compromises that benefit no one. A case in point is George Bush's No Child Left Behind Act, where both the Democrats and the Republicans are on the wrong side as they work to close down tens of thousands of public schools to the detriment of children from Anchorage to Tallahassee.

Perhaps the director's most important achievement has been documenting the way politicians put their campaign contributors' immediate needs ahead of what's best for constituents. At the same time, Michael Moore has been unable to remain true to a single political movement. Like any good performer, he knows how to hold the interest of a crowd. But his short attention span is glued to the headlines, the next big thing, whether it's the Columbine High School killings, the 9/11 attacks, or Hurricane Katrina. Because he seizes on convenient issues, Moore, like any good politician, remains a newsmaker. But his inability to stick with a winning concept like Crackers the Crime Fighting Chicken or a supportive network like NBC demonstrates that he has difficulty remaining part of any campaign that is not built around him.

Moore's reportorial gift, illuminating the weaknesses of our political and corporate life through satire, reminds us that entertainment is a core value in a democracy. If we can't laugh at our leaders and get away with it, we might as well be living in a police state. But there is a big difference between telling a good joke and being one. While this director is better at providing colorful answers than asking questions, there is no doubt that in the years ahead he will remain one of the most important figures on the American political scene. Or to borrow a post-Katrina phrase from New Orleans writer Chris Rose, he would rather be part of the problem than part of solutions that don't work well.

Driving past his imposing home on Michigan's Torch Lake at the end of a Labor Day holiday, I thought about what Michael Moore has done for and to America. Secure in an uncertain economy, living in one of the nation's finest resort areas, not far from Ernest Hemingway's boyhood vacation home on Walloon Lake, he was no doubt working hard on his film about the American health care industry. Like every other story he has worked on, it will doubtless be rich with villains and victims. Finding someone to blame for your difficulties remains his unique artistic achievement.

NOTES

Looking for Michael in All the Wrong Places

1. Listen, a picture: Gabler, Neal. *An Empire of Their Own* (New York: Anchor Books, 1988), p. 189.
1. My first conversation: Author's interview with Douglas Urbanski, Los Angeles.

A Kodak Moment with the Dixie Chicks

2. I want to take out an ad: U.S. Comedy Arts Festival, Aspen, Colorado, March 3, 2003.
4. For United Artists chief . . .: Author's interview with John Pierson, Austin, Texas.
5. As he began walking down: Michael Moore, Paul Wellstone Award Ceremony Flint, Michigan Nov. 20, 2005.
5. He began hearing voices: *Ibid.*
6. Backstage Moore heard: Michael Moore, Toronto Film Festival, Elgin Theater, Sept. 8, 2006.
7. Signs had been plastered: Paul Wellstone Award Ceremony Acceptance Speech, Flint, Michigan Nov. 20, 2005.
7. For one thing: Binelli, Mark, "Michael Moore's Patriot Act," *Rolling Stone,* Sept. 16, 2004.
8. Believe me these media: *Bowling For Columbine* DVD commentary, 2003.
9. Moore denied rumors: *Los Angeles Times,* Dec. 22, 2004.
9. Maybe you've just been told: *Mike's Letter,* Feb. 3, 2006. http://www.michaelmoore.com/words/message/index.php?messageDate=2006-02-03.
9. We have an image problem: *Los Angeles Times,* Dec 22. 2004.
11. It's no fun being targeted: *Ibid.*
11. Why would you be afraid: Paul Wellstone Award Ceremony.
11. On a single October day: *Ibid.*
12. *Canadian Bacon* fan: Author interview with Josh Bricker.

Father Doesn't Know Best

18. What is good: Hirsch, E.D., et. al., *The New Dictionary of Cultural Literacy,* second edition (Boston: Houghton Mifflin, 1998), p. 457

18. Moores of Dublin: *Mike's Letter,* June 6, 2000. http://www.michael-moore.com/words/message/index.php?messageDat e=2000-06-06.

19. In 1947 she met Frank: *Ibid.*

19. Dressed in full bishop regalia: Reeves, Thomas. *America's Bishop* (San Francisco: Encounter Books, 2001), pp. 224-231.

20. Like Soupy: Sales, Soupy, *Soupy Sez* (New York: M. Evans, 2001, p.140)

20. They began a program to adopt: Moore, Michael. *Downsize This.* (New York: Crown, 1996).

20. Equally important, the nuns: Author's interview with Sister Mary Ellen Gondeck and Sister Janet Kurtz, Nazareth, Michigan.

21. At St. John The Evangelist: *Ibid.*

21. He is a special child: *Ibid.*

21. One of the sisters marched the children: Moore, Michael, *The Awful Truth: The Complete DVD Set* (New York: New Media Group, 2003)

22. A friend, Doug Crim: *Michigan Voice,* Oct. 1984.

22. He also decided: Moore, Michael. Stupid White Men (New York: Reagan Books, 2002), pp. 95-100.

22. He attempted to produce: *Ibid.*

23. During St. John's faculty meetings: Author's interview with Sister Mary Ellen Gondeck, Nazareth, Michigan.

23. Moore's English teacher: Author's interview with John Sinclair, Davison, Michigan.

24. While Detroit was famous: *Ibid.*

24. The high-powered: Loren, Cary in *John Sinclair and The Culture of The Sixties* (Ann Arbor: Bentley Historical Library, 2004) pp. 13-23.

25. Michael Moore has frequently claimed that he decided to leave St. Paul's seminary because the fathers would not let him listen to Detroit Tigers baseball games, including the World Series. In a Saginaw, Michigan, interview with the author, Monsignor Francis Murray, who taught at St. Paul's during Moore's seminary year, explained that the students were allowed to listen to Tigers games on weekends.

25. Another challenge was: Michael Moore, Toronto Film Festival, Elgin Theater, September 8, 2006.

25. He gets the point across: *Flint Journal,* June 22, 1970.

25. Not long after: Associated Press, June 27, 1971.

26. And at Davison High: Moore, *Stupid White Men,* pp. 95-100

26. Lennon, making his: Weiner, Jon. *Gimme Some Truth* (Berkeley: University of California Press, 2000)

26. After he died: Moore, *Stupid White Men,* pp. 95-100.

27. Another problem: *Flint Journal,* Feb. 6, 1974.

28. Critics peppered him: *Flint Journal,* Mar. 27, 1979.

28. The citizens of Davison: *Mike's Letter,* Dec. 12, 1999. http://www.mich-aelmoore.com/words/message/index.php?message Date=1999-12-12.

28. One of his critics: Marchese, John, "Me: The Continuing Adventures of Michael Moore," *Esquire,* January 1993.

29. You know in my: *Arcata Eye,* Mar. 3, 2002.

30. He didn't work well: Author's interview with Rachel Haneline, Davison, Michigan.

30. In any dynamic society: Author's interviews with Dan Kildee, Flint and Muskegon, Michigan.

32. But attempts to relocate: *Flint Journal,* Jan. 11, 1977.

32. We are tired: *Flint Voice,* Sept. 16, 1977

33. Davison is a fairly: Author's interviews with Dan Kildee.

34. Where do you think: *Free To Be,* Mar. 22, 1977 and *Michigan Voice,* July 17, 1981.

35. Al Hirvela: *Michigan Voice,* April 1986

37. When I was going . . ." Author's interviews with Dan Kildee.

38. When a check: *Flint Voice,* Sept. 24, 1977 and author's interviews with Dan Kildee.

38. I make my living: Hamper, Ben. *Rivethead* (New York: Warner Books, 1991), p. xi.

39. When I hear: *Flint Voice,* Mar. 14, 1981.

40. Every time the Detroit Tigers: *Michigan Voice,* Aug. 1985.

41. Moore's decision to go: Author's interview with John Sinclair.

42. One evening in the: Author's interview with Wallace Rose, Flint.

43. To him weeklies: Michael Moore's letter of application to *Mother Jones* magazine Dec. 26, 1985.

43. The government paid him $25,000: *Michigan Voice.*

43. What this place lacks in ambiance: Hamper, *Rivethead,* p. 103.

44. I'd make sure: Hamper. *Rivethead,* p.184.

44. We came from Michigan: *Michigan Voice,* July 1985.

45. We are told once again: *Michigan Voice,* Oct. 1984.

46. I started the *Voice: Michigan Voice,* Aug. 1985.

46. Eager to explain why: Democrats: *Ibid.*

47. In the last ten minutes: *Michigan Voice,* Sept. 1985.

"They Have Planted A Microphone In My Bra And I Can't Get It Out"

49. Stewart complained: Author's interview with Stewart Mott, North Salem, New York.

49. Unhappy with his son's politics: *Ibid.*

49. Are you kidding: *Ibid.*

50. Nixon hated Stewart Mott: Author's interview with Conrad Martin, Washington, D.C.

50. Stewart has half the brains: Author's interview with Stewart Mott.

50. One morning in 1984: Author's interview with Anne Zill, New York.

51 The low point: *Ibid.*

52. They have planted: Author's interview with James Ridgeway, New York.

53. The writer's: Ridgeway, James, "Car Design and Public Safety," *The New Republic,* Sept. 19, 1964.

54. When Mussleman released: Author's interviews with Jim Musselman, Philadelphia and West Chester, Pennsylvania.

57. I told Michael: *Ibid.*

57. Armed with a bullhorn: *Oakland Press,* Sept. 28, 1985.

58. We went to his home: Author's interview Jim Musselman.

Thank's (sic) for Asking If I'm Interested in Being Editor of *Mother Jones*

59. Muckraking is like: Paul Jacobs comment to author, San Francisco, 1974.

60. When the new editor: Author's interview with Bruce Dancis, Sacramento, California.

61. You have been publishing: Author's interviews with Bernard Ohanion, Washington, D.C.

62. At it's best: Hochschild, Adam: "The Second Decade Begins," *Mother Jones,* July/August 1986.

63. Sometimes people are less heard: Author's interviews with Jim Musselman.

63. Dear Adam: Michael Moore's letter of application to *Mother Jones.*

65. We had an hour: Author's interview with Bruce Dancis.

66. Michael Moore will miss: *Flint Journal,* Feb. 27, 1986.

67. I'm drowning: *Flint Journal,* Feb. 10, 1986.

67. As an agnostic: *Michigan Voice,* April 1986.

68. Who ya gonna call: Michael Moore's letter of application to *Mother Jones.*

69. I have got Michael Moore: Author's interview with Anne Zill.

70. Moore subsequently rendezvoused: Author's interviews with Kevin Rafferty and Anne Zill in New York.

70. We went out to talk: Author's interview with James Ridgeway.

71. A hospitable Midwesterner: Author's interviews with Anne Bohlen, Yellow Springs, Ohio, Kevin Rafferty and James Ridgeway.

72. On his final night: Hamper, *Rivethead,* p. 199-203.

72. On his flight: Moore, Michael, "A Room With A View," *Mother Jones,* October 1986,

73. It is also: Michael Moore's letter of application to *Mother Jones.*

74. He had a lot: Author's interview with Bruce Dancis. 1986.

77. We had a lead time: Author's interview with Bernard Ohanion.

78. There is only one story: *Ibid.*
78. Another way to attract: *Michigan Voice,* April, 1986.
80. Am I the only person: Author's interviews with Bernard Ohanion and Bruce Dancis.
81. She brought my stash: Laura Fraser, *San Francisco Bay Guardian,* Jan. 17, 1990 and author's interviews.
81. I remember him: Author's interview with Bruce Dancis.
81. San Francisco was on the other side: *Roger & Me* DVD, (Burbank: Warner Bros, 2003)
82. Just hours before: Hamper, *Rivethead,* p. 218.
83. We sent Paul Berman: Author's interview with Bruce Dancis.
83. He really had it in: Author's interview with Bernard Ohanion.
87. By September it was clear: Hochschild, Adam, *Mother Jones,* Dec. 1986.
88. A lot of people: Michael Moore interview.
90. He was full of shit: Author's interview with John Sinclair.
90. Presumably he said this: Laura Fraser, *San Francisco Bay Guardian,* Jan. 17, 1990.
90. *Mother Jones* Communication Director: Author's interview with Richard Reynolds, San Francisco.
91. The real reason: *San Francisco Chronicle,* Sept. 13, 1988.
91. According to the *Village Voice:* Oct. 14, 1986.
91. In another paper: *Metro,* Jan. 11, 1990.
91. And readers of the: *International Herald Tribune,* Jan. 17, 1990.
91. I was practically driven: Hamper, *Rivethead,* p. 220.
92. Paul Fahri said: Deposition, Michael Moore and Kathleen Glynn *vs.* Foundation for National Progress, San Francisco Superior Court Case # 863824. Feb. 25, 1987.

The Nader Evader
93. It was a bad time: Author's interview with Ralph Nader, Washington, D.C.
93. I knew something was: Author's interviews with Jim Musselman.
93. I belong in Flint: *Ibid.*
95. My father warned be: Author's interview with Ralph Nader.
96. He kept it completely secret: *Ibid.*
96. I wondered about Michael's name: *Ibid.*
99. We stay away from: *Moore's Weekly,* Jan. 25, 1988
99. He was outraged: *Moore's Weekly,* Feb. 8, 1988.
100. Who are you: *Moore's Weekly,* Jan. 25, 1988
101. The occupation: *Moore's Weekly,* Jan. 18, 1988
101. It is a method: *Moore's Weekly,* Feb. 8, 1988
102. Assistant Editor: Author's interview with Andrew Morehouse, North-

ampton, Massachusetts.
103. What does it take: *Moore's Weekly,* June 13, 1988.
104. The first Washington couple: *Moore's Weekly,* June 13, 1988.
104. Another grand prize: *Moore's Weekly,* June 6, 1988.
105. He was obviously: Author's interview with Andrew Morehouse.
106. Nader agrees: Author's interview with Ralph Nader.

You Can Take Mike Out of Flint but You Can't Take Flint Out of Mike
108. It was not: Author's interviews with Jim Musselman.
109. Sent in a proposal: *Ibid.*
109. Developed a proposal: Working draft of Flint (film) proposal.
110. While the Westfall inspired film project: Author's interviews with Jim Musselman.
113. Give a lie: *Mike's Letter,* Jan. 12, 1990. http://www.michaelmoore.com/words/message/index.php?messageDate=2000-01-12
113. I enjoy documentaries: Author's interview with Ed Bradley.
114. Moore, who had: *Flint Journal,* June 11, 1981.
114. She had been nominated: Author's interview with Anne Bohlen.
114. His story sense: Author's interview with Kevin Rafferty.
114. Similar advice: Author's interview with Conrad Martin.
115. They felt like castor oil: *David Letterman Show,* Dec. 28, 1989.
115. On the third day: Author's interview with Kevin Rafferty.
115. Michael didn't know much: Author's interview with Anne Bohlen.
116. When he ran out: Author's interview with Dan Kildee.
116. Thanks to a $58,000 settlement: Author's interview with *Mother Jones* attorney Guy Saperstein.
117. Roger, he told: General Motors Annual Meeting, May 22, 1987.
117. The night before: Author's interviews with Jim Musselman.
119. You always know: Jim Musselman's video of Open Public Meeting, Mott Community College, Flint, Oct. 10, 1995.
120. In January 1988: Author's interviews with Jim Musselman.
122. In Washington, Nader: Author's interview with Ralph Nader.
124. Sometimes in history: Open Public Meeting, Mott Community College.
125. The civil rights movement: Author's interview with Jim Musselman.
126. Like a lot of people: Author's interview with Gini Reticker, Yonkers, New York.

Driving a Stake Through the Heart of Reagan's America
129. John Pierson, a New York: Author's interview with John Pierson, Austin, Texas.
130. Pierson was appalled: *Ibid.*
131. Out of money: Michael Moore's commentary, *Roger & Me* DVD.

131. It's amazing: Author's interview with Kevin Rafferty.
132. When the *Detroit Free Press:* Author's interview with John Pierson.
133. Another rave came in: *Ibid.*
134. General Motors is going to have you killed: Michael Moore, Toronto Film Festival, Sept 8, 2006.
134. Setting up a command post: Author's interview with Conrad Martin.
133. I'm from Flint: Author's interviews with Stewart Mott and John Pierson.
133. It was Stewart: Author's interview with Stewart Mott.
133. America has an irrepressible: *New York Times,* Sept. 27, 1989.
134. Standing in front of the dinner party: Author's interviews with Anne Bohlen and Kevin Rafferty.
134. I've just seen: Author's interview with John Pierson.
134. I like films: *Detroit Free Press,* Oct. 1, 1989.
135. I wanted to give: Author's interview with John Pierson.
136. I had tired out: *Ibid.*
137. In their contract: Pierson, John, *Spike, Mike, Slackers and Dykes* (New York: Miramax, 1995), pp. 154-157.
138. During the making: Michael Moore commentary, *Roger & Me* DVD.
138. If these evictions: *Flint Journal,* Jan. 12,1990.
139. Moore refused: *Mike's Letter,* Jan. 12, 2000 http://www.michaelmoore.com/words/message/index.php?messageDate=2000-01-12
139. It made Flint look: Author's interview with Wallace Rose.
141. You got a lot of help: Phil Donahue show transcript, Jan. 29, 1990, Mike Westfall Collection, University of Michigan Flint, Francis Wilson Thompson Library, Genesee Historical Collections Center, The Michael Moore *Roger & Me* Film Controvesy
141. Our movie was not: Mike Westfall Collection.
142. It never occurred: Author's interviews with Jim Musselman.
143. Ralph Nader demanded: Author's interview with Ralph Nader.
143. He's a Nader Raider: *Flint Journal,* Jan. 20, 1990.
144. Her scene appeared: *Flint Journal,* Feb. 13, 1990.
144. People really need: *Flint Journal,* Oct. 1, 1989.
145. The film was a classic: Author's interview with John Pierson.
145. I'm still looking: *Ibid.*

Not Bringing Home the Bacon
146. Even suits against Moore: *Flint Journal,* Jan. 12, 1994.
146. Anyone who knows me: *Flint Journal,* June 30, 1993.
146. Another litigant: *Flint Journal,* June 15, 1990.
147. It was clear: Ingrassia, Paul and White, Joseph. *Comeback* (New York: Simon and Schuster, 1994), p. 20.
148. Undeterred by 38 consecutive: *Hollywood Reporter,* May 30, 1995.

148. Uh sure!: Moore, Michael and Glynn, Kathleen. *TV Nation* (New York: Harper Perennial, 1998) p. 2.

149. Pilot Performance Weak: NBC Program Test Report, *The Seinfeld Chronicles,* Oct. 26, 1989.

151. We borrowed money: Author's interview with Warren Littlefield, Burbank, California.

154. Would be a cross: *TV Nation,* p. 4.

154. That's the funniest: Author's interview with Warren Littlefield.

155. We were stunned: *TV Nation,* p. 12.

156. In New York: *Ibid.*

157. It is amazing: Author's interview with David Wald, New York.

160. An initial verdict: United States Court of Appeals, Fifth Circuit. No. 96-50253. Peter Scalamandre & Sons, Inc., Merco Joint Venture, et. al. *vs.* Hugh B. Kaufman, TriStar Television, Inc., *et. al.* June 3, 1997.

160. The last-minute programming: *TV Nation,* p. 185.

160. Michael had a lot: Author's interview with David Wald.

161. I think the: Author's interview with Warren Littlefield.

163. An audience of 9 million: *Ibid.*

163. One was a piece: *Ibid.*

164. Actually says Littlefield: *Ibid.*

164. Producer Wald believes: Author's interview with David Wald.

164. I was overwhelmed: Author's interview with Warren Littlefield.

166. General Motors, General Electric: *TV Nation,* p. 200.

We Bombed in Toronto

167. It was the true: Michael Moore, Toronto Film Festival, Sept. 8, 2006.

168. Unfortunately the screening: Author's interview with David Brown, New York.

169. 72 years-old and slightly bitter. *Georgia Straight,* Dec. 7, 1995.

169. They almost came to blows: Author's interview with David Brown.

169. Are we going to: Michael Moore, Toronto Film Festival, Sept. 8, 2006.

169. I can barely breathe: *Ibid.*

169. We needed Candy: Author's interview with David Brown.

169. I wish I said: Michael Moore, Toronto Film Festival.

170. But as Haskell Wexler: *Who Needs Sleep* (2006) directed by Haskell Wexler, The Institute For Cinema Studies.

170. Was too political: *Hollywood Reporter,* May 30, 1995.

170. I thought people were: Author's interview with David Brown.

171. Unfortunately we never even saw: *Ibid.*

172. I never talk about: Author's interview with Douglas Urbanski.

174. When I worked for Michael: *Ibid.*

175. We tried to keep him focused: *Ibid.*

Thinking Big
177. Proud to wear: The *Playboy* Interview, July 2004.
178. Unfortunately the film only grossed: Exhibitor Relations Co. and *Hollywood Reporter* as reported on IMDBpro.com
179. In feature films: Author's interview with Meg Reticker.
180. When I worked: *Ibid.*
181. I think Michael believes: *Ibid.*

No Republicans Were Harmed In The Making of This Show
182. The glove didn't fit: Author's interview with John Derevlany.
183. Clearly I suffer: London Guardian, Nov. 11, 2002.
183. Everyone acted as if: Author's interview with Gideon Evans, Brooklyn, New York.
183. I read what you wrote about: *Mike's Letter*, Dec. 12, 1998, http://www. michaelmoore.com/words/message/index.php?messageDate=1998-12-18
184. I've been a big fan: *Ibid.*
184. Black, white, men, women: *Ibid.*

Cracking Up
187. But he was intercepted: Author's interview with John Derevlany, Culver City, California.
188. It was the first time: *TV Nation,* p. 57.
188. But that didn't hurt: Author's interview with John Derevlany.
188. It could get: *Ibid.*
189. One of Moore's: *Ibid.*
190. One of the problems: *Ibid.*
190. One of Moore's great contributions: *Ibid.*
191. That's a ridiculous: *Ibid.*
191. One performer, unable to pay: Author's interview with Gideon Evans.
191. We have a situation: *Ibid.*
192. We have all this: *Ibid.*
192. It's as cool as: *The Awful Truth Complete DVD.*

The Firing Line
193. Barbara he asked: Author's interview with Barbara Moss, New York.
193. Moore believed that too much: Author's interviews with Alan Edelstein, New York and John Derevlany.
193. It was almost as if: Author's interview with John Derevlany.
195. I did enjoy: Author's interview with Alan Edelstein.
196. It was a very thin premise: *Ibid.*
197. I was sincerely angry: *Ibid.*
198. Later that day Moore called: *Ibid.*

198. Call my office: *Ibid.*
198. I guess it was illegal: *Ibid.*
199. So I guess: *Ibid.*
199. When Edelstein showed up: *Ibid.*
199. He lied: *Ibid.*
200. My film is: *Ibid.*

"You Are the Only Person I've Ever Seen Dive Into a Mosh Pit and Come Out with His Tie Straight"
201. If you're listening: *Muskegon Chronicle,* July 3, 2006.
201. The masterminds: Author's interview with Ralph Nader.
202. There are so few places: *Ibid.*
203. But after his daughter: *The Awful Truth Complete DVD.*
204. We just didn't know: *Mike's Letter,* Jan. 28, 2000. http://www.michael-moore.com/words/message/index.php?messageDate=2000-01-28
204. I was a little surprised: Republican presidential primary debate, Manchester, New Hampshire, January 26, 2000.
205. As the band played on. *Mike's Letter.* Jan. 28, 2000.
205. She discovered that: *Mike's Letter,* June 11, 2000.http://www.michael-moore.com/words/message/index.php?messageDate=2000-07-11.
205. Bush and Gore: *Mike's Letter,* July 19, 2000. http://www.michaelmoore.com/words/message/index.php?messageDate=2000-07-11.
206. I will go so far: *Mike's Letter,* July 18, 2000. http://www.michaelmoore.com/words/message/index.php?messageDate=2000-07-18.
207. He told me he couldn't: Author's interview with Ralph Nader.
208. I support the death penalty. Video of Nader super rally, Boston, October 3, 2000.
211. He brought us youthful credibility: Author's interview with Matt Zawisky, Baltimore.
212. While personally committing: *Stupid White Men,* p. 247.
212. Mike, said one of Nader's advisers: *Stupid White Men,* p. 254.

How Much Is That Uzi In the Window?
213. Don't write me: *Mike's Letter,* Dec. 11, 2000. http://www.michael-moore.com/words/message/index.php?messageDate=2000-12-11.
213. Another victim, Barbara Olsen: *Mike's Letter,* Sept. 19, 2001. http://www.michaelmoore.com/words/message/index.php?message Date=2001-09-19
214. Another 5,000 were turned away: *London Guardian,* Nov. 11, 2002.
214. I am sure: *Mike's Letter,* Sept. 15, 2001. http://www.michaelmoore.com/words/message/index.php?messageDate=2001-09-15
214. I think I know: Sept. 17, 2001. http://www.michaelmoore.com/words/

message/index.php?messageDate=2001-09-17.

214. Unfortunately publication: *Mike's Letter,* Sept. 19, 2001. http://www.michaelmoore.com/words/message/index.php?messageDate=2001-09-19.

214. Keep crying, Mr. Bush: *Mike's Letter,* Sept 14, 2001. http://www.michaelmoore.com/words/message/index.php?messageDate=2001-09-14.

214. I have absolutely zero interest: *Mike's Letter,* Sept. 19, 2001. http://www.michaelmoore.com/words/message/index.php?messageDate=2001-09-19.

214. Moore balked: *London Guardian,* Nov. 11, 2002.

215. You must not fight back: *Stupid White Men,* p. 184.

216. In the summer of 2002: *London Guardian,* Nov. 14, 2002.

217. Bob, he replied: *Mike's Letter,* Aug. 29, 2002: http://www.michaelmoore.com/words/message/index.php?messageDate=2002-08-29.

217. Hey, said one of the crew members: *London Guardian,* Nov. 11, 2002.

220. His suggestion: *London Guardian,* Nov. 13, 2002.

220. One of the things: Eyewitness accounts of Moore's performance provided by audience members.

221. Whose quote is it: *London Guardian,* Nov. 11, 2002.

221. It's trying to take: *Ibid.*

221. Guys like me: U.S. Comedy Arts Festival, Aspen, Colorado, March 3, 2003.

When You Whiz Upon A Star

224. The reason it's a hit: Associated Press, July 24, 2004.

224. On hand were: Imdbpro.com, June 12, 2004, http://pro.imdb.com/title/tt0361596/photo gallery.

225. Veteran author: "Paranoia For Fun and Profit, The Hollywood Economist," Slate.com, May 3, 2005. http://www.slate.com/id/2117923/. Edward Jay Epstein, has also published *The New Logic of Money & Power in Hollywood* (New York: Random House, 2005).

225. Moore's former colleague: Author's interview with Bruce Dancis.

226. On hand to cover: *New York Sun,* Aug. 31, 2004.

227. For example Chris Moore: Author's interview with Chris Moore, Davison, Michigan.

228. Here's the way to stop: Moore, Michael, *Dude Where's My Country?* (New York: Warner Books, 2003), pp. 121-122.

A Message From Michael

230. I never danced once: Michael Moore's speech at Central Michigan University, Mt. Pleasant, Michigan, Sept. 27, 2004.

233. I never thought: Michael Moore Toronto Film Festival, Sept. 8, 2006.

236. In Michigan angry Republicans: Associated Press, Oct. 6, 2004.

237. A comedian portraying: *Saturday Night Live,* Oct. 30, 2004.

237. On Real: *Real Time With Bill Maher,* July 30, 2004.

237. He told me: Author's interview with Ralph Nader.

238. He claims that: *Ibid.*

You Can't Get Into Heaven Without a Permission Slip from the Poor

239. To much of corporate America: U.S. Comedy Arts Festival.

239. Remember, America: *Mike's Letter,* Nov. 5, 2004, http://www.michael-moore.com/words/message/index.php?messageDate=2004-11-05.

239. I'm just not sure: Bachrach, Judy, "Michael Moore Speaks," *Vanity Fair,* March 2005.

240. He also received a confidential: Michael Moore, Toronto Film Festival, Sept. 8, 2006.

241. Something happened overnight: *Ibid.*

241. I feel a kind of strange kinship: *New York Times,* Jan. 11, 2005.

241. Do you think: Michael Moore, Paul Wellstone Award Ceremony acceptance speech, Flint, Michigan, Nov. 20, 2005.

242. On Valentine's Day: *Washington Post,* Feb. 13, 2005.

242. Some people think: Author's interview with Kay Shepherd.

242. The same thing happened: Author's interview with Ed Bradley.

243. I thought *Fahrenheit 9/11*: Author's interview with Greg Fiedler.

243. The bible is very clear: Paul Wellstone Award ceremony.

244. I get along fine: Author's interview with Wallace Rose.

246. The people in *Roger & Me*: *Ibid.*

249. From the very beginning: Author's interview with Sister Mary Ellen Gondeck and Sister Janet Kurtz, Nazareth, Michigan.

250. When we started: *Roger & Me* DVD.

250. It cost us $150,000: Author's interview with Dan Kildee.

259. In 1963, 22-year-old: Loren, Cary in *John Sinclair and The Culture of The Sixties* (Ann Arbor: Bentley Historical Library, 2004) pp. 3-23.

259. Thank you, said Sinclair: Author's interview with John Sinclair.

Afterword

264. Leader of the pack: *New York's Free Weekly,* Nov. 12–18, 1997.

266. Television never precludes: Author's interview with Warren Littlefield.

267. Michael Moore style: Author's interview with Conrad Martin.

270. The conservatives seized control: Author's interview with Kevin Rafferty.

271. I've got my reputation: Author's interview with Wallace Rose.

272. A Nader/Moore ticket: Author's interview with Matt Zawisky.

273. Interested in the: Author's interview with Anne Zill.

Think About What You've Done

274. I want people to worry: *Detroit Free Press,* Oct. 1, 1989.

BIBLIOGRAPHY

Epstein, Edward J. *The New Logic of Money and Power in Hollywood*. New York: Random House, 2005.

Gabler, Neil. *An Empire Of Their Own: How The Jews Invented Hollywood*. New York: Crown Publishers, 1988

Hamper, Ben. *Rivethead: Tales From The Assembly Line*. New York. Warner Books. 1991.

Hardy, David T. and Jason Clarke. *Michael Moore Is A Big Fat Stupid White Man*. New York: Regan Books, 2004

Ingrassia, Paul and White, Joseph, *Comeback*. New York: Simon and Schuster, 1994

Nader, Ralph. *Unsafe At Any Speed: The Designed-in Dangers of the American Automobile,* expanded edition. New York: Grossman, 1972.

Martin, Justin. *Nader: Crusader, Spoiler, Icon*. New York: Perseus Publishing, 2002.

Moore, Michael. *The Official Fahrenheit 9/11 Reader*. New York: Simon and Schuster, 2004.

Moore, Michael, and Kathleen Glynn. *Adventures in a TV Nation*. New York: Harper Perennial, 1998.

Moore, Michael. *Downsize This: Random Threats From An Unarmed American*. New York: Crown Publishers, 1996.

Moore, Michael. *Dude, Where's My Country?* New York: Warner Books, 2003.

Moore, Michael. *Stupid White Men: And Other Sorry Excuses For the State of the Nation*. New York: Regan Books, 2002

Moore, Michael. *Will They Ever Trust Us Again*. New York: Simon and Schuster, 2004.

Pierson, John. Spike, Mike, *Slackers & Dykes: A Guided Tour Across A Decade of American Independent Cinema*. New York: Miramax Books/Hyperion, 1995.

Schultz, Emily. *Michael Moore: A Biography*. Toronto: ECW Press. 2005.

Rampell, Ed. *Progressive Hollywood: A People's Film Histsory of the United States*. New York: The Disinformation Company, 2005.

Tanner, Robert T. *Michael Moore's Fahrenheit 9/11: How One Film Divided A Nation*. Lawrence: University Press of Kansas, 2006.

INDEX

ACKNOWLEDGMENTS

JUST LIKE GEORGE W. BUSH, authors can't work in a vacuum. We need thinkers, enablers, handlers, gofers and of course, people who help us finish our sentences. Backing up the characters who populate these pages is a behind the scenes cast that has been heroic in its devotion to the untold, unauthorized, unbelievable story of Citizen Moore. Alphabetizing is a democratic way to credit those who patiently shared their knowledge and insights. But I also want to single out a few people who made my own journey a pleasure.

My wife Martha Ferriby, who grew up minutes from Flint, has been a guiding light on this project. Her intimate knowledge of the region's history, culture and religious traditions informs these pages. Richard Harris, my friend and colleague, has guided many authors who appreciate his patience and sense of humor, not to mention his own writing skills. My brother Ron, the first writer I ever met, made many valuable suggestions. I also appreciate the support of my father Dan Rapoport, a pioneer in a Michigan industry that is not downsizing, aerospace and my sister Carla who was a great help on events in the United Kingdom. Calvin Goodman and Florence Goodman were two indispensable allies on this project, as were Ken and Yetta Goodman. I am also grateful to my daughter Elizabeth, my son Jonathan and stepson William Ferriby. Sterling Lord remains the best friend a writer could ask for. Colleen Weesies, Megan Trank, Elizabeth Hasse, Paula Morrison, Casey Sodini and Phil Stoffan all lent their talents to this project, as did the staffs of the Hackley Public Library, the Flint Public Library, the Genesee District Library, the Elk Rapids District

Library, the *Flint Journal,* the *Muskegon Chronicle,* the *Davison Index,* the *Traverse City Record-Eagle, Mother Jones* magazine, and the Center For Study of Responsive Law.

From Northampton, Massachusetts to beautiful downtown Burbank, California, I was fortunate to work with a gifted and talented group of filmmakers, producers, directors, editors, journalists, artists, agents, managers, philanthropists and clerics who offered a birds-eye view of their days with Michael Moore. My friends in the book publishing community were also a great support group. So here's a tip of the baseball cap to Paul Berman, Anne Bohlen, Ed Bradley, Jennifer Braham, Jason Chambers, Conrad Erb, Bruce Dancis, John Derevlany, Alan Edelstein, Gideon Evans, Greg Fiedler, Robert Fields, Sister Mary Ellen Gondeck, David Hogue, Robert Guinsler, Paul Keep, Dan Kildee, Sister Janet Kurtz, Dave Larzelere, Sallye Leventhal, Warren Littlefield, Patty Mann, Conrad Martin, Andrew Morehouse, Barbara Moss, Laura Mortensen, Stewart Mott, Monsignor Francis Murray, Jim Musselman, Ralph Nader, Bernard Ohanion, John Pierson, Janet Pierson, Kevin Rafferty Gini Reticker, Meg Reticker, John Richard, Eileen Rieger, James Ridgeway, Fred Ross, Wallace Rose, Guy Saperstein, John Sinclair, John Tewsley, Douglas Urbanski, Craig and Shari Whittaker, Jean Wollan, Jennifer Wollan, Matthew Zawisky and Anne Zill. Finally to you the reader, thanks for your support of the bookselling community, your local public library and authors you've never met. It's your enthusiasm that makes books like this one a labor of love, most of the time.

ABOUT THE AUTHOR

A VETERAN INVESTIGATIVE JOURNALIST AND AUTHOR, Roger Rapoport has worked with many of the people who have been at the center of Michael Moore's career.

Rapoport has written about the automobile industry for the *Wall Street Journal*, worked on an automotive assembly line for Ford and published a *Mother Jones* cover piece on the FBI undercover agent who burned down the Watts Writers Workshop. He has also written about nuclear weapons for the *Los Angeles Times*, for-profit hospitals in *Harper's Magazine*, automobile salesmen in the *Atlantic Monthly* and the California earthquake threat in *Esquire*. His newspaper work has appeared in the *San Francisco Chronicle, San Jose Mercury-News, Oakland Tribune, Dallas Morning News* and many other papers.

He is the author, co-author or editor of 17 books including *Hillsdale: Greek Tragedy in the American Heartland*, the story of the mysterious death of the editor of Michigan's conservative Hillsdale College Press, and *California Dreaming: The Political Odyssey of Pat and Jerry Brown*. Most recently, he co-edited *Saving Our Schools*, a study of George Bush's No Child Left Behind law, which threatens to close more than 27,000 American public schools.

Rapoport graduated from the University of Michigan, where he edited the *Michigan Daily*. After residing in California for many years, he returned to his home state in 2004 and now lives in Muskegon, the largest deep water port on Lake Michigan.

His wife, Martha Ferriby, is the director of the Hackley Public Library, a Richardsonian Romanesque National Historic Landmark where much of this book was written. He is the father of Jonathan and Elizabeth Rapoport and the stepfather of William Ferriby.

ABOUT RDR BOOKS

Founded in 1993, RDR Books has been named by *Book Marketing Update* as one of America's top 100 independent presses. The publisher of such distinguished authors and illustrators as Michael Rosen, Quentin Blake, Alec Le Sueur, Ken and Yetta Goodman, Joseph Pell, Fred Rosenbaum, Carol Polsgrove and Richard Harris, the company has received many literary honors. Based in Michigan and California, RDR's authors and editors have been widely praised by reviewers. Many titles are published in translation around the world. In addition to well known authors and illustrators, RDR has also introduced many promising new talents such as Michael Kohn, Burt Dragin, Milly Moguloff, Ron French, Christopher Rush and Brice Smith.

RDR's adult titles include biography, memoirs, history, the environment, travel literature, Judaica, health, criticism, sports and guidebooks. The company also publishes a distinguished children's line. Many RDR titles focus on important political issues including George Bush's No Child Left Behind Act, outsourcing of American industry and the case against nuclear power plants. The company is well known for humor titles including the worldwide bestselling *I Should Have Stayed Home* series.

For more information, visit www.rdrbooks.com or email us at read@rdrbooks.com. Our mailing address is 960 West Sherman Blvd., Muskegon, Michigan 49441.